CompuServe Information Manager Keyboard Shortcut Commands

F1	Help
F2	Save As
F4	Print
F10	Menu Bar
↵	Do
Esc	Cancel
Ctrl-D	Disconnect (from CompuServe)
Ctrl-F	Filing Cabinet
Ctrl-G	Go
↓	Move Down
↑	Move Up
Alt-X	Exit (to DOS)

Prodigy Keyboard Shortcut Commands

F6	Jump (to a service feature or database)
F5	Contents (displays a list of 13 categories that span the entire Prodigy service)
F7	Index (lists all available features and subjects in a window, with redundant entries eliminated)
F8	X-Ref (cross-reference tool that finds all content related by subject to a given feature)

Exploring the World of Online Services

Exploring the World of Online Services

ROSALIND RESNICK

SYBEX®

San Francisco
Paris
Düsseldorf
Soest

ACQUISITIONS EDITOR: Dianne King
DEVELOPMENTAL EDITOR: David Kolodney
EDITOR: James A. Compton
TECHNICAL EDITOR: Maryann Brown
PRODUCTION ARTIST: Lisa Jaffe
SCREEN GRAPHICS: John Corrigan
DESKTOP PUBLISHING SPECIALIST: Dina F Quan
PROOFREADER: David Silva
INDEXER: Liz Cunningham
COVER DESIGNER: Ingalls + Associates
COVER PHOTOGRAPHER: Mark Johann

The photographs on pages 20 and 21 appear by permission of Practical Peripherals.

Screen reproductions produced with Collage Plus.

Library of Congress Card Number: 93-83101
ISBN: 0-89588-798-3

Manufactured in the United States of America
10 9 8 7 6 5 4 3 2 1

To Julia, who already knows how to reboot Mom's computer, and to Caroline, who undoubtedly will before long.

ACKNOWLEDGMENTS

As every author knows, writing a book is a team endeavor. First of all, I'd like to thank the folks at SYBEX—Dianne King, David Kolodney, Jim Compton, John Corrigan, Lisa Jaffe, Dina Quan, David Silva, Liz Parra, and Maryann Brown—for the months they spent helping me make this a useful, timely, and accurate book; and Matt Wagner, my agent, for his help in bringing my first book project to fruition.

I'd also like to thank Robert Bixby, my editor at *Compute* magazine, who prodded me to write this book in the first place. A special thank-you, too, to Susie Archer, my computer guru, who knew me back before I knew my bauds from my bits.

In addition, I'd like to thank the helpful folks at CompuServe and Prodigy, especially Dave Kishler, Debra Young, and Steve Hein, who patently answered all my questions about their services. I'd also like to thank the community of on-line users who generously offered their insights, suggestions, and time.

My thanks also go to my editors at *PC Today*, *Home Office Computing*, and *International Business*, who gave me the opportunity to report on the world of online services and to enhance my understanding of that world.

And, last but not least, I'd like to thank my family—my husband, Bill Grueskin, and my daughters, Julia and Caroline—for their tireless encouragement and support.

Contents at a Glance

	Introduction	*xix*
PART I	**THE BASICS**	**1**
Chapter 1	The Wide World of Online Services	2
Chapter 2	Separating the Bauds from the Bits	16
Chapter 3	Getting Started	38
Chapter 4	Getting Around	52
Chapter 5	The Bottom Line	68
Chapter 6	E-Mail	84
Chapter 7	Uploading and Downloading	102
Chapter 8	Forums and Bulletin Boards	120
Chapter 9	Tapping into Databases	138
Chapter 10	Logging On Overseas	156
PART II	**THE ONLINE WORLD**	**172**
Chapter 11	The Big Guns	174
Chapter 12	Dollars and Sense	192
Chapter 13	Working the Room	220
Chapter 14	Stocking Your Office	236
Chapter 15	Trains, Planes and Automobiles	254
Chapter 16	Technical Support for Non-Techies	272
	Conclusion	*289*
Appendix	The Rest of the Pack	294
	Index	*305*

Table of Contents

INTRODUCTION . . . . **xix**

PART I **The Basics** **1**

Chapter 1

THE WIDE WORLD OF ONLINE SERVICES **2**

What's Out There 4
Why It's Worth Getting 5
Paying the Price 6
Knowing Before You Go 6
Doing Business Online 12
  The Online Detective 12
  The Mail-Order Retailer 12
  The International Trader 13
  The Information Broker 13
  The Online Investors 14
Summary 15

CHAPTER 2

SEPARATING THE BAUDS FROM THE BITS **16**

Setting Up Your Modem 19
  Internal versus External Modems 19
  Hayes Compatibility 21
  Modem Speed 22
Communications Software 23
  Multipurpose versus Front-End Software 24
  Off-the-Shelf Programs versus Shareware 26
  Logging on through Windows 28
Setting Up Your Communications Software 32

Making Contact 34
Troubleshooting Your Modem and Software 36
Summary 36

CHAPTER 3
GETTING STARTED **38**
Logging On 40
Logging On with a Multipurpose Program 41
Logging On with a Front-End Program 43
Protecting Your Password 46
Weighing the Costs 47
Basic Service Plans 48
Off-Peak Plans 48
Customized Plans 49
Surcharged Databases 50
Membership Fees 50
Summary 51

CHAPTER 4
GETTING AROUND **52**
The Main Menu 54
Making Your Way Around Prodigy 54
Making Your Way Around CompuServe 55
Saving Time with Shortcut Commands 57
Using the Go Command 57
Using the Find Command 58
Customizing the Service to Fit Your Needs 59
Creating a Prodigy Pathlist 59
Creating a CompuServe Favorite Places List 61
Saving Time with Abbreviated Menus 61
Putting on the Brakes 64
Getting Online Help If You Get Lost 65
Summary 65

CHAPTER 5

THE BOTTOM LINE 68

How Online Services Can Get Expensive 70
Connect Charges 71
Surcharges 72
Network Charges 73
Pay-As-You-Go versus Flat-Fee Plans 75
Pay-As-You-Go Plans 75
Flat-Fee Plans 76
Saving Money with Off-Line Options 76
WinCIM versus TAPCIS 77
How To Ask About Your Bill 79
Getting Billing Information on Prodigy 79
Getting Billing Information on CompuServe 81
Summary 81

CHAPTER 6

E-MAIL 84

Sending and Receiving Messages 86
Sending an Electronic Message 86
Retrieving an Electronic Message 92
Saving Time with an Address Book 94
Creating an Address Book with CompuServe 95
Creating an Address Book with Prodigy 96
Online Networking: Private and Public Messages 97
E-Mail Lingo and "Etiquette" 99
Summary 101

CHAPTER 7

UPLOADING AND DOWNLOADING 102

Making Your Files Fly 104
Uploading a Text File 104
Uploading Program and Graphics Files 106

Bringing Your Files Home 107
Downloading a Text File 107
Downloading Program and Graphics Files 113
Choosing a File Transfer Protocol 115
Printing Text from the Screen 118
Summary 118

CHAPTER 8

FORUMS AND BULLETIN BOARDS **120**

Hanging Out at the Online Bulletin Board 122
Putting Online Bulletin Boards to Work for You 123
The Message Board 125
The Library 129
The Conference Room 130
Finding Kindred Spirits 132
Tuning In to Online Chat Boards 133
CompuServe's CB Simulator 134
Summary 137

CHAPTER 9

TAPPING INTO DATABASES **138**

Online Access versus Online Overload 140
Doing Your Homework with Online Bulletin Boards and Encyclopedias 142
Targeting Your Market 143
Mining Your Modem for Money 145
Full-text Databases: Black and White and Read All Over 145
IQUEST 149
Tracking People Trends 150
Paging through Business Directories 152
Summary 154

CHAPTER 10

LOGGING ON OVERSEAS 156

Know Before You Go: Disasters That Await You 158
  Braving the Risks 159
Preparing for Pitfalls 160
Pinching Pesos on Phone Calls and Access Charges . . 167
Logging onto CompuServe in Europe 168
Summary 169

PART II

The Online World 172

CHAPTER 11

THE BIG GUNS 174

The Evolution of Prodigy and CompuServe 176
  The Compuserve Connection 177
  Prodigy Is Born 178
How the Big Two Stack Up 180
  Features and Options 181
  Pricing 186
  Ease of Use 187
  Speed 187
  Accessibility 188
And the Winner Is 188
Looking Ahead: The Future of Prodigy and CompuServe 189
Summary 190

CHAPTER 12

DOLLARS AND SENSE 192

A Wealth of Financial Data Just a Phone Call Away . . . 194
Tapping into Financial Databases via the Big Two 195
  Getting Financial Information with Prodigy 195

Getting Financial Information with CompuServe . . 196
Using More Specialized Financial Services 198
Dialog 200
Dow Jones News/Retrieval 201
Newsnet 203
Data-Star 204
I/PLUS Direct 206
The Internet 207
Cost-Cutting Tips 209
Downloading Data to Your Spreadsheet 210
Online Brokerages: Trading Stocks Where You Buy Your Socks 212
Making a Trade 213
How the Online Brokerages Stack Up 215
The Financial Meet Market 216
Investor Bulletin Boards 216
Online Investment Clubs 218
Summary 219

CHAPTER 13

WORKING THE ROOM **220**

Online Networking for Fun and Profit 222
Help for Home Business Owners 222
Looking for Jobs in All the Right Places 224
Professional Advice: Is There a Doctor (or Lawyer, or CPA) in the House? 228
Legal Advice 228
Tax Advice 229
Getting Health Advice: An Ounce of Prevention . . 230
Summary 234

CHAPTER 14
STOCKING YOUR OFFICE 236
The Hassle-Free World of Online Shopping 238
The Pros and Cons 239
Cruising the Electronic Malls 241
Compuserve 242
Prodigy 244
Comparison Shopping 246
Searching Consumer Reports 246
Searching PC Catalog 249
Online Ordering 249
Ordering through Prodigy 250
Summary 251

CHAPTER 15
TRAINS, PLANES, AND AUTOMOBILES 254
Online Travel Services: Your Ticket to Ride 256
Travel Clubs 257
Travel Databases 258
Reservations Systems 260
Eaasy Sabre 262
Accessing Eaasy Sabre on Prodigy 262
Accessing the Official Airline Guide on CompuServe 265
Ticket Deliveries 269
Summary 270

CHAPTER 16
TECHNICAL SUPPORT FOR NON-TECHIES 272
Technicians Who Never Sleep 274
How to Get Help 276
Where to Start 276

Working the System 279
Pros and Cons 280
Technical Support Databases 281
Bulletin Board Messages and Libraries 282
The Microsoft Knowledge Index 282
Advice Columns 283
Shopping for Help Online 284
Prodigy 285
CompuServe 285
GEnie 287
America Online 288
Summary 288

CONCLUSION 289

APPENDIX

THE REST OF THE PACK 294

GEnie 294
America Online 296
Delphi 299

INDEX 305

INTRODUCTION

If you're in business—as an executive, an entrepreneur or an investor—you're well aware that time is money. You know by hard-won experience that the sooner you can get your hands on the vital business information you need, the better your chances of besting your competition in the marketplace.

The trouble is, until recently, up-to-date business and financial information was difficult to find and frustratingly slow to retrieve. Gathering government export statistics, for example, often meant trekking to far-away libraries and sifting through huge volumes packed with tiny print. Compiling mailing lists required manually combing obscure trade association directories and other hard-to-find books. And doing market research to find out which part of the country buys the most chocolate bars or which company is expected to emerge as the leader in the global biotechnology industry by the year 2000 could take weeks—not to mention dozens of expensive long-distance phone calls.

Wouldn't it be great if you could have a world of business information at your fingertips—any time of day or night? Now, thanks to the magic of computer technology, you can.

If you have a personal computer and a modem, the information you need to stay on top is only a local phone call away. By tapping into easy-to-use on-line services like Prodigy and CompuServe, even a computer novice can instantly access the kind of business and financial information that once was the exclusive domain of Wall Street professionals and Fortune 500 executives. The bottom line: Without leaving your chair, you can bring the world to your desktop 24 hours a day, seven days a week.

Imagine the possibilities: With the touch of a key, you can access the latest industry data, trademark filings, and stock market quotes and even get the inside line on your competition's upcoming advertising campaign. If you want to store that information for future reference, simply print it out on your computer's printer or save it as a text file on your hard drive or floppy disk. You can also use on-line services to shop for office supplies, chat with potential clients, and even book a seat on the next flight to Tokyo.

If this sounds like just the sort of thing you need to put you and your business ahead of the pack, it is. The trouble is, tapping into on-line databases isn't as simple as dialing a phone or slipping a videocassette into your VCR—although it probably will be in the not-too-distant future. On the other hand, it's not nearly so difficult as your friends, colleagues, and some computer manuals may have led you to believe—especially if you already know something about using a personal computer. In fact, many of the on-line services now offer Windows (or Windows-like) software interfaces that let you use lots of the same commands and key combinations you already use with other programs. You can even use your mouse!

This book is a beginner's guide to on-line services—a book designed show you, the time-conscious business person, how to tap into, navigate and profit from the ever-expanding world of on-line information. Through easy-to-follow instructions, plain-English explanations, and real-life stories from dozens of successful on-line users, you'll quickly master tips and tricks that will help you reap cost savings that far outweigh this book's purchase price. Throughout the book, you'll find dozens of step-by-step examples of how to access information on the two biggest mass-market on-line services—Prodigy and CompuServe. Chapter by chapter, you'll build your knowledge until, by the end of the book, you'll possess all the tools you need to grab hold of the information you need now—quickly, painlessly, and without busting your budget.

To help you save money, this book also provides a wealth of comparative pricing information, pointing out online bargains and steering you away from online money pits. You'll learn about all-you-can-eat plans, pay-as-you-go plans, network access fees and database surcharges. You'll also find out how the major online services compare—which ones offer the cheapest e-mail, which ones let you make free travel reservations, and which ones include free stock quotes as part of the basic package.

This book is divided into two parts—the basics of using on-line services and a guide to what's available on-line for the financial and business user.

In Part I, the Basics, Chapter 1 offers an overview of "the wide world of on-line services"—what on-line services are, the kind of information that's out there and why it's worth getting—plus short profiles of savvy business people who use on-line services to make a living. Chapters 2 through 10 teach you the basic skills you'll need to know to access any on-line service—setting up your modem and communications software, logging onto the service with your password and ID, zipping from main menus to submenus and back again, sending and receiving electronic mail and files, chatting with other users on on-line bulletin boards, tapping into databases, and logging on overseas.

Part II, The Online World, gives you a quick tour of what's out there. Chapter 11 compares Prodigy and CompuServe—two very different kinds of on-line services. Chapters 12 through 16 fill you in on everything from ferreting out investment information to networking, shopping, making travel reservations on-line, and getting technical help. The book concludes with a brief look at the future of electronic information retrieval, and an appendix highlighting three smaller but worthwhile on-line services—GEnie, America Online and Delphi.

Now, let's log on and get started …

PART 1

The Basics

If you have a personal computer and a modem, the information you need to stay on top of your business and personal finances is only a phone call away. By tapping into easy-to-use on-line services like Prodigy and CompuServe, even a computer novice can gain instant to the kind of cutting-edge information that once was the exclusive domain of Wall Street professionals and Fortune 500 executives. Without leaving your chair, you can bring the world to your desktop 24 hours a day, seven days a week.

But before you play the game, you've got to learn the rules. That's what Part 1: The Basics is all about. With the help of plain-English explanations and step-by-step instructions, you'll learn everything you need to know about logging on, sending electronic mail, posting notes on online bulletin boards and tapping into databases. You'll even learn how to go online overseas.

CHAPTER 1

The Wide World of Online Services

This chapter introduces you to the wide world of online services. If you've heard a little about these services but aren't sure exactly what they offer, it may be helpful to visualize them as giant electronic libraries—though they're actually much more than that. Online services are book stores, newspapers, encyclopedias, bulletin boards, clipping services, department stores, travel agencies, and automated teller machines all rolled into one. And, unlike stores and libraries that generally close in the evening, online services are available any time of night or day—without your ever having to leave your home or office.

The purpose of an online service is to help you get the information you want when you want it. Though there are thousands of different online services and bulletin boards nationwide, they all offer two basic kinds of services—information retrieval and interactive communications. Information retrieval is a fancy term for access to online information, the kind of newspaper articles, financial statistics and other data that, until recently, were available only in printed form. Interactive communications is the ability to send messages, known as *electronic mail*, to other online subscribers and to buy products, make travel reservations, bank by computer and *download*, or copy to your computer, software at bargain prices.

These days, the two most popular mass-market online services are Prodigy and CompuServe, each with more than 1 million subscribers. Other popular online services include America Online, GEnie and Delphi. There are also a number of specialized online services such as Dow Jones News/Retrieval, Dialog, NewsNet, and Data-Star, which are popular among large corporations but too expensive for the average individual. While no two online services operate exactly the same way, the skills you learn on one can be easily transferred to the rest with a little effort.

What's Out There

Unless you live in a major city like New York or Washington or Chicago, your friendly online service is likely to offer you much more information than you could ever hope to find at your local library, newsstand, or bookstore. At last count, there were some 5500 online databases out there, and the number is growing daily. These databases give you everything from stock quotes and interest-rate predictions to the latest articles from *PC* magazine and *The Wall Street Journal*.

Looking for the latest trends in Japanese sushi consumption? Online services offer access to hundreds of newspapers worldwide, letting you instantly retrieve news stories from Oregon to Osaka. Traveling out of town on a business trip? Online services can tell you which restaurants are the best and the toll-free number to call to reserve a table. And, unlike browsing through traditional newspapers and magazines, browsing online doesn't require you to waste time taking notes by hand or making photocopies. Simply press a few keys, and you can print out a copy of the article on your computer printer or store it on a disk.

Why It's Worth Getting

The real value of online services is instant access—access to people, places, and information. That's because online services are not merely electronic substitutes for the same information you can find on paper. They're electronic communities where you can make contacts, meet new customers, and even find the best deal on a PC, laser printer, or fax modem.

Thinking of quitting your job and starting a home business? Simply tap into CompuServe's Working from Home Forum and meet others who are in the same boat. Read about a hot stock in *The Wall Street Journal* but aren't sure whether to take the plunge? Join Prodigy's Money Talk bulletin board and check out what your fellow investors think. Planning your next business trip? Almost all the major online services offer access to Eaasy Sabre, American Airlines' online reservations system that not only books your flight but also delivers the tickets to your door.

Simply sign up, log on, and explore...

Paying the Price

Of course, online access isn't free—or even cheap, in many cases. And, if you're not careful, online availability can quickly turn into information overload. With hundreds of online services and thousands of databases currently available, where do you begin? And, once you've logged on, how do you get the biggest bang for your buck?

Despite the many advantages of using online services, going online can cost a small fortune if you don't know what you're doing. Individual databases such as Dialog's Agrochemicals Handbook, for example, costs $345 an hour to search, and many services require mastery of a complex set of search commands and procedures. Some services, such as Dialog and Dow Jones News/Retrieval, now offer easy-to-operate menus, but this convenience generally will end up costing you more: Not only can these front-end programs slow down your search, but, in Dialog's case, you can pay an extra 75 cents a minute to use the menu feature instead of the commands.

Note: As you read this book, be aware that all prices quoted here are current as of January 1, 1993, and subject to rapid change. After all, the goal of this book is not to be a buyer's guide—there are plenty of computer magazines that serve that function perfectly well—but to give you a general idea of the difference in pricing between one online option and another.

Knowing Before You Go

Navigating the world of online services doesn't have to be difficult or expensive—as long as you do a little homework ahead of time and understand what you want to get out of them.

Ask yourself the following 10 questions before you start dialing for data:

1. **What am I really looking for?** An online service is no place to browse. Since many online services charge by the minute and hit you with surcharges for accessing specialized databases, the meter is always running. Depending on

the speed at which you want your data sent out and received, CompuServe will charge you up to $12.80 an hour, or 22 cents a minute (at the highest speed, it's $22.80 an hour or 38 cents a minute). Logging onto Dow Jones News/Retrieval can cost as much as $200 an hour depending on the time of day.

So, before you log on, jot down a few notes to remind yourself what you're going to be looking for. The more narrowly you can define your search on paper ahead of time, the less time and money you'll end up spending online. For example, typing the search words "photocopiers" and "industry" into an online database can easily turn up dozens or even hundreds of articles, many of which will be irrelevant to your needs. Rather than waste your time and money sifting through a mountain of data, narrow your search as much as possible. Add a few more words to your search string, such as "competition" and "Canon" and "Sharp," and you stand a much better chance of retrieving more specific market information.

2. **How quickly do I need this stuff, anyhow?** In the online world, the faster you want the information, the more it's going to cost you. If you need an immediate price quote on 100 shares of IBM stock, for example, you can log onto Dow Jones News/Retrieval, pay $14.59 and get it right away. (This minimum fee for accessing a single stock quote includes $1.95 for one minute of connect time, $1.14 for accessing up to 1000 characters and an $11.50 monthly service charge.) If you can afford to wait a little longer, you can log onto CompuServe at 22 cents a minute and get a 20-minute delayed quote. If you're the patient type who can wait until the market closes, you can dial up GEnie and get free closing stock quotes as part of your $4.95 monthly fee.

   Surprised? Just like airlines that offer cheap flights to Europe in the winter, many online services charge lower rates at night and on weekends when few business people use them. For instance, Dialog offers its Knowledge Index service, which gives you access to more than a hundred Dialog databases during evenings and weekends at a reduced rate. Dow Jones News/Retrieval discounts access to its full selection of databases during off-peak hours. (Prodigy and CompuServe, which target both consumers and business users, do not offer off-peak discounts.)

3. **Can I get what I'm looking for off-line, too?** Again, this comes down to a question of priorities—your money or your time. If you live in or near a big city, your local library probably houses much of the same information you can find online (although the online information is often more current). You'll have to get up out of your chair to go there, of course, but, once you arrive, the information is free and the reference librarians are usually helpful. Many libraries now contain not only printed materials but information on CD-ROM, such as government census and trade statistics. Many state and federal agencies will send you economic and demographic information for free in a week or so—if you can afford to wait that long.

4. **Can I get everything I want from just one online service?** Many online services overlap when it comes to the more popular business databases such as Disclosure, D&B Dun's Market Identifiers, and ABI/Inform, to name a few. Since there is so much duplication, you can save on annual subscription fees by limiting the number of online services you join. (Fortunately, many online services offer free software and sign-up plans that let you "try before you buy." This allows you to sample their service for several hours before the meter starts running.)

   There's another drawback to signing up for multiple online services. Though the commands you need to make your way around the various services are similar—for example, typing the letter "m" at a command prompt gets you back to the previous menu on CompuServe, whereas, on Dow Jones News/Retrieval, you type "/m"—there are numerous tiny differences that take time to master. Rather than learning a handful of "words" in each online "language," pick one or two services and become fluent.

5. **How much time do I plan to spend online each month?** Some of the major online services, such as Prodigy, CompuServe and GEnie, offer flat-fee plans that let you pay $4.95 to $14.95 a month in return for unlimited access to their basic services. Prodigy, for example, charges $14.95 a month ($9.95 a month if you sign up for a year) for access to a wide variety of databases and other services including news, weather, sports, financial information and an online travel agency. CompuServe's $8.95-a-month plan includes an electronic mail allowance of $9, which entitles you to send up to the equivalent of 60 messages as long as 7500 characters (about three typed double-spaced pages) each.

   The bottom line: If you plan to spend a lot of time online, spring for a flat-fee plan that won't penalize you for heavy usage. If you only plan to go online every once in a while, choose the option that lets you pay as you go. Generally speaking, if you plan to spend at least half an hour online each month. it pays to invest in a flat-fee plan.

6. **How much money do I want to spend online?** Like any business expense, the cost of going online must be weighed against the potential return on your investment. While spending several hundred dollars a month on an online service may sound like a lot of money, it may actually be a pittance compared to the cost of photocopying research materials at your local library, sending out reports and computer diskettes via overnight mail, and going to industry trade shows to hobnob with potential customers. At the same time, it's important to recognize that online networking and research are no guarantee of future customers or profits—and that the most you may ever get back is a tax break from the IRS.

7. **How much time do I want to spend learning about online services?** If you're like most business people, the answer is

"as little as possible." After all, you can't bill your clients for time spent learning to use an online service.

But if you're planning to use online services as your primary research tool, it makes sound business sense to devote some time to getting to know the ins and outs of the services you use most often. Not only will your online services bills be lower at the end of the month, but you'll also have more time to do what you do best—run your business. If you don't plan to spend a lot of time online, consider signing up for a service that offers pull-down menus and a plain-English command structure (like Prodigy), even though it may cost you a little more.

8. **How much of my day do I expect to spend online?** That's an important question to ask if you're thinking of taking advantage of one of the online world's most popular services—electronic mail. Just as it wouldn't make much sense to rent a post office box if you never stopped by the post office to pick up your letters, it doesn't make sense to send out lots of e-mail if you rarely go online to check your messages.

   Remember: The only way to find out if you have electronic mail waiting is to log on to the online service, an activity that's almost certain to cost you money. So, before you scrap the US Postal Service for the convenience of swapping messages online, weigh the costs and benefits of retrieving the answers from your online mail box.

9. **What type of information will I need most often?** When choosing which online service or services to subscribe to, it's important to know what kind of information you'll need most. While many of the major services like CompuServe and Prodigy offer access to a wide variety of business and financial databases, it may be worthwhile to subscribe to a specialized service if your business requires it.

   For example, few people who make their living trading stocks would want to be without a subscription to Dow Jones News/Retrieval, the only online service that offers real-time stock quotes, the full text of *The Wall Street*

Journal, *Barron's*, *Business & Finance Report*, and *American Demographics*, and up-to-the-minute reports on SEC filings. If you do business in global markets, think about signing up for Data-Star, a service of Switzerland's Radio-Suisse. Data-Star features more than 300 databases offering worldwide financial information on business, medicine, science, pharmaceuticals, and technology. Data-Star also offers Tradstat, a unique database containing official government import/export information on more than 60,000 commodities from Europe, Japan, Canada, Taiwan, South America, and the United States.

10. Do I just want to search for information online or do I want to send it, too? Though most of the online services offer access to similar (and sometimes identical) databases, it's important to know that not all services offer the same ability to send and receive electronic files and messages. CompuServe, for example, allows you to send and receive messages—no matter how long—and to send files not only to other CompuServe members but to anyone in the world who has a fax machine, a telex machine or even an ordinary postal mail box. Prodigy, by contrast, lets you send e-mail only to other Prodigy members and does not allow you to send text files that you create off-line with your word processor. (Prodigy has promised to add this capability, for a fee, sometime in 1993).

The ability to send and receive messages is especially important for sales reps and other business people who are frequently on the road. Unless you have a fax modem attached to your portable computer, you'll need to subscribe to at least one service like CompuServe that gives you the freedom to touch base with your home office and send e-mail and faxes to colleagues and customers. Otherwise, you may find yourself standing in line at the hotel fax machine.

Doing Business Online

If all this sounds a bit futuristic, it's not.

Below are some real-life examples of how business people like you are using online services to make their companies more profitable and efficient.

THE ONLINE DETECTIVE

Nate Lenow, a private investigator in Memphis, is no ordinary gumshoe. A seasoned veteran of CompuServe and other online services, Lenow makes his living, in part, by scouring online databases for business information and reselling it to corporate clients in search of a marketing edge.

Tapping into online databases, Lenow says, reduces the time he needs to spend in libraries or government offices and helps him expand his client base.

"Being online, I can handle cases all over the country without having to be there," Lenow says. "I don't use [online services] in every case, but it is another tool I can use in an investigation."

Lenow also uses online services to help him market his business. He's picked up a number of clients, he says, through his high-profile position as manager of CompuServe's Private Investigator's Forum.

THE MAIL-ORDER RETAILER

Jeff Freeman of Front Porch Computers in Chatsworth, Georgia, says his fledgling business never could have taken off the way it has without the help of online networking and advertising. Started as a home business in May 1991, Front Porch expected to rake in gross revenues of more than $500,000 for 1992 and sell its homemade IBM clones to customers as far away as Europe and South America. Freeman, who says he has met many through CompuServe's Working from Home forum, spends less than $200 a month on an ad in the CompuServe classifieds and reaches more than 1 million people worldwide. It's hard to top that kind of return on investment.

Take away his online connections, Freeman says, and his booming business would be "nowhere." Chatsworth, population 5000, is 100 miles north of Atlanta, he explains, and his computer store is the first and only one the town has ever had—and is ever likely to. "With a store in a town like this, you may sell one computer at a time, but on CompuServe you may meet somebody who wants to buy multiple computers for his business. Our store is a small thing here, but with CompuServe I can reach the world."

THE INTERNATIONAL TRADER

Ed Shore, a former US Commerce Department official who lives in Columbia, Maryland, used online databases to start a home-based business called the Trade Data Exchange. Every day, Shore uses his computer to retrieve dozens of online trade leads—items such as a request by a foreign government for bids on supplying machine parts—from his old department's Economic Bulletin Board. Then he loads them into a simpler menu-driven system that allows his subscribers in the international trade community to search for topics with simple query words such as "apparel," "footwear," or "computers."

That's far more efficient, Shore says, than trudging off to the local library or one of the Commerce Department's district offices and sifting through trade data contained in weighty tomes or on CD-ROM diskettes. And, although Shore's customers could log onto the government's electronic bulletin board directly if they wished, they'd have to wade through a maze of arcane terms and, in the case of trade leads, retrieve the entire file, print it out or store it on their hard disk, and sort through it manually.

THE INFORMATION BROKER

Similar to people who deal in stocks, real estate, and other valuable items in the off-line world, Susan Rugge of Oakland makes her living as an information broker. Charging fees as high as $125 an hour, Rugge and her international network of "searchers" sift through thousands of online databases to help corporate clients find the latest information on everything from semiconductors to BMWs. One recent project involved helping a patent lawyer locate evidence of prior art to challenge a competing patent; another search helped the American Heart Association survey the use of corporate wellness programs.

Rugge says that, because online databases can be time-consuming and expensive to search, businesses and professionals are often willing to hire trained searchers rather than try to hunt down the information themselves. As a result, the number of US information brokers has soared from fewer than 300 in 1984 to over 900 now. Rugge, one of the pioneers of the information brokerage business, says she expects to rack up sales of roughly $500,000 for 1992.

THE ONLINE INVESTORS

Then there are the folks who started the online investment club. Organized in August 1991, the Pioneer Online Investment Club is one of the first investment clubs in the United States to conduct business online, meeting not in someone's living room but in CompuServe's NAIC Forum. While the Pioneer Club is still in its infancy, it's off to a good start. The club has already invested in such stocks as McDonald's, and its 25 or so members range from recent college graduates to retirees and include a Washington lobbyist, a volunteer firefighter from Nashville, an English professor who teaches in Japan, and an engineer from Seattle.

"With most clubs, you meet on the third Thursday," says club member Sammye Baker, who runs a lighting manufacturing company in Indianapolis with her husband. "This one meets all the time."

And the list goes on. As computers and modems continue to proliferate, it's possible that the day will come when online networking, marketing, investing, conferencing, and messaging will become as common as attending staff meetings, business lunches, trade shows, and office parties. In the future, "What's your fax number?" may well give way to "What's your sign-on?"

For now, online communications and information-gathering offers a unique opportunity to extend your circle of contacts to an ever-expanding universe of computer-literate colleagues and find a customer, colleague, or contact with common interests, problems, or goals. From a venture capitalist to a new sales manager, there's probably someone in front of a computer somewhere waiting to link up with you.

Summary

In this chapter, you learned what an online service is, what it offers, and why it's worth signing up for. You also learned how to get the biggest bang from your buck by "knowing before you go" and met some savvy business people who are using online services to make their companies and investments more productive and profitable.

In the next chapter, you'll learn how to set up your modem and communications software to go online.

CHAPTER 2

Separating the Bauds from the Bits

In the previous chapter, you got your first glimpse of the wide world of online services—what's out there, why it's worth getting, and how to get the biggest bang for your buck without busting your budget. You also met some successful users of online services—the online detective, the mail-order retailer, the international trade bulletin board operator, the information broker, and the online investors.

In this chapter, you'll learn about the tools you need to get started. Because most online services and the databases they offer reside in giant mainframe computers far away from your home or place of business, you'll need a way to connect with them.

Generally speaking, this requires four things:

- A personal computer
- A phone line
- A modem
- A communications program

If you're like most business people these days, you probably already have the first two. If you haven't bought a computer yet, don't worry. Even the most basic IBM-compatible, Apple or Tandy models will do just fine when it comes to accessing online services. There's no need to rush out and buy a brand-new 80486 machine. And just about anything will do for phone lines, too—even if the phone service you have is old-fashioned pulse, rather than touch-tone, dialing.

Two things you'll probably need to buy—that is, if they didn't come with your computer when you bought it—are a modem and a communications program that, together, let your computer "talk" to the giant host computer on the other end.

If you're not sure what a modem is, think of it as a foreign-language translator, converting the digital 0's and 1's produced by your computer into analog sound waves capable of winging their way across conventional phone lines. They're called "modems" because, in the world of electronics, computer-to-telephone translation is called *modulation* and telephone-to-computer translation is called *demodulation*.

Setting Up Your Modem

Hooking up a modem can be as simple as plugging in a toaster. Simply insert one end of an ordinary modular phone cord into the back of the modem and plug the other end into your phone's wall jack. Then, for an external modem, connect the cable from the modem to your serial port. Understand, though, that when your computer is "talking" to an online service, your phone line will ring busy—just as if you were making an ordinary phone call. That's why, if you plan to use online services on a regular basis or during business hours, it may be worth your while to install a second line.

How does a modem work? Explaining that would take a while, but, fortunately, it's not something you'll need to know to go online—after all, you don't have to be an auto mechanic to drive a car. In fact, there are only three things you need to know about modems to go online: 1) whether you want an internal or an external modem; 2) whether the modem you're buying is Hayes-compatible; and 3) how fast you want your modem to send and receive data.

INTERNAL VERSUS EXTERNAL MODEMS

Internal and external modems both do the same thing, though there are pros and cons to each. An internal modem, soldered to a card inside your computer's chassis, usually costs less—these days, you can pick up a reliable modem for about $50 at your local computer superstore—and won't clutter up your desk. (If you have, or plan to add, various peripheral devices such as a sound board, extra memory, and so on, you should be aware than an internal modem does occupy one of the expansion slots inside your computer.) Unless you're comfortable rooting around under the hood of your PC, though, you'll probably want the people at the computer store to install it for you.

An external modem, which comes in its own case and plugs into the serial port at the back of your computer, tends to cost a little more and definitely hogs more desk space. On the other hand, external modems feature lights and other visual aids that tell you what the modem is doing and can easily be moved from PC to PC—a cost-saving feature if you like to take a portable PC on the road. In addition to the modem you plug into your desktop computer at work, you may also want to buy a smaller "pocket modem" for your laptop or notebook computer.

Figures 2.1 and 2.2, which illustrate two modems currently available from Practical Peripherals, show you how internal and external modems typically look. Both operate at the same speed and offer fax capability.

FIGURE 2.1:

An internal modem, the PM2400EFX from Practical Peripherals

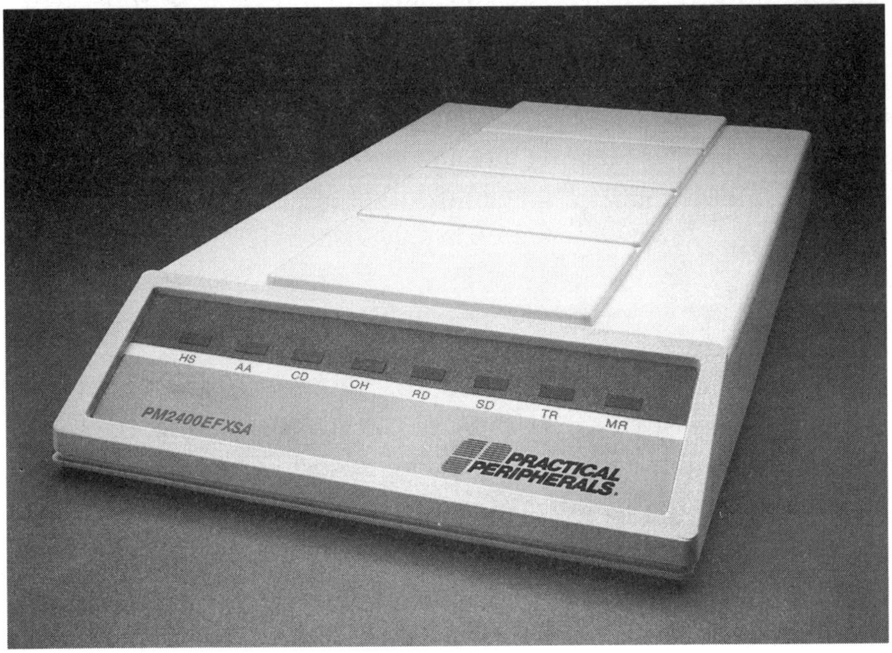

FIGURE 2.2: An external modem, the PM2400EFXSA from Practical Peripherals

HAYES COMPATIBILITY

Fortunately for first-time modem buyers, the question of Hayes-compatibility isn't really an issue any more. These days, it's hard to buy a modem that *isn't* compatible with modems made by Hayes Micro-computer Products, which long ago developed a common language, or "command set," for personal computer communications devices. A "Hayes-compatible" modem is one that uses this command set. There's a powerful reason to buy a Hayes-compatible modem: If you don't, there's a good chance that the communications software you buy to operate it won't work.

But don't feel obliged to buy a modem manufactured by Hayes—just like IBM PC's, Hayes modems cost more than the "clones" and, for a beginner's purposes, may not have any real advantages.

A note of warning: Just because a modem is Hayes-compatible (or claims that it is) doesn't mean that you'll be able to log onto any online service or bulletin board without a hitch. High-speed modems that contain error correction and data compression features may require some fine-tuning—often the insertion of a new "modem initialization string," or series of command codes, into your communications software—before you can make the connection. If you're a beginner, it's a good idea to ask for help from the company that sold you the modem or from the online service you're trying to reach.

MODEM SPEED

Probably the most important thing to think about when buying a modem is how fast you want it to go. Generally speaking, the faster the modem you buy, the more it's going to cost you—not unlike the difference between pinching pennies by buying a clunky but dependable Volkswagen and splurging on a sexy Lamborghini. And, because online services typically charge by the minute (though some charge more for faster modems), your best bet is to buy the speediest modem you can afford.

These days, most personal computer users have 2400 bps modems, devices that are capable of sending and receiving data at speeds of 2400 bits, or characters, per second. Just a few years ago, the standard speed was 1200 bps, and now many people are upgrading to the 9600 bps and 14,400 bps levels. If all this sounds Greek to you, think of it this way: To send a 40 kilobyte file to another computer at 300 bits per second would take about 23 minutes. The same file would take just six minutes to send with a 1200 bps modem and less than three minutes with a 2400 bps modem. A 9600 bps modem would speed that file along in an incredible 42 seconds—freeing your phone line and slashing your online services bills dramatically.

So choosing a modem really comes down to a tradeoff between what you pay up front and how much you save in the long run. For an internal 2400 bps modem, you can expect to pay about $50 at your local computer superstore. A fax modem, which lets you send and receive faxes with your computer at 9600 bps in addition to logging you onto an online service at speeds of up to 2400 bps, can be had for under $100 now, too. Unfortunately, 9600 bps and 14,400 bps modems are still expensive—though they are coming down in price—retailing even at a discount stores for $200 to $500. (Prodigy members can buy a 9600 bps modem for $199.95.)

A word of caution: Despite the conventional wisdom that you should buy the most technology you can afford, it may be wise to hold off buying a 14,400 bps modem—at least for now. No online service currently lets you zoom full-throttle at this speed, and there are also a number of technical adjustments you may need to make to get your super-fast modem to log on even at slower speeds. If you're a beginner, a 9600 bps modem is probably your best bet for now—even though you'll have to pay $2 a month extra to use it on Prodigy and more than $22 an hour to use it on CompuServe.

On the other hand, if you want to save a little money up front and don't mind sacrificing some speed, there are still a few 1200 bps and 300 bps modems available. But beware: With a service like Prodigy, which contains graphics files that typically take longer to transmit than plain text files, operating at speeds this slow can be a painful experience for all but the most patient of users.

Communications Software

To operate a modem, you'll need communications software—the kind of program that lets you dial up the online service and send and receive electronic information. At a minimum, the communications software you buy should include two basic features that virtually all of the leading programs have: 1) an automated dialing directory (similar to the speed dial on your telephone), and 2) an easy way to send and receive files (known in the online world as *uploading* and *downloading*).

These days, there's a dizzying array of communications software available. You can buy a front-end software program specially designed to log you onto a particular online service, or a multipurpose program capable of dialing up many services. You can buy an off-the-shelf program at your local computer store, or you can download "shareware" (the kind of program that lets you try before you buy) when you go online. And, finally, you can buy a text-based program that sends the data to your computer in ordinary letters and numbers, or you can use a program that takes full advantage of Microsoft's graphical Windows environment.

Your first choice is between multipurpose and single-purpose software.

MULTIPURPOSE VERSUS FRONT-END SOFTWARE

All communications software is designed to do two things: (1) dial a phone number; and (2) establish communication with the computer at the other end of the line. The second task consists of passing along various communication codes, or settings, which will be discussed later in this chapter. Multipurpose programs handle these operations for many online services but can be tricky for beginners to use; "front-end" programs designed for a single online service tend to be much easier. For example, while a multipurpose program requires you to enter detailed information about each service you want to communicate with, a front-end program would already have that information programmed in.

So is it simply a choice between flexibility and ease of use? Not entirely; there are a number of pros and cons to consider:

1. **Cost:** Both multipurpose and front-end software programs cost money, but front-end programs typically cost less—after all, the idea isn't to make money off the software but to get you to use the service. Procomm Plus 2.0, for example, retails for about $70 at computer superstores, while Prodigy and CompuServe start-up kits sell for less than half that price. Therefore, if you're only planning to use one online service and have no other need for communications software, it's probably a good idea to buy a front-end program and forget about mastering Procomm.

If, on the other hand, you're thinking of signing up for more than one online service, it's wise to opt for a multipurpose program that lets you dial up as many services as you like. A word of caution: Some services, such as Prodigy and America Online, can only be accessed through front-end programs. In other words, you can't get to Prodigy from Procomm.

Before you plunk down your money for a multipurpose program, check to see whether your computer already has a communications program. Some computers come prepackaged with a shareware version of Procomm (mine did), and both Windows 3.0 and 3.1 feature an accessory program called Terminal that's easy to program and perfectly capable of dialing online services and sending and receiving files. In Chapter 3 you'll see how to log onto a service using Terminal.

2. **Time:** Just as important as saving money is saving time. Because multipurpose programs can connect with online services in "TTY mode" (a blank screen that simulates what you'd see on a giant mainframe), an experienced user can zip through the service without waiting for pull-down boxes, instructions, or other graphics to appear on your screen. Until you've developed some online expertise, however, it may be faster to let the service prompt you where to go rather than trying to figure out the exact command syntax to use. In the long run, though, taking the direct route saves time, and on a "pay-as-you-go" plan, it saves money, too.

   On the other hand, if you're just getting used to navigating online, front-end software can save you time by making executing commands as simple as clicking a mouse. To log on and check your mail on CompuServe Information Manager, for example, simply select Mail and then Get New Mail button, and a box will open with a list of messages that you can read simply by clicking the Get button. From there, you can click other boxes that let you reply, file the message away or delete it. To do the same thing using multipurpose software, you'd have to choose the correct commands from a series of online menus.

3. **Disk Space:** Unless you've got plenty of space left on your hard disk (and if you're a Windows user like I am, you probably don't), installing a front-end program may only add to the space crunch. Both Prodigy and CompuServe Information Manager take up slightly over 1 megabyte of hard disk storage space (the Windows version of CIM takes about 2 megabytes). Not only does this leave less room for your other software, it can also slow down the speed at which your computer accesses programs and files. Multipurpose programs, by contrast, generally take up far less space. The shareware version of Procomm, for example, takes up only 245,000 bytes of storage. Remember: Each front-end program you install means less space for anything else you want to do.

4. **Ease of Use:** Until you've mastered the various commands that get you around the online service of your choice, it's hard to argue with the fact that using a front-end program makes your online life much easier. But, as you progress, you may find yourself growing impatient and longing to take the direct route to the parts of the service you need and use the most. By then, you may not mind sacrificing some ease of use for a little more cost-efficiency.

   In Chapter 3 you'll get a good idea of how significant the ease-of-use issue is for you, as we try logging on first with a multipurpose program and then with a front-end program.

OFF-THE-SHELF PROGRAMS VERSUS SHAREWARE

If you decide to buy a front-end program for a single online service, such as CompuServe or Prodigy, you simply call the service and order it directly or pick up the program at your local computer store. But if you want multipurpose software, you have a more difficult choice to make.

Popular off-the-shelf multipurpose programs include the latest versions of Procomm Plus, Crosstalk, Smartcom and Carbon Copy. Expect to pay about $100 at a computer superstore or mail-order house.

But you don't have to pay big dollars to get a reliable communications program. For a lot less, you can pick up a "shareware" program that does the trick just as well. The drawback to shareware programs is that they don't always come with a manual, and they don't always come with all the bells and whistles off-the-shelf programs do. Procomm version 2.4.3, for example, lacks many of the features that come with Procomm Plus version 2.01, such as an enhanced dialing directory, full mouse support and context-sensitive help. With shareware, if you like the program, you're honor-bound to send in a contribution to the program's author; if you don't like it, you simply delete it from your computer's hard drive. Procomm's shareware program, which is perfectly serviceable once you get the hang of it, costs $50 to $89.

Shareware is not usually sold in stores, and you often need a modem and communications software to download it. If you're an online novice, your best bet may be to contact your local computer user group.

Built-In Programs—A Third Choice

As noted earlier, you may not need to buy a multipurpose communications program at all. Such programs are also included in inexpensive integrated software packages such as Microsoft Works and Microsoft Windows. See Chapter 3 for details on using the Terminal program in Windows 3.1.

LOGGING ON THROUGH WINDOWS

Until now, front-end programs such as those offered by Prodigy, CompuServe and America Online have gone about making their services easier to use by featuring Windows-like pull-down menus and dialog boxes. But there were limits to how friendly the programs could be under DOS.

These days, there's another option—logging on through Microsoft Windows. Generally, these Windows programs come in two varieties: (1) Text-based software such as Windows' built-in Terminal program, which lets the host computer at the other end send letters and numbers to your screen just like Procomm Plus, and (2) Graphical programs such as WinCIM 1.0 (see below) which let you shortcut complex menus and commands by clicking pictorial icons. Both types of programs allow you to copy online information to the Windows Clipboard for insertion into other Windows applications.

WinCIM—A Window into CompuServe

As this book goes to print, CompuServe has just unveiled a Windows version of CompuServe Information Manager—WinCIM 1.0. America Online has also released a Windows version, and Prodigy and Dow Jones News/Retrieval are expected to do so later this year.

"The growing popularity of Windows has produced a strong demand for a Windows-CompuServe interface," said Barry F. Berkov, executive vice president of CompuServe's Information Services Division. "While the functionality in WinCIM is based on that of the CompuServe Information Manager for DOS Version 2.0, WinCIM is a true Windows application and contains a number of unique features."

Structurally, WinCIM and CIM for DOS bear a strong family resemblance. Both offer an introductory menu that lets you select from a variety of popular topics, including Computers, News, Forums, Investments, Shopping and Games. Both also offer a number of automated features that make using the system easier: a Sessions

Settings box that stores your ID and password so you won't have to type it in every time you log on, a Favorite Places list that takes you to your favorite forum or database with the click of a mouse, an off-line text editor that lets you create messages to be sent later, and a Mail command that retrieves your mail, ships off any messages you've typed up off-line and logs you off once the job is done. In addition, both programs offer an Address Book, In-Basket, Out-Basket and Filing Cabinet and other "desktop" features.

WinCIM takes the basic elements of CIM for DOS and transforms them into the kind of program that millions of Windows users have come to know and love. The most obvious difference is the presence of icons capable of issuing online commands. Though WinCIM has many of the same pull-down menus available in the DOS and Mac versions, it also features a button bar across the top of the screen containing icons that let you access Favorite Places, the GO command, Weather, Quotes, Filing Cabinet and other popular destinations with the click of a mouse. You can also click icons to disconnect from the service and exit the program. WinCIM also features a "toolbox"—a floating palette of icons—that lets you perform common functions in CompuServe's forums, Executive News Service and CB Simulator. Click the picture of a hand holding a pen, for example, and a template appears that lets you create a forum message.

And that's not all. Even more so than CIM for DOS, WinCIM lets you customize your access to the service with multiple sessions-settings and allows you to perform numerous functions off-line, saving you time and money. While online in a forum, for example, you can mark forum messages for retrieval to the Filing Cabinet to be read off-line at your leisure or select forum library files to be downloaded to your hard drive. And, as with your e-mail, WinCIM can be set to automatically disconnect when the forum message-retrieval and/or file-download has been completed. WinCIM also includes a context-sensitive Help feature that can be accessed from any part of the service plus a searchable off-line version of the CompuServe Directory, which provides a brief description of each of the more than 1700 services on CompuServe. Figure 2.3 illustrates the

WinCIM Services menu; Figure 2.4 shows the equivalent menu in DOS CIM.

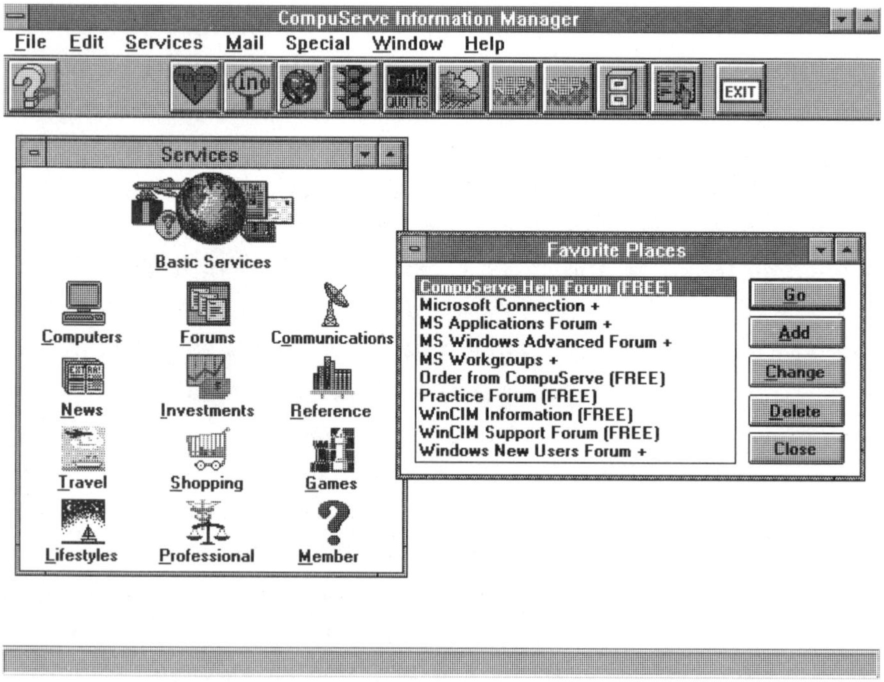

FIGURE 2.3:

The Services menu in WinCIM

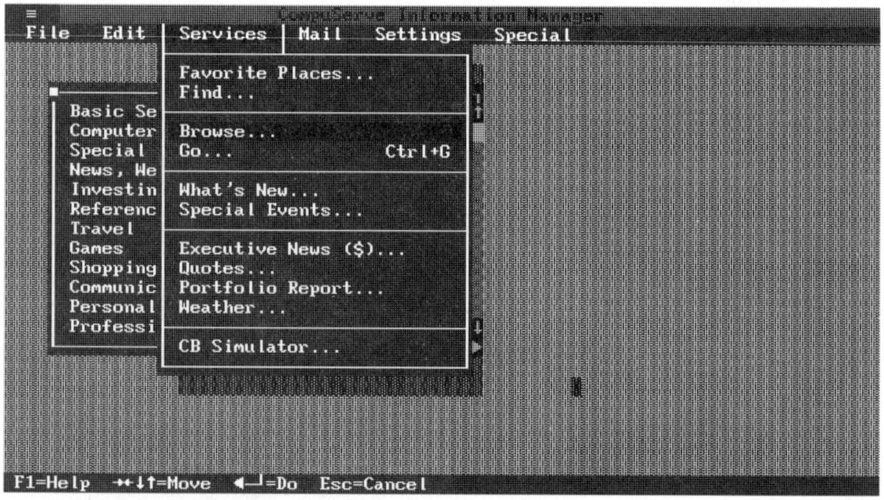

FIGURE 2.4:

The Services menu in DOS CIM

WinCIM also makes excellent use of the Windows environment. Two special features on the Edit pull-down menu, Copy To and Paste From, let you compose mail and forum messages using text from on-line articles, messages in your In-Basket or Filing Cabinet, and text files on your hard drive. WinCIM also takes advantage of Windows' multitasking abilities; you can minimize WinCIM while retrieving a long file, freeing your computer to work on other applications. WinCIM also features a built-in decoder for the Graphics Interchange Format (GIF), the CompuServe-developed standard for exchanging online images. Members can view GIF images online or off and copy images to the Windows clipboard for importation to a graphics program.

And, best of all, WinCIM is practically free. As this book was going to press, CompuServe was offering a WinCIM prerelease kit to its members for $15.00 (plus $4.00 shipping and handling) with a $15.00 usage credit applied to your CompuServe account once the kit has been shipped. The program's first production version, WinCIM 1.0, was released in February, 1993.

Does WinCIM have its drawbacks? Of course. For one, even CompuServe admits that there are still some programming bugs to work out. And users of CIM for DOS will be disappointed to learn that they'll have to upgrade to DOS CIM 2.1 before they can use a special command permitting shared access to their CompuServe Address Book, In-Basket, Out-Basket, Filing Cabinet, and other desktop features. Also, like any Windows program, WinCIM is much bigger than its DOS counterpart—in this case, more than twice the size (2.3 megabytes versus about 1 megabyte). And, finally, unless you have a fairly powerful computer with lots of memory, CompuServe may run more slowly in Windows than it does in DOS.

My advice to Windows users who already have CIM for DOS: Don't delete DOS CIM from your hard drive just yet, but go ahead and give WinCIM a try. You may never have to click that DOS prompt icon again.

Setting Up Your Communications Software

Now that you've assembled the necessary equipment, the next step is to set up your communications software so that it will dial the online service you want to reach. Once you get the hang of it, it's really no tougher than programming the speed dial on your office telephone and a whole lot easier than programming your VCR. And, once you've set up your software to do what you want it to, there's no need to reprogram it ever again—unless you want to dial another online service, that is.

Learning the Lingo

Mastering a few words of modem lingo can spare you hours of frustration—just as it makes sense to learn the French phrase for, "Could you point me in the direction of the train station?" before setting off for France. Knowing a bit of lingo really comes in handy when trying to get help from your software company's technical support gurus—many of whom speak Techie, not English, as a native language.

Though the various communications programs are all a little different, most feature some kind of on-screen autodial directory that lets you to type in certain vital statistics about the online service you want to call. The most important of these are the service's phone number, bps rate, parity, number of data bits and the presence or absence of a stop bit. The dialing directory may also ask you to select either "full duplex" or "half duplex" mode and turn the "local echo" on or off.

The communications software asks for this information not to bore or confuse you but to let you set it up to match the settings used by the computer that houses the online service you're trying to call. It's just like traveling overseas: If you and the cab driver can't find a common language with which to communicate, you won't be able to get where you want to go.

As you've just learned, the *bps rate* is the speed, measured in bits per second, at which your modem receives and transmits data. The *parity bit* checks for errors in data transmission, the *data bits* represent blocks of data or characters, and the *stop bit* is there to tell the online service's computer that you have completed your transmission of a particular data block. *Full duplex mode* allows data to flow in two directions at once, while *half duplex mode* allows information to flow in one direction only. Switching *local echo* to the "on" setting displays characters on your screen as they are being sent or received; switching it to "off" hides those characters.

You may also have heard about something called the *baud rate*. *Baud* and *bps* are often used interchangeably to describe the speed of a modem, but, actually, they're two slightly different animals. That's because the bps rate refers to the number of bits that can be transferred in one second. (An ASCII text character is a block of seven bits; a binary number, a block of eight bits.) The baud rate refers to the number of signal changes that occur in one second. Sometimes, more than one bit is sent in each signal change.

If all this sounds technical and confusing, it is. So don't sweat it. The truth is that you don't really need to know a baud from a bit to get your modem up and running, anyway. That's because the manual that comes with the online service you've signed up for will probably tell you how to set up your software to dial in, and many services that sell their own software already have the correct settings preprogrammed. And if, for whatever reason, the online service you're trying to dial doesn't specify which settings to use, give one of these a try: 2400 bps, even parity, seven data bits and one stop bit, or 2400 bps, no parity, eight data bits and one stop bit.

(Even if you program your settings incorrectly, you may still be able to connect to the online service. However, instead of a request for your user identification number, you may end up with "garbage"—line after line of unrecognizable characters swimming across your screen.)

Making Contact

Now that you know the lingo, let's try dialing up an online service using a multipurpose communications program. For the sake of example, I've chosen two mainstays of the old-line world—CompuServe and Procomm Plus 2.01 for DOS. While you may have different software or be logging on to a different online service, the following example is designed to give you a general idea of what to do.

1. Install Procomm Plus on your hard drive, following the instructions in the Procomm Plus manual. At the C:> prompt, type **cd\pcplus**. Then press ↵ and type **pcplus** again. Press ↵ and wait for the screen with the Procomm Plus logo to appear.

2. Press any key to exit the Procomm Plus screen and enter terminal mode. Next you'll see a screen that says *Procomm Plus Ready!*

3. Press Alt-D to pop up the autodial directory on your screen.

4. Type **R** to revise Entry No. 1. A pop-up box will appear in the middle of your screen to allow you to change the settings.

5. At the *Name:* prompt, type **CompuServe**. Then press ↵.

6. At the *Number:* prompt, type the CompuServe local access number for your area. Then press ↵. (To get your local access phone number, look in the membership booklet that CompuServe provides. If it's not listed there, call CompuServe at 1-800-63LOCAL.)

7. Continue down the list of prompts, filling in the appropriate settings for CompuServe. The correct settings are even parity, seven data bits and one stop bit. If you already have a mouse or other peripheral device plugged into serial port 1 (COM1) in the back of your computer, be sure to change the Procomm Plus setting to COM2 (communications port 2) so you'll be able to dial out.

8. When you are finished programming the settings, another box will appear asking if you want to *clear last date and total?* Press **N** for no. Then press **Y** (yes) to accept the entry, and press **Y** again to save the entry to your hard disk.

Figure 2.5 shows what the dialing directory will look like when you're finished.

To connect with CompuServe, simply highlight Entry No. 1 and press ↵. Your modem will then dial CompuServe. Once the connection has been made, you'll hear a high-pitched screech and see a message that reads *Connect 2400*. Press ↵ twice to "wake up" the CompuServe system. You'll then be prompted to type in the name of your host computer.

Now you're ready to go online, which will be explained in detail in Chapter 3. For now, however, press Alt-H to hang up your modem and Alt-X to exit Procomm Plus and return to the DOS prompt.

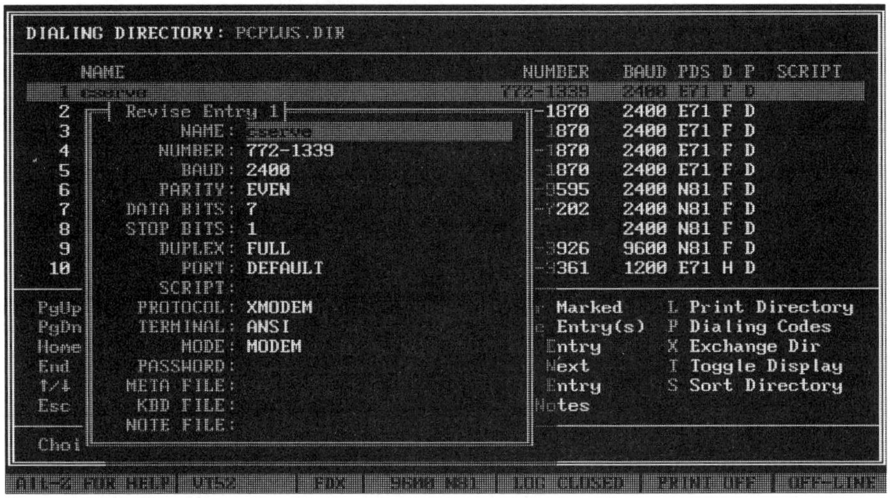

FIGURE 2.5:

The Procomm Plus dialing directory

TROUBLESHOOTING YOUR MODEM AND SOFTWARE

Sometimes when you dial up an online service, you'll get a message that says *No Carrier* or *Busy*. If you try and try and still can't connect to the online service, it probably means one of three things: 1) The online service's phone lines are temporarily busy; 2) your phone cord is unplugged from the wall, your modem, or both; or 3) your communications software is set for a communications port (the same as a serial port) that's being blocked by a mouse, optical scanner, or other device you've installed.

Before you pick up the phone and call technical support (and fumble your way through those bauds and bits you just learned about), try a few of these home remedies: 1) Wait a few minutes, then redial your modem; 2) check to see if the phone plug is connected, then plug it in if it's not; and 3) change the software's communications settings to a serial port that is not blocked by a peripheral device —for example, to COM2 instead of COM1.

Once you get the hang of it, online communications will save you time, not waste it. And, if you don't let the jargon scare you away, you'll soon be as comfortable using your modem as you are faxing out for sandwiches from the local deli.

Summary

In this chapter, you learned the basics of setting up your modem and communications software, and you looked at the pros and cons of various types of software. You also learned how to shop for the communications tools that best fit your needs and how to cut through "modem lingo" to program the settings in your autodial directory. And you learned, step-by-step, how to dial up CompuServe using Procomm Plus, a multipurpose communications program.

In the next chapter, you'll learn how to log onto an online service, how to change your password and how to pick the most cost-effective service option for your business.

CHAPTER 3

Getting Started

In Chapter 2, you learned about the tools you need to go online—a computer, a modem, communications software, and an available phone line. You also acquired the basic skills you need to program your autodial directory to connect with the online service of your choice.

Now you have everything you need to proceed to the next step—logging on.

In this chapter, you'll learn how to put your key in the ignition and get your online vehicle out of "park" and onto the road. You'll also learn how to enter your password and user ID code—and how to stop someone else from swiping them.

Finally, you'll learn about the various service options offered online—how much it costs to sign up for a basic service plan, an off-peak plan, and a customized plan—and how to choose the right one for you.

Logging On

No matter which online service you choose, you're going to have to log on before the service will allow you access to its many products and services. Logging on typically involves dialing up the service and typing in your correct user identification number and password. The reason for this is simple: Since the account is in your name, the online service doesn't want anyone logging on as you and not sticking around to pay the bills—and you shouldn't, either. In fact, many online services even suggest that you change your password every couple of months just to prevent someone else from accessing your account.

Fortunately for beginners, most online services make logging on a snap. Assuming that you found out about an online service through an article or an ad in a magazine, simply pick up the phone and dial the toll-free number listed. (To reach Prodigy, call 1-800-284-5933; for CompuServe, call 1-800-848-8199.) In a couple of weeks, your start-up kit will arrive in the mail along with your user ID, password, user manual, and any software you need to access the service. Some services, such as Prodigy and America Online, require special software in order to tap into them. Others, such as CompuServe, GEnie and Dow Jones/News Retrieval, can be accessed using any communications software package.

LOGGING ON WITH A MULTIPURPOSE PROGRAM

For starters, let's look at logging onto an online service that does not require any special software. Here's how to log on to CompuServe using Procomm Plus:

1. Log onto CompuServe the way you learned in Chapter 2. Once the connection has been made, you'll be prompted to type in the name of your host computer. Type **CIS** (for CompuServe Information Service).
2. Next, you'll be asked for your user ID. Type in the temporary ID that appears in the CompuServe Introductory Membership manual that you received in the mail. This number will be 177000 followed by a comma, followed by two, three, or four more digits. Then press ↵. At this point your screen should look something like Figure 3.1.

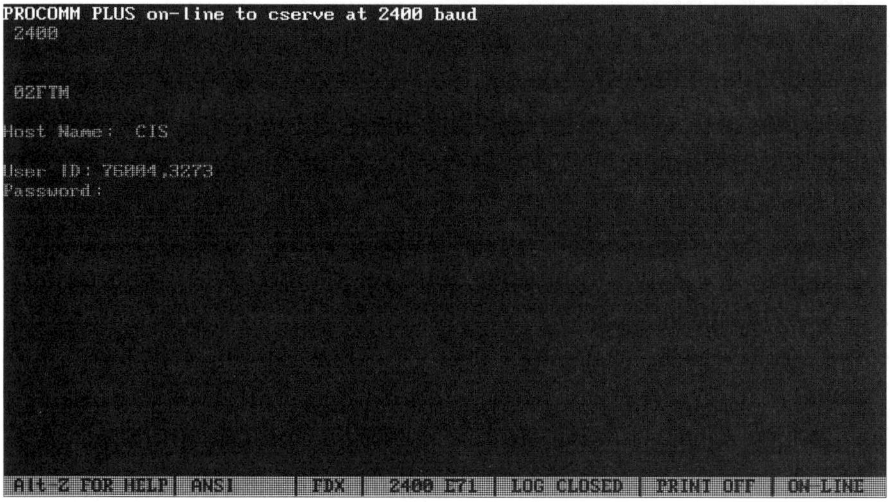

FIGURE 3.1: Using Procomm Plus to log onto CompuServe

3. Next, type in your temporary password (also included in your start-up kit) and press ↵. (You'll get your permanent password by mail in about 10 days.) You'll then be prompted to enter the agreement and serial numbers that appear in your startup kit.

4. After a few seconds, you'll start seeing screenfuls of information explaining CompuServe's rules and regulations and how to sign up and pay for the service. You won't be charged during this initial session.

5. To log off or end your online session, simply type the word **off** at the nearest prompt and wait for the service to disconnect. You'll see a message that says something like, *Thank you for using CompuServe! Off at 15:11 EDT 10-Sep-93 Connect time = 0:15.*

6. Then press Alt-H to hang up.

A Multipurpose Alternative—Logging On with Terminal

If you have Windows 3.0 or 3.1, you can log onto any online service using the Terminal accessory program.

Here's how to log onto CompuServe using Terminal:

1. Double-click on the Terminal icon in the Accessories window of Windows' Program Manager.

2. Once the Terminal window appears on your screen, click File and then New to begin programming the settings for CompuServe.

3. Click Settings, then choose Phone Number from the pull-down menu to type in CompuServe's local access number. Click OK.

4. Click Communications from the Settings menu to enter the correct bps rate, data bits, stop bits, flow control and

communications port settings in the Communications dialog box that appears. (The settings for CompuServe are 7 data bits, even parity, and one stop bit.) Once you are finished, click OK.

5. To save the settings for another session, click Save from the File menu. Then type CompuServe in the dialog box that appears on your screen and press OK.

6. To log onto CompuServe, click Dial from the Phone menu. Terminal will call the CompuServe host computer. Once the connection is made, press Return twice and you will be prompted for the host name (enter **CIS**), your user ID, and your password.

7. When you want to log off the service, click Hangup from the Phone menu. To close the Terminal window and exit the program, press Alt-F4 or click Exit from the File menu.

LOGGING ON WITH A FRONT-END PROGRAM

For novice users, one of the most daunting aspects of going online is the fear of getting lost in a maze of unfamiliar menus and commands—and wasting time and money in the process. That's why, as you saw in the last chapter, several major online services—Prodigy, CompuServe, and America Online—have created front-end programs that let you work with pull-down menus, dialog boxes, and often toolbar icons.

CompuServe's front-end program is CompuServe Information Manager (CIM), available for DOS, Macintosh, and Windows. This program makes it much easier to maneuver your way around the service, and for that reason the Windows version is used in the examples of CompuServe procedures throughout this book.

Here's how to install WinCIM and log onto CompuServe:

1. Turn on your computer and start Windows. If you haven't already installed WinCIM, insert the WinCIM disk marked Diskette 1 in your diskette drive (if WinCIM is already installed, skip ahead to step 5). Click Run from the Program Manager screen that appears and type **a:setup**. Click OK. Follow the on-screen instructions to install WinCIM on your hard drive.

2. During the "sign-up" portion of the installation, you'll read about CompuServe's rules and regulations and be prompted for information about your payment preference (credit card, electronic transfer, or corporate billing). You will also be asked to provide your agreement and serial numbers as well as personal information such as your name, address, and phone number. (Your temporary user ID and password will already be in there.) If you are already a CompuServe member, you can skip all this sign-up stuff and, once you're loaded in the program, click Special, then Session Settings to make any changes to CompuServe's standard log-on instructions.

3. WinCIM's installation program automatically programs the correct settings (7 data bits, even parity, no stop bits) for you unless you prefer to do it manually. Later, you may want to change the baud rate from 2400 bps to 9600 bps, for example, or change the communications port from COM2 to COM3. To save your settings, click OK.

4. Click Exit from the File menu to quit the sign-up program.

5. To access WinCIM, double-click the WinCIM icon on the Program Manager screen. After a few seconds, you'll see the Windows screen shown in Figure 3.2, with a row of commands across the top such as File, Edit, Services and Mail. You'll also see a toolbar of icons that let you access Favorite Places, the GO command, Weather, Quotes, Filing Cabinet

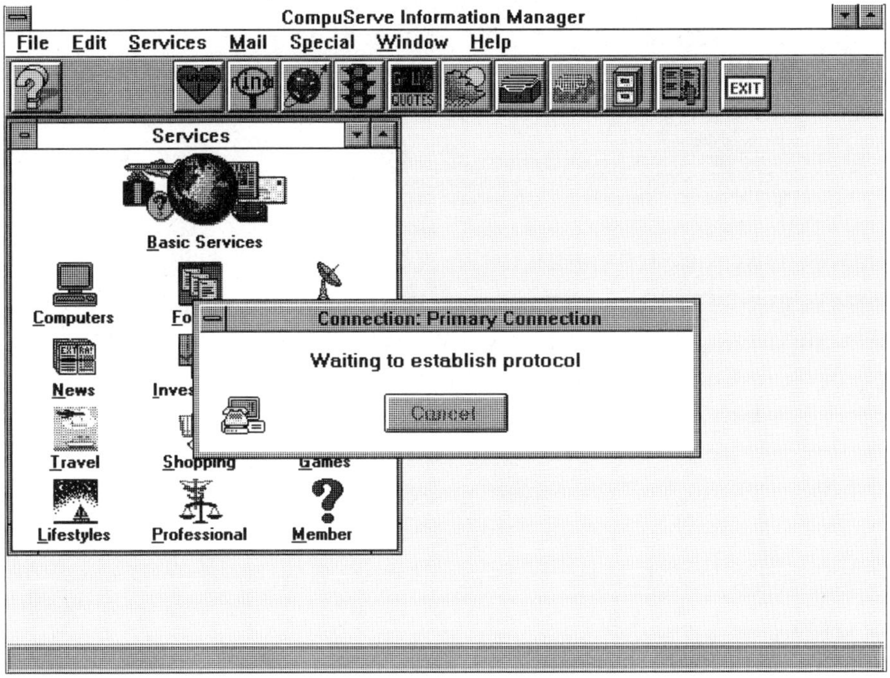

FIGURE 3.2: Logging onto CompuServe with WinCIM software

and other destinations with the click of a mouse. A large box on the left side of your screen has icons representing Basic Services, Computers, Forums, News, and Investments.

6. To log on, simply click one of the on-screen icons, such as Computers or News, or click a command from one of the pull-down boxes, such as Get New Mail. You can also log on by clicking the Go icon and typing in the keyword for the service feature you want to go to. WinCIM will automatically dial CompuServe's local access phone number and enter your user ID and password. When the connection is complete, a *Connected* message will appear in the upper-left corner of your screen.

7. To log off, or end your online session, click the Disconnect icon (a picture of two separated cables) on the toolbar at

the top of your screen. You'll see the message *Disconnecting from Network*, and, after a few seconds, your connection with CompuServe will be dropped. To exit the program, click the Exit icon, also located on the toolbar.

Protecting Your Password

Just because a certain password came with your start-up kit doesn't mean you've got to keep it forever. In fact, for security reasons, you probably shouldn't. Changing your password every few months or so reduces the chance that anyone else will be able to access your online service subscription without your knowledge or permission.

Most online services make changing your password a snap. (Remember to write your new password down, though, or else you won't be able to log back on.) Prodigy even lets you restrict which on-line bulletin boards the other members of your household can gain access to—an important feature if you work at home and have young children.

Here's how to change your password using WinCIM:

1. Log onto CompuServe. (If you change your password off-line—before logging on—you won't be able to connect to CompuServe when you load in the WinCIM software.)
2. Click the Go icon, then type **password**. You will be prompted to enter your old password and then asked to type in a new one.
3. Type your new password once more to verify it, then log off.
4. Once you've disconnected from CompuServe, click Session Settings from the Special menu and click the Password asterisk farthest to the right in the dialog box shown in Figure 3.3. Then hit the backspace key until all the asterisks disappear.

5. Type in your new password. It can contain as many as 14 letters, digits, and/or special keyboard characters.

6. Click OK to save your new Session Settings.

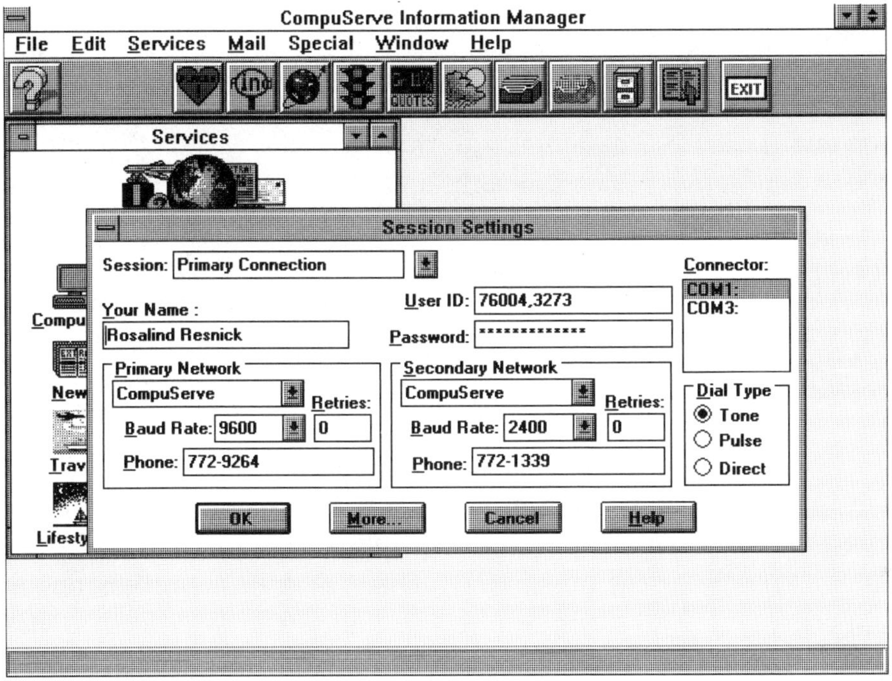

FIGURE 3.3:
Changing your password on CompuServe

Weighing the Costs

Now that you know how to log onto an online service, you're probably wondering how much all this is going to cost. As you learned in Chapter 1, how much money you end up spending will depend on three things: 1) the amount of time you spend online, 2) how quickly you need the information, and 3) the type of information you need to obtain.

Fortunately, most online services are savvy enough to realize that one size does not fit all. That's why many of them allow you to select from several service options that let you pick what you want.

Note: All prices here are current as of February 1993 and are subject to change. As noted in Chapter 1, the goal of this book is not to be a buyer's guide (plenty of computer magazines are available for that purpose), but to give you a general idea of the difference in pricing between one online option and another.

BASIC SERVICE PLANS

Basic service plans typically allow you unlimited access to general-interest databases containing information such as news, weather, sports, and movie reviews in addition to interactive services such as shopping, online travel reservations and electronic mail. Typically, online services charge a flat monthly fee for access to these basic services with additional surcharges for specialized services and databases. Some of the major online services, such as Prodigy, CompuServe, America Online, and GEnie, offer flat-fee plans that let you pay $4.95 to $14.95 a month for basic services.

Not all basic service plans are alike, however. GEnie, for example, charges only $4.95 a month for its basic services plan but charges additional fees for accessing those services during daytime hours. Prodigy, on the other hand, charges $14.95 a month but does not charge more for daytime access and allows flat-fee access to virtually all its services. (A note about Prodigy: As this book was being written, Prodigy announced plans to offer electronic mail functions such as fax, postal delivery, and off-line mail, and to charge an additional fee for access to them.)

OFF-PEAK PLANS

Some online services, primarily those that target mainly business users, offer off-peak plans that charge lower rates at night and weekends. Dialog, for instance, has a Knowledge Index service that gives you access to more than 100 Dialog databases during evenings and weekends at a reduced rate. Dow Jones News/Retrieval discounts its full selection of databases during off-peak hours.

A few services even combine off-peak plans with flat-fee packages. Dow Jones, for example, now offers three flat-fee plans for people who log on between 9:01 P.M. and 6 A.M. Eastern Time. Tier 1 ($25 a month) offers news and stock-market quotes, Tier 2 (also $25 a month) offers financial forecasts and analyses, and Tier 3 ($12.95 a month) offers an online encyclopedia, career-management advice, book reviews, and several other general interest databases. You can also purchase any combination of these plans.

CUSTOMIZED PLANS

Some online services offer customized plans for executives, investors, and people with special interests. Typically, these plans cost more than the fees charged to access the basic services.

Prodigy, for example, offers what it calls Custom Choices—in-depth databases and interactive services on topics such as investments, baseball, and even an electronic version of Sesame Street. Strategic Investor, the investment database, costs an extra $14.95 a month and offers reports on more than 4,500 individual stocks and 3,000 mutual funds plus market news, charts, and columns from *Investor's Business Daily*. CompuServe's Executive Service Option carries a minimum usage charge of $10 a month, toward which all connect-time charges and database surcharges apply. By signing up, you gain access to sophisticated financial databases such as Disclosure II (company reports), the Institutional Brokers Estimate System (earnings forecasts) and Ticker Retrieval, which helps you find all the information pertinent to a certain stock issue.

Signing up for a customized plan is easy. On Prodigy, simply choose the Jump button at the bottom of your screen and type **Custom Choices** in the box that appears. CompuServe lets you request the Executive Service Option during your initial sign-up session, though you can join any time by typing **Go Executive** at any prompt.

SURCHARGED DATABASES

Many online services offer databases that carry surcharges. These surcharges—extra fees tacked on to what you ordinarily pay for accessing the service—generally are based on three factors: 1) how much time you spend searching the database, 2) how many records, or "bibliographic citations," you request, and 3) whether you want to see the full text of an article or just a summary (full text usually costs more).

For example, CompuServe's Computer Database Plus, an online library stocked with articles from more than 200 magazines, newspapers and industry journals, charges 25 cents a minute to connect to the database plus $2.50 for each article retrieved and $1.50 for each summary. After you're through with your search, an itemized bill will flash up on your screen. Any surcharges will charged to your CompuServe account at the end of the month along with your connect-time charges.

Remember: Accessing databases like these can get expensive, so be sure to take a good look at pricing information that flashes up on your screen before you start your search. (You can also lower your costs by narrowing your search as much as possible to find only the information you're really looking for.)

MEMBERSHIP FEES

Finally, some online services charge membership fees. Dow Jones News/Retrieval, for example, charges an annual membership fee of $18—whether you log on or not. CompuServe charges a $2 per month membership support fee that comes to $24 per year. (CompuServe waives this fee if you sign up for its $8.95 per month flat-fee plan.) That's why it's wise to sign up only for those online services you actually intend to use.

Summary

In this chapter, you learned how to log onto an online service, both with multipurpose communications software and with front-end programs unique to a particular service. You also learned how to enter your password and user ID code—and how to stop someone else from swiping them. Finally, you learned about the various service plans—basic services, off-peak, customized—and how to choose the best one for your needs.

In the next chapter, you'll learn how to make your way through the online world by using menus, submenus, and short-cuts.

CHAPTER 4

Getting Around

In the previous chapter, you learned about getting started with online services—how to install communications software and log on, using both front-end and multipurpose programs. You also learned about using passwords and user IDs and weighed the various service plans available online.

In this chapter, you'll learn to navigate the services themselves, exploring the highways and byways of the online world through main menus, submenus and pathways. You'll also learn valuable online shortcuts that get you where you want to go more efficiently and discover ways to customize your service to make it work the way you want it to.

The Main Menu

The kind of menu that you see online is not so different from the kind the waiter hands you in a restaurant. Like its paper counterpart, an online menu is simply a list of choices—some with tastier descriptions than others—that lets you pick from a variety of databases and other online offerings.

On most online services, the main, or introductory, menu is easy enough to spot. Immediately after you log on, the main menu will pop up on your screen with a list of that day's selections—a special deal on fax modems, for example, or a news bulletin about the latest developments in the Middle East.

MAKING YOUR WAY AROUND PRODIGY

The main menu can take many forms. When you log onto Prodigy, for example, the menu that greets you reads *Prodigy Service Highlights* and lists about 10 items that typically include news, politics, sports, shopping, travel, and other topics of user interest. If you want to learn more about one of the items featured, simply click the number to the left of the item with your mouse or press the ↑ or ↓ key to highlight the number and press ↵.

If you want to find a topic other than one of those listed, use your mouse or keyboard to select the Jump button at the bottom of your screen and type in a topic that interests you. (You can find a list of topics by selecting Index of JumpWords in the JumpWindow that appears on your screen.)

Let's say that you'd like to find out more about what happened today in the world of business. Type **Money High** in the JumpWindow and a submenu will appear that reads *Prodigy Highlights Money*. This submenu, shown in Figure 4.1, lets you choose from a

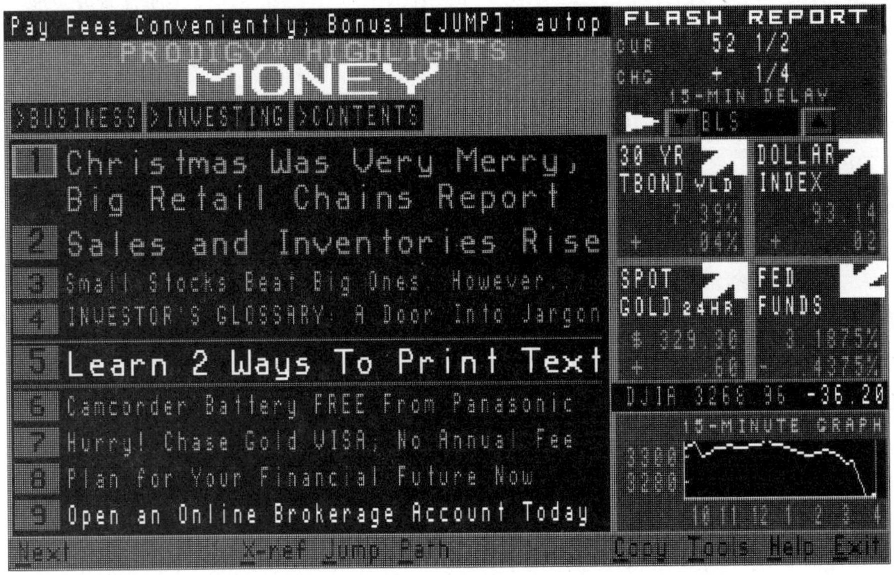

FIGURE 4.1:
Prodigy's Money Highlights menu

list of topics that pertain to business and finance. Once you find a topic that interests you, simply select the number to the left of it and click your mouse or press ↵.

If the article you've selected runs longer than a single screen, choose the Next button at the bottom of your screen to see the following page. Choose the Back button (also at the bottom of your screen) to see the previous page. To return to the Money Highlights menu, choose the Menu button. To get all the way back to the Prodigy Service Highlights menu, choose Menu again.

It's that simple.

MAKING YOUR WAY AROUND COMPUSERVE

Other online services offer menu and command structures that are similar to Prodigy's but a little more complicated. Remember that each main menu is a door that leads you through a series of other doors, or submenus, that eventually lead you to your destination.

The online commands—such as Jump on Prodigy and Go on CompuServe—are the directional signals that tell the service where to take you.

CompuServe can be navigated in any of four ways, or any combination. By logging on interactively through a multipurpose program such as Procomm Plus, you can type commands after the ! prompt and press ↵. If you log on through a front-end program such as CompuServe Information Manager for DOS, you can select commands from pull-down menus at the top of your screen. You can also use macros, or key combinations. And, if you use CIM for Windows (WinCIM) or the Macintosh, you can use the pull-down menus and macros, too, but you also have the option of clicking pictorial icons with your mouse.

For the purposes of this book, we'll primarily be navigating CompuServe the WinCIM way. It's easier, faster and, for Windows users, much more convenient than clicking the DOS prompt every time you want to check your e-mail.

Here are some of the basic commands that will help you make your way around CompuServe if you log on with multipurpose software or connect with a database that CompuServe Information Manager doesn't support. With any version of CIM, you can simply select a menu with your mouse or, if you've gone into one of the submenus, press Esc until the menu you want to return to reappears on the screen.

T (top)	Returns you to the menu of the main groups of services that appeared when you logged onto CompuServe.
B (back)	Brings you back to the previous page or screenful of text in a multiple-page menu or article.
M (menu)	Returns you to the previous menu.

N (next)	Takes you to the next choice on the same menu where you last made a selection. For instance, if you had selected Choice 5, you could enter **N** to move to Choice 6.
R (resend)	Repeats the current page or menu displayed.

Saving Time with Shortcut Commands

Once you learn your way around an online service, there's no need to trudge through every submenu to get to where you're going. You can compare the process to making your way to the top of a 36-story office building: you can walk up 36 flights of stairs, or you can take the elevator. It all depends how much of a hurry you're in—and, since time is money with online services—how much you want to spend.

USING THE GO COMMAND

Fortunately, most online services offer plenty of shortcuts to make your journey speedier. Prodigy, as you just learned, lets you zero in on the databases you want by using Jump words. CompuServe offers a Go command that lets you zip to the database of your choice. Using CompuServe interactively (without CIM), you type **go** and the keyword, or abbreviated name, of the database at any prompt. Examples of Go commands include **go mail** (CompuServe Mail), **go work** (Working from Home Forum), **go apo** (Associated Press Online), **go compdb** (Computer Database Plus), and **go directory** (CompuServe's Membership Directory). If you don't know the command for the database you're looking for, try typing in the first few letters of the database or type **go index** at any prompt. Using WinCIM, you click the Go icon from the toolbar or select Go from the Services menu. A dialog box appears, as shown in Figure 4.2, prompting you to type in the keyword for the service you want.

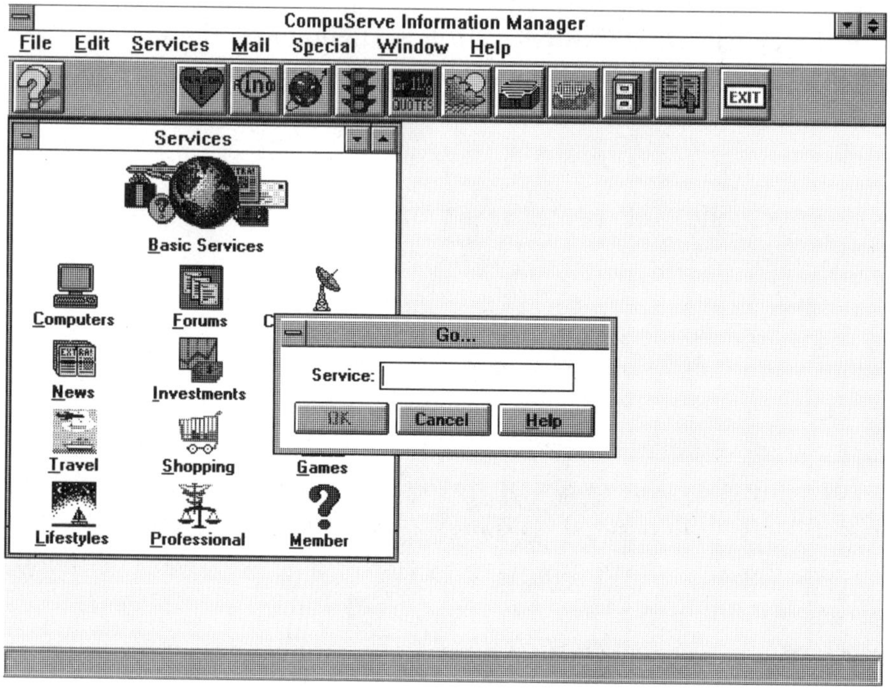

FIGURE 4.2:
The screen that appears when you select Go in CompuServe Information Manager

(Notice that you can also select a service category from the Browse list if you remember the keyword; but you'll then have to select the exact service from another list, so this method is less direct.)

USING THE FIND COMMAND

In addition to the Go command, CompuServe also offers a Find command that lets you locate databases and interactive services by topic.

Here's how to locate information about travel reservations using WinCIM:

1. Click the Find icon from toolbar at the top of your screen.
2. In the middle of your screen, a box will appear that prompts you to identify a topic. At the *Topic:* prompt, type the word **travel**. Click OK.

3. A box containing a list of travel databases will appear. Choose the travel service you prefer—say, Eaasy Sabre—and click the GO button below the box.

4. A new screen will appear that says *Eaasy Sabre* followed by explanatory material and access information.

Customizing the Service to Fit Your Needs

Many online services let you customize the service by creating lists of the databases and other features you use most often. Prodigy, for example, lets you create a Pathlist. CompuServe allows you to compile a list of Favorite Places.

The beauty of Prodigy's Pathlist is that it lets you skip directly to those services and features you use most often—in the order you typically use them—first checking your mail, then the weather, then stock quotes, or whatever. (You may want to wait until you've established a working routine before creating a Pathlist.) Once you've compiled your list (see "Creating a Prodigy Pathlist" below), all you have to do is click the Path button at the bottom of your screen whenever you're ready to move to the next topic. That way, you don't waste time using the Jump command or searching for Jumpwords in the index.

By contrast, CompuServe's Favorite Places feature is less automated. Once you've made your list (see below), you have to select Favorite Places from the Services pull-down menu, then highlight the name of the feature and choose Go. CompuServe has no equivalent of Prodigy's Path button.

CREATING A PRODIGY PATHLIST

Here's how to create a Pathlist using Prodigy:

1. Select Jump from the bottom of your screen. Press ↵.

2. Select Viewpath from the JumpWindow (or view the default Prodigy pathlist from the Selection List), then press ↵.

3. Select Changepath, then press ↵.
4. Select Add from the bottom of the box, then press ↵.
5. Select Other Location from the box that opens at the bottom of your screen, then press ↵.
6. After the word *Add,* type in a Jump word—say, **Computer Ex**. Then press ↵.
7. After *To position #*, type in any available position on the Pathlist—say, 20. Then press ↵.
8. To add more items to the list, repeat steps 4 through 7 as often as needed.
9. To leave the Changepath window, highlight a topic and select Goto.

Figure 4.3 shows a Pathlist being created.

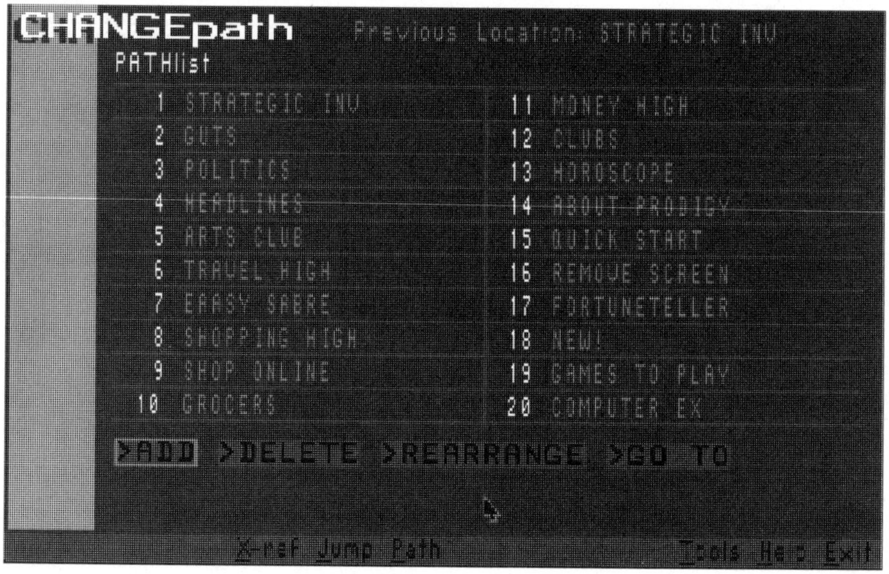

FIGURE 4.3: Creating a Pathlist in Prodigy

Once you've created the list, you can either work through the list in order using the Path button or go directly to a topic from any window by clicking Viewpath from the JumpWindow, highlighting the topic on the Pathlist, and pressing ↵.

CREATING A COMPUSERVE FAVORITE PLACES LIST

Here's how to compile a list of Favorite Places on CompuServe:

1. Using WinCIM, click the Find icon from the toolbar at the top of your screen.
2. When the *Topic:* box appears, highlight the database or service you want and click the Add button at the bottom of the Favorite Places box to the right.
3. Click OK.
4. Repeat steps 2 and 3 to add more items to the list.

Figure 4.4 shows a topic being added to the Favorite Places list.

To find any topic in the future, simply select it from the Favorite Places box before you log on. Then select Go from the box below it to go there automatically.

SAVING TIME WITH ABBREVIATED MENUS

Once you get comfortable with using an online service, you may grow tired of seeing the same menus pop up on your screen—and wasting time and money going through the same repetitive motions to get where you want to go. Fortunately, some online services such as CompuServe give you the option of using abbreviated menus or skipping menus altogether in favor of one-word commands.

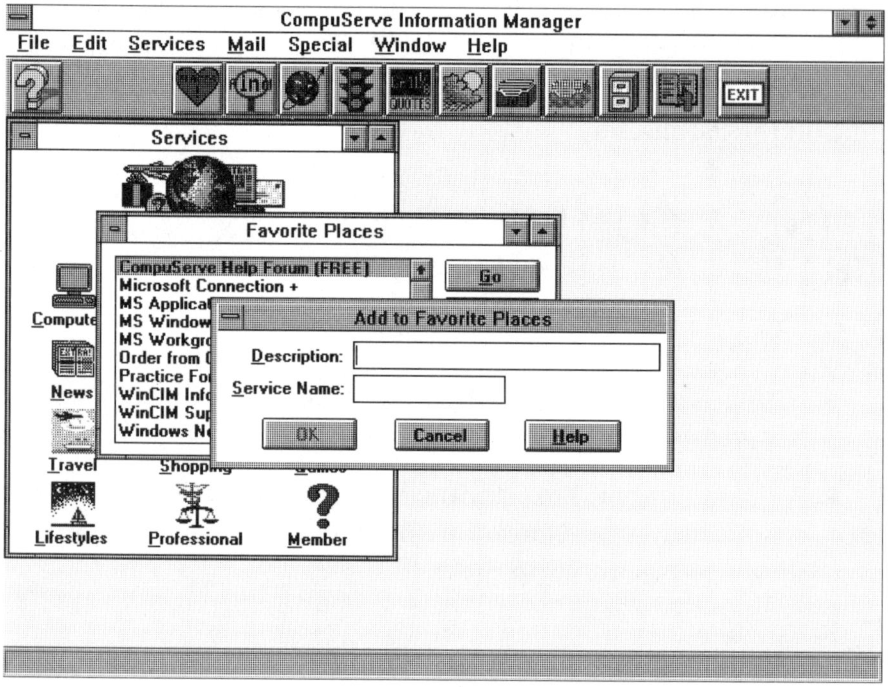

FIGURE 4.4: Adding to CompuServe's Favorite Places list

This feature is especially helpful if you're using a multipurpose program like Procomm Plus rather than front-end software like CIM, which replaces CompuServe's text-based menus with pop-up boxes that let you choose your options with a mouse. The only drawback to the no-menus approach—and it's a big one for beginners—is that you'll need to memorize your most frequently used commands or keep them handy on a piece of paper. If you forget a command or two while you're online, type **H** for "help" at the nearest ! prompt.

Here's how to change from Menu mode to Command or Prompt mode to speed up access to CompuServe Mail:

1. Log onto CompuServe using Procomm Plus or another multipurpose communications program.
2. Type **GO MAIL** at the ! prompt.

3. Type **SET** to change your menu options. When the Options menu appears on your screen, type 2 to go to the Mode menu, shown in Figure 4.5. Then press ↵.
4. Type 3 to choose Command mode, which replaces the online menus with one-word prompts such as *Mail!* and *Send!* If you'd like a bit more help, type **2** to select Prompt mode, which gives you a brief list of commands. Press ↵ after each selection.
5. To save even more time, choose 1 from the Options menu to get rid of the line numbers that appear when you create a message online. You can also choose 3 from the Options menu to view your messages in one continuous stream rather than page by page.
6. When you finally have your settings the way you want them, type **log** at the ! prompt and press ↵.
7. Type **Y** (for yes) to save your changes for all future CompuServe Mail sessions.

You can use the same procedure to return to Menu mode at any time.

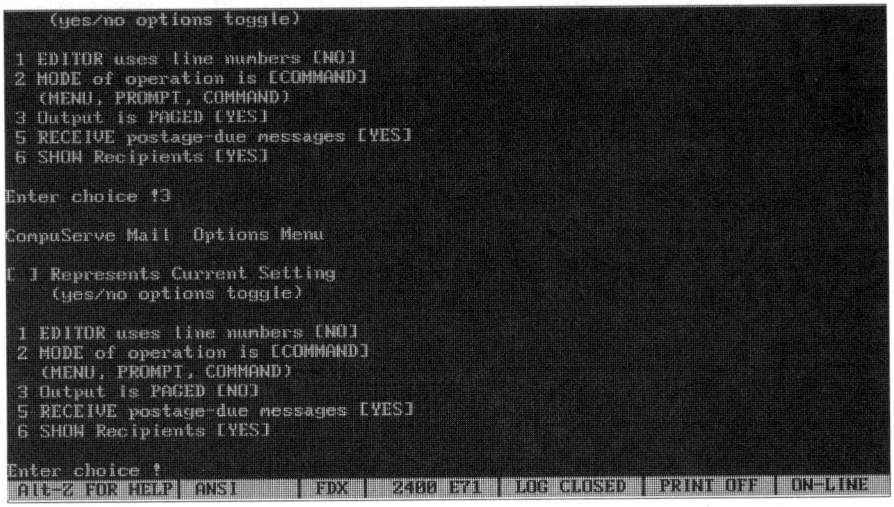

FIGURE 4.5: Switching CompuServe's settings to Command or Prompt mode

PUTTING ON THE BRAKES

For beginning users, the easiest way to get around an online service is through a front-end program like Prodigy or CIM. But, as you progress, you may find yourself straying into databases that aren't supported by the user-friendly boxes and pull-down menus you've grown accustomed to.

On CompuServe, for example, many of the more sophisticated financial and videotext databases are only available on what is called *terminal emulation mode*—a name that's not really as grim as it sounds. In terminal emulation mode, your PC screen turns into the video equivalent of a blank chalkboard, and the text that appears there can come pouring at you in reams—sending many novice users into a panic. Like Mickey Mouse in the animated version of *The Sorcerer's Apprentice*, you may find yourself scurrying around just trying to make the darn thing stop!

Master this handful of helpful commands, and put your fears to rest:

Ctrl-C	Otherwise known as the "panic button," Ctrl-C stops an online operation dead in its tracks and returns you to a comforting ! prompt. You may have to press Ctrl-C several times, though, before the operation comes to a complete halt. Press Ctrl-C too many times, and you may get disconnected.
Ctrl-S	Stops CompuServe from transmitting text to your screen. This is important if you want to read the text online rather than just print it out or save it on your hard disk.
Ctrl-Q	Tells CompuServe you are ready to resume receiving text to your screen.

Ctrl-O	Tells CompuServe to skip the remainder of the report or article currently being displayed. This command is useful if you want to cut short a long display after seeing those parts that interest you.
Ctrl-U	Erases (or undoes) anything you've typed online but have not yet sent to CompuServe by pressing ↵. This is helpful if you're participating in an online conference (see Chapter 8).

Getting Online Help If You Get Lost

Despite the recent attempts by online services to make their menus and command structures friendlier, it's still entirely possible to get lost online. The key is not to panic: Not only won't it do you any good, but you may dig yourself in deeper, wasting even more time and money.

With online services, the best way to get help is to ask for it. On Prodigy, this means selecting the HELP button at the bottom of your screen. On CompuServe, click the Help button in WinCIM, press F1 in DOS CIM, or type **H** if you're in terminal emulation mode. CompuServe also gives you the option of typing **T** (for top) at any ! prompt, which automatically brings you back to the first menu that you saw when you logged on.

The best place to get help, though, is off-line. If you're having a serious problem or need a question answered, it's best to log off the service and call the service's toll-free technical support number. That way, the meter isn't running. CompuServe also gives you a chance to sharpen your skills in its free Practice Forum before getting in over your head elsewhere on the service.

Summary

In this chapter, you learned how to navigate online services using menus, submenus, and pathways. You also learned valuable shortcuts, such as the Jump, Go, and Find commands that quickly get you where you want to go, saving you time and money. Finally, you learned how to customize the service to make it work the way you want it to.

In the next chapter, you'll learn why online services can get expensive and how to save money with flat-fee plans and off-line options such as automated programs like TAPCIS.

CHAPTER 5

The Bottom Line

In Chapter 4, you learned how to navigate your way around online services using menus, submenus, and pathways. You also learned valuable shortcuts, such as the Jump, Go, and Find commands that quickly get you where you want to go, saving you time and money. Finally, you learned how to customize the service to make it work the way you want it to.

In this chapter, you'll learn the various ways online services can get expensive—through connect charges, surcharges, and network charges—and how to save money with flat-fee plans and automated software programs like TAPCIS. You'll also learn how to analyze your monthly online services bill and how to get billing help.

The bottom line: The best way to save money with online services is to stay off-line as much as possible.

How Online Services Can Get Expensive

An online service costs you money every time you use it—and sometimes, in the case of online services that charge you flat fees and membership fees, even when you don't. Like the parking meters that swallow your quarters when you park in front of your favorite downtown restaurant for lunch, online services typically charge you fees based on how much time you spend online and, unlike the major long-distance phone companies, rarely offer volume discounts.

That's why, while it may feel like you're getting a free ride while you're navigating your way around an online service, you may end up with a bad case of sticker shock when your monthly bill arrives. Heavy users of online services can rack up charges of several hundred dollars or more in a single month.

"It's not unusual for us to run up bills of $300 a month on CompuServe," says Chuck DeFiore, who runs a home-based consulting and desktop publishing business in Rancho Cordova, California, with his wife, Sue. "We know some people who spend $700 to $800 a month."

At $12.80 per hour (the going rate for 2400 bps service on CompuServe's pay-as-you-go plan), users who incur bills like that are spending about 60 hours a month on forums, which are not included in CompuServe's flat-fee plan.

Unless you sign up for a flat-fee plan (see below), you'll generally end up paying as you go. Most online services divide their charges into three categories: 1) connect charges, or fees based on how much time you spend online; 2) surcharges, or fees you pay to log onto specialized databases the online service offers access to; and

3) network charges, or fees you pay to access an online service through a communications network such as TYMNET or SprintNet. Some services also charge annual membership fees.

CONNECT CHARGES

Connect charges are the per-minute charges you pay to access an online service such as CompuServe. It's just like when you make a long-distance phone call on AT&T or MCI—you're billed by the amount of time you spend communicating with the party on the other end, in this case the CompuServe computer. But, unlike phone services, in the online world, you pay the same price whether you're sending a message to someone in Paris or to the computer enthusiast who lives next door. That's because, when you dial an online service, you're actually calling the service itself, not the person who receives your message and sends one back.

Connect time can get pricey, though, if you choose to access the online service at higher speeds. CompuServe, for example, charges users of its $8.95 flat-fee plan $6 an hour to dial in at 300 bps (300 characters per second), a relatively slow speed, but boosts the price to $8.00 an hour for 1200 and 2400 bps access. If you log on at 9600 bps, CompuServe will charge you $16.00 an hour. (For pay-as-you-go users, the connect-time charges are higher: $6.30 an hour at 300 bps, $12.80 an hour at 1200 and 2400 bps, and $22.80 at 9600.)

Which speed to log on at depends on what you're trying to do online. If you're logging to participate in a real-time conference with other users, dialing in at 300 baud will be more than sufficient for all but the speediest typists. On the other hand, if all you want to do is get your e-mail or download a long file and log off, a super-fast 9600 baud connection may be your best bet. To read a file online, you're better off at a medium speed such as 1200 or 2400 baud.

CompuServe magazine recently worked up some extremely useful comparisons of the total costs of different operations at various baud rates. Here's what it cost to read a 25 KB text file (roughly 20 double-spaced pages) online:

BPS	TIME	COST PER MINUTE	TOTAL COST
9600	4 min.	$.38	$1.52
2400	4 min.	$.2133	$.85
1200	4 min.	$.2133	$.85
300	14 min.	$.1050	$1.47

To download a 1 MB file (roughly the size of the CIM for DOS program), the costs were as follows:

BPS	TIME	COST PER MINUTE	TOTAL COST
9600	17 min.	$.38	$6.46
2400	1 hr. 8 min.	$.2133	$14.50
1200	2 hrs. 16 min.	$.2133	$29
300	9 hrs. 4 min.	$.1050	$57.12

The cost-per-minute figures in these comparisons are based on the pay-as-you-go hourly rate; on the flat-fee plan, the connect-time charges are lower but the relative differences are similar.

SURCHARGES

Many of the bulletin boards and databases offered through online services are free—you pay the standard connect charges but nothing more. Others, usually the more specialized databases dealing with law, medicine, and business, carry a surcharge, or additional access fee. Typically, an online service will hit you with a surcharge when there's some extra processing involved or because the service acts as a gateway for another electronic information vendor that wants to make a profit, too.

Surcharges vary in price, and most online services will warn you in advance about the cost. CompuServe, for example, puts a dollar sign next to all surcharged services and flashes an on-screen price list that tells you how much to expect to pay. Generally, surcharges are priced based on three factors: 1) how much time you spend searching the database; 2) how many records, or "bibliographic citations," you request; and 3) whether you want to see the full text of an article or just a summary (full text usually costs more).

Here are some examples of how much a surcharge can add to your online bill: CompuServe's financial surcharges range from 1½ cents for current and end-of-the-day stock and options quotes to $5 to $25 per report for access to its Disclosure II database, which provides information compiled from 10K forms and other disclosure statements that publicly traded companies are required to file with the Securities & Exchange Commission. On CompuServe, newspaper and magazine databases such as Magazine Database Plus, Business Database Plus, and Health Database Plus cost $15 an hour plus additional charges for access to articles and summaries.

NETWORK CHARGES

Network, or communications, surcharges are the fees you pay to access an online service from a telecommunications network. While people who live in major population centers can generally dial into national services such as CompuServe and Prodigy through local access numbers, you may have to call long-distance if you live in a remote area without such a node.

That's why, if you live on a farm in rural North Dakota, for example, and there's a local TYMNET number you can call, it may be less expensive to dial in that way than to call CompuServe long-distance in Minneapolis. It costs $11.70 an hour to connect to CompuServe through TYMNET during the day but only $1.70 on nights and weekends. CompuServe also offers 1-800 service anywhere the United States for $8.70 an hour. Logging on outside the United States, where local access numbers are few and far between, often requires dialing in through a third-party network such as Infonet (see Chapter 10).

As Figure 5.1 shows, pricing information is readily available on CompuServe. To get current rates, type **go rates** at any prompt, or click the Go icon from the WinCIM toolbar and then type **rates** and click OK.

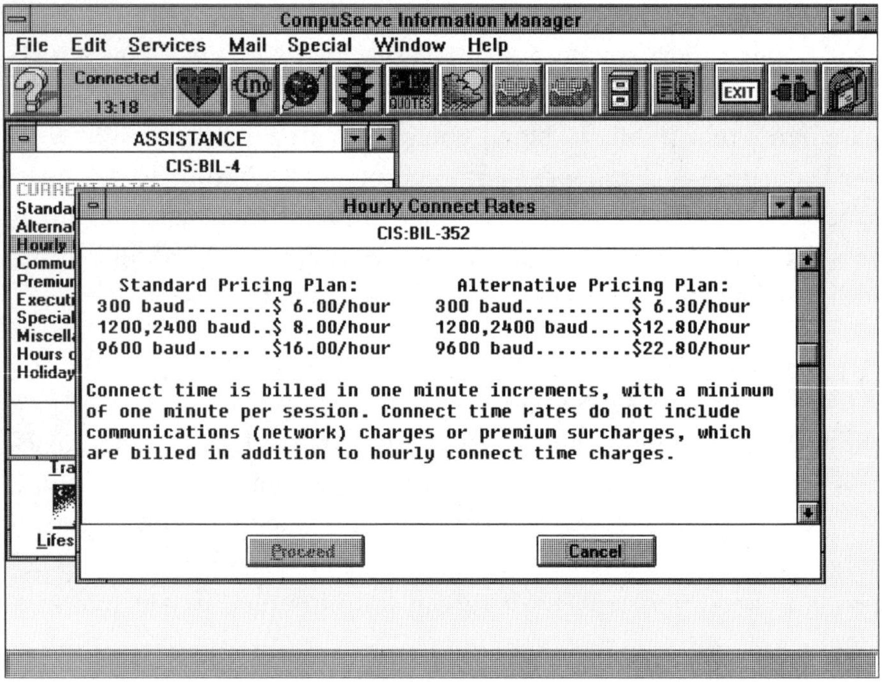

FIGURE 5.1: Getting rate information on CompuServe

Pay-As-You-Go Versus Flat-Fee Plans

As you learned in Chapter 3, the choice between a flat-fee and pay-as-you-go plan really depends on how often you're going to use the service and what you're going to use it for. Flat-fee plans, also known as basic service plans, typically allow you unlimited access to databases containing general-interest topics. These include news, weather, sports, and movie reviews in addition to interactive services such as shopping, online travel reservations, and electronic mail. The trouble is, if you're logging on for business rather than personal use, these all-you-can-eat plans may overload you with information you don't need and fail to give you access to the specific data you really want.

Pay-as-you-go plans, on the other hand, charge you only for those services you actually use. But, just like ordering a la carte in a restaurant, you may end up paying much more than if you had ordered the Blue Plate Special and simply ignored the boiled green beans that came in the little bowl next to your plate. Pay-as-you-go plans can also get expensive if you send a lot of e-mail. CompuServe's $8.95-a-month flat-fee service lets you send up to 60 e-mail messages of about three typed double-spaced pages each month—which may alone be worth the monthly fee. Signing up for a flat-fee plan also means you don't have to watch the meter—a small price for a little peace of mind.

PAY-AS-YOU-GO PLANS

Pay-as-you-go is the tried-and-true way to pay for online services. One big advantage to this option is flexibility: You can roam over hundreds of online offerings, picking and choosing the ones you want, paying only for those services you use and only the time that you actually spend. Typically, online services bill you in one-minute increments, even though front-end services like CompuServe Information Manager will clock your online time in seconds.

Pay-as-you-go plans are also a good idea if you use an online service primarily for business purposes and want your clients to reimburse you for any charges you rack up online. With a flat-fee plan, that's impossible to do.

FLAT-FEE PLANS

Flat-fee plans typically charge you a flat monthly fee for access to the basic services described above, with additional surcharges for specialized services, databases, and bulletin boards. Some of the major online services, such as Prodigy, CompuServe, America Online, and GEnie, offer flat-fee plans that let you pay $4.95 to $14.95 a month for basic services.

Before signing up for a flat-fee plan, though, it's important to find out what it *doesn't* include. GEnie, for example, charges only $4.95 a month for its basic services plan but charges additional fees to access those services during daytime hours. CompuServe's flat-fee plan does not include access to its hundreds of specialized bulletin boards, or "forums," probably the service's most popular feature. (You'll still have to pay about 22 cents a minute for forum access, depending on modem speed.) And even Prodigy, which started out with a flat fee of $9.95 for all its services, has recently raised its monthly fee to $14.95 and announced plans to charge extra for specialized databases and mail functions.

Saving Money with Off-Line Options

When it comes to saving money using online services, choosing the right options packages is not enough. The best way to save money online, experienced users say, is to stay off-line as much as possible. It's a cost-effective strategy that makes a lot of sense. Unless your business plan is to make the online services rich, it pays to learn how to use a front-end program that can check your messages, retrieve your e-mail, and let you compose your messages and files off-line. Otherwise, you'll spend a fortune typing and sending your mail on-line while the meter is running.

WINCIM VERSUS TAPCIS

CompuServe Information Manager for Windows, or WinCIM as it's called, is one of the easiest automated programs available and one of the best for beginners to use. WinCIM lets you create, store, and reply to messages without spending a penny on-line. Another nifty feature lets you log onto CompuServe, send messages to other CompuServe members, retrieve any e-mail that has been left for you, and log off—all in a matter of minutes. WinCIM also lets you mark and retrieve any forum messages that you'd like to read later—again saving you time and money. Best of all, WinCIM is a true Windows application which not only lets you click icons and select commands from pull-down menus and dialog boxes but also lets you copy and paste information to and from any other Windows program.

The only drawback to WinCIM—or its DOS or Mac equivalents—is that it's a little slower at retrieving mail and messages than an automated program like TAPCIS. TAPCIS, a $79 shareware program, offers many of the same features as WinCIM but executes them faster. With its sophisticated navigation system, TAPCIS will take you online with a single keystroke and you won't have to press another key until TAPCIS has sent your messages, received your new ones, retrieved your files, and logged you off CompuServe. TAPCIS is especially useful for accessing CompuServe's many forums: The program displays forum section numbers and names in a pop-up window, and you can configure it to retrieve large groups of forum messages to be read off-line at your convenience.

Figure 5.2 illustrates TAPCIS in action.

The main drawback to TAPCIS, some users say, is that it takes time to learn and, because it lacks the friendly interface that WinCIM

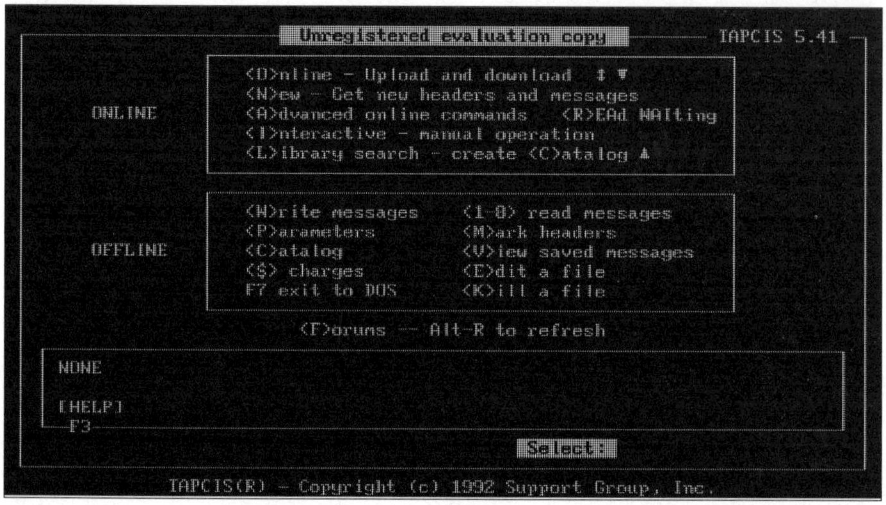

FIGURE 5.2: Accessing CompuServe through TAPCIS

has, can be tricky to use. On the other hand, there are thousands of online users who find that it saves time (and therefore money).

Marty Winston, a home-based publicist in Russell, Ohio, says he cut his CompuServe bill by two-thirds the first month he switched to TAPCIS. Before, he was navigating the service manually.

"CompuServe is the Manhattan of online communities," Winston says. "I go on through TAPCIS, which is the equivalent of having a chauffeured limo."

To get your copy of TAPCIS, simply retrieve it from Library 1 of CompuServe's TAPCIS Forum. TAPCIS requires an IBM PC-compatible computer, 384K of RAM, a more or less Hayes-compatible modem and, for desktop use, a hard disk drive. The program file is called TAP.EXE. The file containing the manual is called TAP-DOC.EXE. To access these files, you'll need to use a process called *downloading*. For more on this, see Chapter 7.

How to Ask About Your Bill

It's hard to keep track of your bottom line if you don't know what it is. That's why it's a good idea to check your bill periodically and see if your online services charges are under control. Fortunately, most online services offer readily accessible billing information online and let you look at it free of charge.

GETTING BILLING INFORMATION ON PRODIGY

Finding out about your bill is a snap on Prodigy. Here's how to do it:

1. Select TOOLS at the bottom of your screen and press ↵.
2. Select Account Menu in the pop-up box that appears. Press ↵.
3. Choose from Statement, Latest Payment, Statement Help, Payment Method, Prodigy Term, and Message Detail.
4. To see your monthly statement, select Statement and press ↵. The screen that appears, illustrated in Figure 5.3, will show you your current charges and the amount due.
5. To see the other selections, select Account Menu again and press ↵. For example, Statement Help (illustrated in Figure 5.4) explains how to read your bill and lets you send a free message to Membership Services to clear up any problems. Message Detail lets you see a list of all personal messages sent by members of your household over the last three months. (Prodigy gives you up to 30 free personal messages a month and charges 25 cents a message for each additional note.)
6. To get back to where you were before you checked your bill, simply select MENU from the bottom of your screen and press ↵.

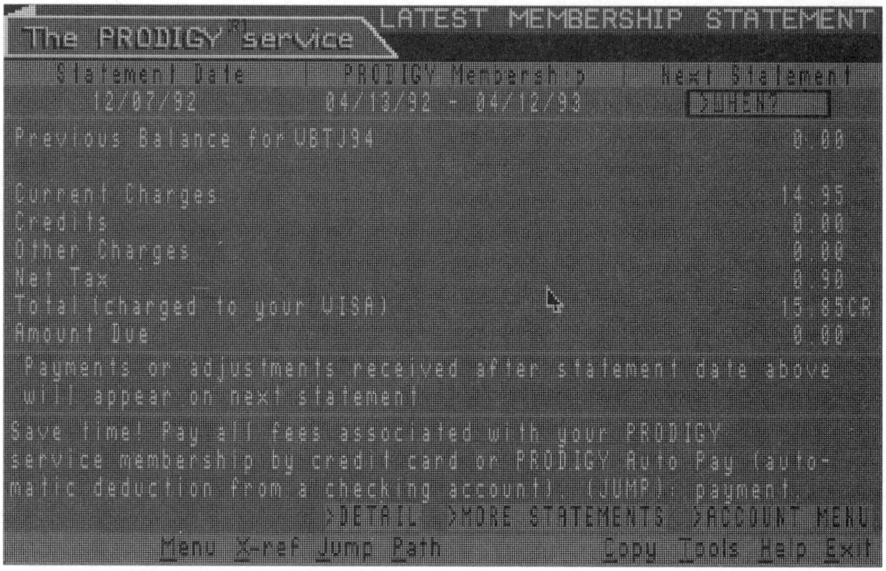

FIGURE 5.3:
A typical monthly statement on Prodigy

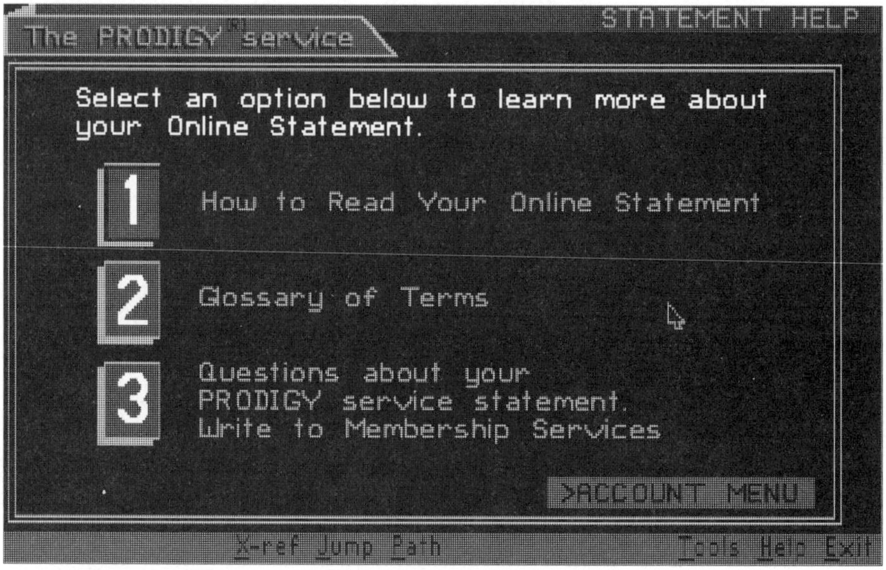

FIGURE 5.4:
Getting billing help on Prodigy

GETTING BILLING INFORMATION ON COMPUSERVE

Checking your bill on CompuServe is easy, too, especially if you're using Compuserve Information Manager. Here's how to do it using WinCIM:

1. Click the Go icon from the toolbar at the top of your screen.
2. At *Service Name:*, type **Charges**. Press ↵ or select OK.
3. From the Terminal Emulation screen that appears next, select 1 (Explanation), 2 (Account Balance), 3 (Billing History), 4 (Current Activity), or 5 (Previous Activity). Once you've made your selection, press ↵. All options are free of charge.
4. To make another selection, press Esc to return to the options list.
5. To learn more about your charges, click the Go icon and type **Bill**. Here, you can change your billing address, switch to a different credit card or ask Compuserve to deduct your monthly charges from your bank account automatically, as shown in Figure 5.5. (There is a $5 a month minimum for Electronic Funds Transfer (direct withdrawal) billing, and this option is available only to members with billing addresses within the United States.)

Summary

In this chapter, you learned why the best way to save money online is to stay off-line as much as possible. You also learned why online services can get expensive—through connect charges, surcharges, and network charges—and how to save money with flat-fee plans and automated software programs like CIM and TAPCIS. And, finally, you learned how to analyze your monthly bill and get billing help online.

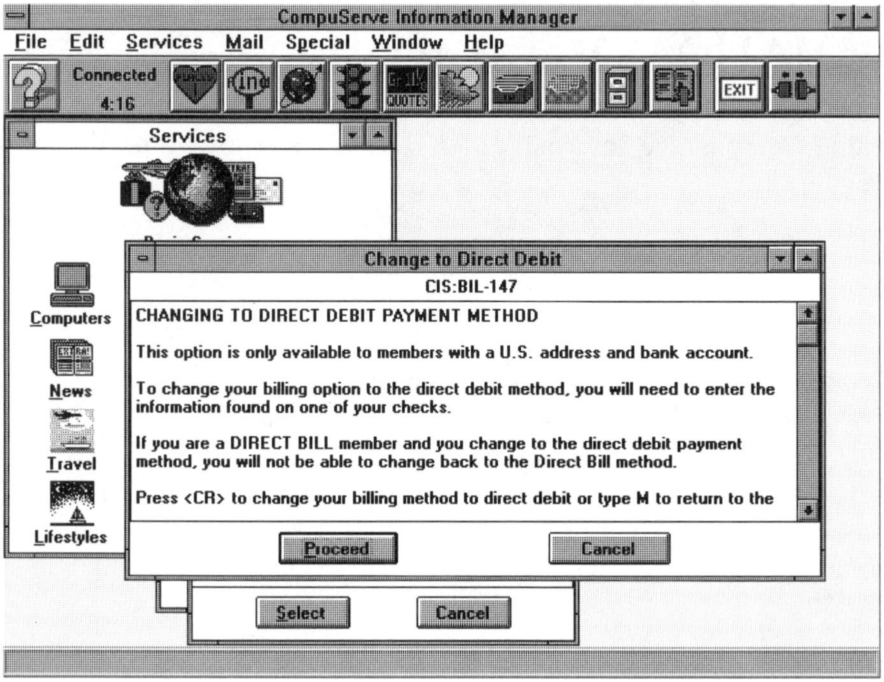

FIGURE 5.5: Direct billing (Electronic Funds Transfer) using CompuServe Information Manager

In the next chapter, you'll learn all about electronic mail, or e-mail as it's commonly called.

CHAPTER 6

E-Mail

In Chapter 5, you learned about saving money online—and why to get the biggest bang for your buck it's a good idea to stay off-line as much as possible. In this chapter, you'll learn about one of the most widely used features of online services—electronic mail, or e-mail. With electronic mail, you can send instant messages to colleagues, friends, or people you've never met. You can even send paper mail to a fax, a teletype machine, or a post office box.

Along the way, you'll also learn how to compile an address book, join in group discussions with other online subscribers, and bone up on the finer points of e-mail lingo and "etiquette." Finally, you'll learn the difference between public and private messages and the pros and cons of using each.

Sending and Receiving Messages

Most mass-market online services allow you to send and receive messages, though some offer more flexibility than others. Prodigy, as noted earlier, only lets you send messages to and receive messages from other Prodigy members. And the service does not currently offer fax, teletype, or US Mail capabilities—although Prodigy has promised to address these limitations in 1993 for an additional fee. CompuServe, on the other hand, lets you send your messages in virtually any format you want—computer-to-computer, fax, teletype, US Mail—even if the recipient is not a CompuServe member. In addition, some online services give you access to MCI Mail, which lets you send electronic messages to the thousands of business people with MCI mailboxes, and lets you tap into the Internet, a global communications link accessed by millions of users worldwide. (You'll learn about financial information available through Internet in Chapter 12. For the most part, however, this network is designed to serve technically advanced users; and even many of them find it difficult to use.)

SENDING AN ELECTRONIC MESSAGE

Once you get the hang of it, sending an electronic message is no more difficult than scribbling a note on a piece of paper—and wastes fewer trees and less of your time. The advantages of e-mail are numerous: There's no need to print out a letter, sign it, and stuff it in an envelope; and, depending on the service plan you sign up for, it may well be cheaper than making a long-distance phone call, sending a fax, or shipping a letter by postal mail. What's more, your online mailbox receives messages around the clock—even when you're not logged onto the service—and you can pick them up at any time. It's like having your own private post office box, except that you never have to leave your desk to drive there.

Like any communications method, though, e-mail has its downside. The chief drawback is that, unless you and your recipients log on every day, it may take a while before the person you're sending your message to gets around to reading it. And it may be several more days before you log on to read the reply. The other disadvantage is that, unless you use a front-end program like WinCIM or TAPCIS, you'll have to type your messages online while the clock is ticking—a costly and inefficient way to draft all but the briefest correspondence.

The bottom line: For business letters, it only makes sense to use e-mail if either (1) you and your correspondents check your online mail boxes on a regular basis, or (2) you're not in any big hurry.

Sending an E-Mail Message on CompuServe

Here's how to send an e-mail message using WinCIM:

1. Click Create Mail from the Mail menu at the top of your screen. A Recipient List will appear in the middle of your screen. The word *To:* will have a black dot in the circle next to it.

2. Type the name of the person to whom you're sending the message.

3. Move to the Address area and type in the person's CompuServe ID number. You send copies of your message to other people by clicking the circles next to CC: (for carbon copy) or BC: (for blind copy).

4. Click Add, and the recipient's name and address will appear in the Recipients window. Click OK when you have finished your list. (CompuServe lets you send the message to up to 50 different people.)

5. At the *Subject:* prompt, type the subject of your message.

6. Then move to the blank area where you will type your message. You can edit your message by using the Delete key, Backspace key and the cut-and-paste commands under the Edit pull-down menu at the top your screen. You can also use the Edit commands to copy and paste text from other Windows applications.

7. To send your message, click the Send Now button at the bottom of the message box. The message will be delivered to your recipient's CompuServe mail box within minutes. Or click the Out Basket box to send it later.

Figure 6.1 shows an e-mail message being created.

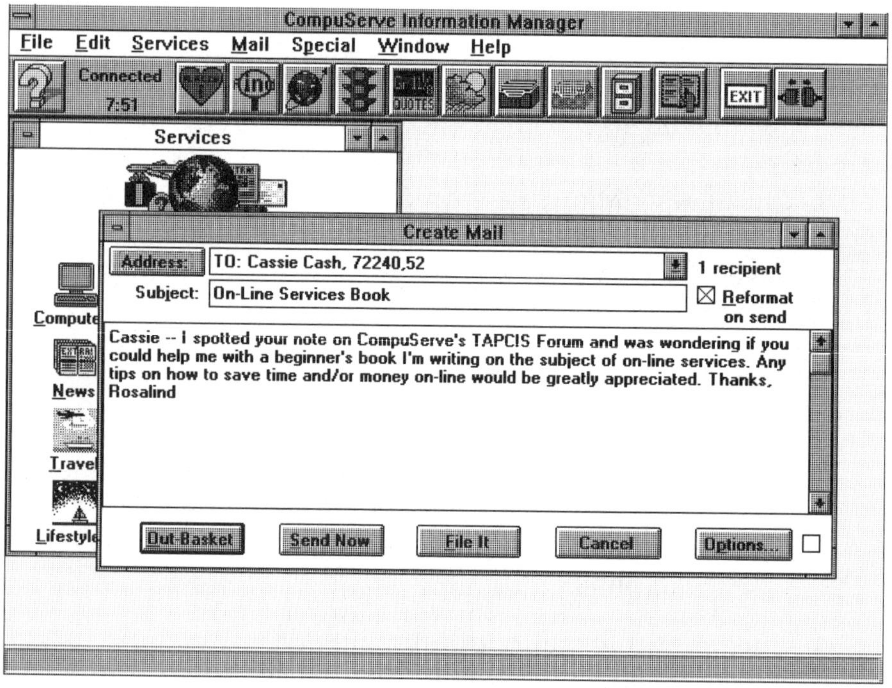

FIGURE 6.1: Creating an e-mail message on CompuServe

Here's a tip: Though WinCIM lets you create messages both on- and off-line, you can save money (if you've signed up for pay-as-you-go service) by using the program's off-line text editor to type and address your messages before you log onto the service. When you're finished, click Send/Receive All Mail from the Mail pull-down menu, then select the Disconnect After Operation option and click OK. CompuServe will automatically log you on, send all your messages, retrieve any messages waiting for you and log off. Depending on how much e-mail is involved, the entire process generally takes less than two minutes—a bargain at 44 cents of connect time (at 2400 bps). The flat-fee Basic Services rate includes e-mail, but you'll probably still find this a more efficient way to work.

Sending a Fax Besides sending e-mail to other online subscribers, CompuServe and most other major online services also let you send your messages by fax. This can be a real plus if your computer didn't come with a fax board or fax modem and you don't send enough faxes to justify buying one. What's more, you won't have to pay long-distance charges if you're faxing a letter out of town. But beware: Most online services charge extra for faxes. CompuServe, for example, charges 75 cents for the first 1000 characters of a US-bound fax plus 25 cents for each additional 1000 characters. Faxes to European destinations cost 90 cents for each 1000 characters sent. (Other online services charge by the page plus any fraction thereof.)

To use WinCIM to send a fax, follow the steps outlined above (Sending an Electronic Message) except for the address. Instead of typing the recipient's CompuServe ID number, type **FAX:** plus the recipient's fax number, as shown in Figure 6.2. Be sure to leave out all hyphens and parentheses between the numbers. For US-bound faxes, be sure to include the number 1 and the area code, for example, **FAX:13055551234**. For international faxes, include the country code and the city code.

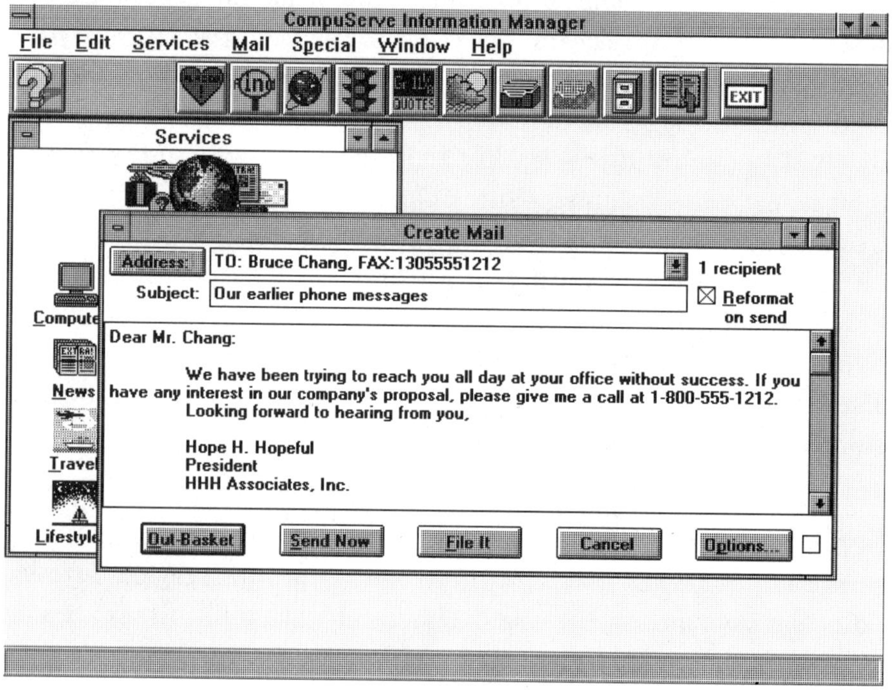

FIGURE 6.2: Using CompuServe to send a fax

Sending a Message to an MCI Mail Box To use WinCIM to send a message to an MCI Mail box, follow the same steps as for a fax but type **MCIMAIL:** plus the recipient's MCI Mail address; for example, **MCIMAIL: 123-4567**.

Sending a TELEX Transmission To send a TELEX, follow the same steps as for a fax or MCI Mail message but type **TLX:** plus the recipient's TELEX machine number; for example, **TLX: 9991234567abcdef**.

Sending Postal Mail You can also use e-mail to send a regular letter. If the letter is short, letting an online service like CompuServe address the envelope and lick the stamp is often more efficient than doing it yourself. On the other hand, mailing letters online can get pretty expensive. While the US Postal Service charges only 29 cents to ship a standard first-class letter anywhere in the United States, CompuServe charges $1.50 for the first page and 20 cents for each page after that. Foreign-bound letters start at $2.50.

To mail a paper letter using CompuServe Information Manager, simply enter the recipient's address in the CompuServe address book (see "Saving Time with an Address book" below) and create a message as explained under "Sending an Electronic Message" above. Once you select the address, CompuServe will automatically print a hard copy of your letter and mail it off.

Sending an E-Mail Message on Prodigy

Even more so than CompuServe Information Manager, Prodigy makes mastering e-mail a snap—the drawback is that Prodigy's e-mail functions are limited. Although you can send messages to other Prodigy members, you can't send a fax, a TELEX, or a note to somebody who's a member of another online service such as CompuServe or GEnie. In addition, you can't send a document that you've composed off-line with your word processor.

1. To send a message on Prodigy, simply log on by typing in your user ID and password. Then choose the Jump button from the bottom of your screen and type **communication** in the blank space in the box that appears. Then press ↵.
2. Select Write a Message (Box 1) from the menu that appears on your screen. Press ↵.
3. At the *To:* prompt, type in the recipient's Prodigy address, tab to the *Subject Matter:* prompt and type a few words that summarize your message.
4. Tab to the text box below the address, and type your message.

5. When your message is complete, tab to the Send button at the bottom of your screen and press ↵.

RETRIEVING AN ELECTRONIC MESSAGE

Now that you've learned how to send an electronic message, it's time to learn how to retrieve one. Virtually all online services maintain electronic mail boxes where incoming messages are stored.

Retrieving a Message from CompuServe

Here's how to retrieve a message using WinCIM:

1. Click Get New Mail from the Mail pull-down menu that appears on your screen. WinCIM will automatically log you on and display the mail box showing your new messages. As an alternative, you can log on by clicking another option (such as the Go or Browse commands). If you have new mail, a Mailbox icon will appear at the upper-right-hand corner of your screen. Click the icon to display your messages.

2. Click Get from the bottom of your mailbox. This will open your message and allow you to read it.

3. Once you've finished reading the message, select one of the following options: In-Basket (to file it away and read later), File It (to store the message in WinCIM's electronic filing cabinet), Reply (to let you compose a quick reply online), Forward (to forward a copy of the message to another CompuServe user, adding comments if you like), Cancel (to return you to the list of messages in your mail box), or Delete (to erase the message and return you to the message list).

4. You can also print and save online messages. To print a message, click Print from the File pull-down menu. To save a copy of the message to a disk, click Save As from the same menu and give the file a name.

Both the Filing Cabinet and the In-Basket are off-line storage options, so when you deposit a message in either of those places, all you're doing is storing it on your hard disk. Therefore, you can store your messages there as long as you like—the CompuServe host computers have nothing to do with it. The difference between the two options is very slight. The CompuServe In-Basket serves the same function as the In basket on the desk in your office—it stores the message until you get around to filing it. The Filing Cabinet, on the other hand, lets you create electronic "folders" so that you can store you messages by subject heading for future reference.

Saving Time with WinCIM's Get All Command Unless you have only one or two brief messages in your mail box, it doesn't make sense to read your mail online. You can save time and money (on the pay-as-you-go plan; Basic Services users will only save time) by clicking Get All from the bottom of the mailbox displaying your new messages. This way, WinCIM will automatically transfer all your messages into your In-Basket so you can read and reply to them offline—when the meter is no longer ticking. To access your In-Basket, click In-Basket from the Mail pull-down menu. You'll see the screen shown in Figure 6.3.

Retrieving a Message from Prodigy

To retrieve a message using Prodigy, simply select the New Mail box that appears in the right-hand corner of your screen when you first log on, or choose the JUMP button at the bottom of your screen and select Read Your Mail from the box that appears.

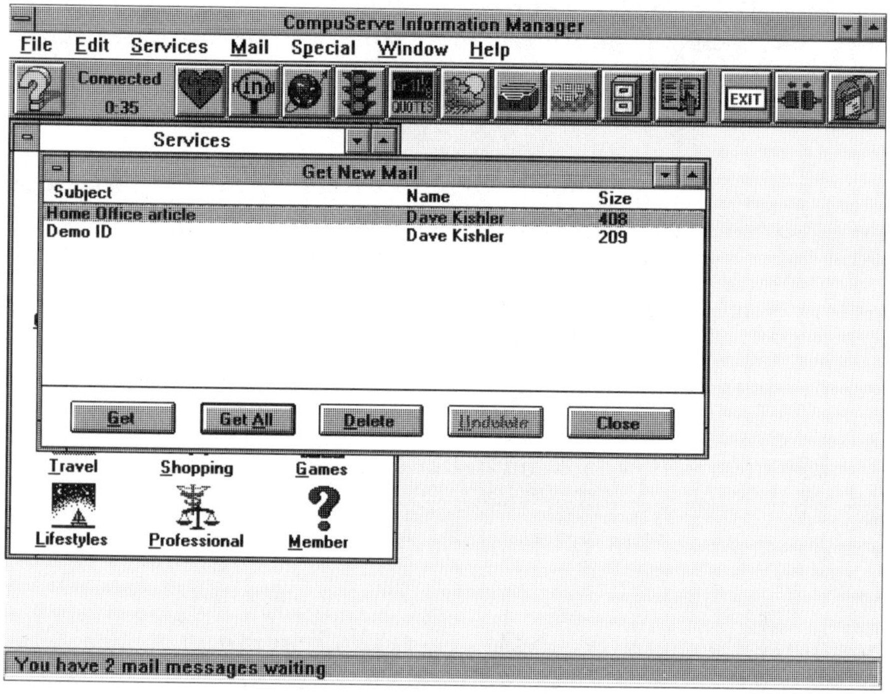

FIGURE 6.3: Receiving messages with WinCIM's Get All command

Saving Time with an Address Book

Some online services, including both Prodigy and CompuServe, feature electronic "address books" that make it quicker and easier to send e-mail. Like their paper counterparts in the off-line world, the address books offered by online services let you store names, online addresses and other pertinent information so you won't have to look them up every time you want to send a letter. Address books are also a plus when sending the same e-mail message to more than one person.

CREATING AN ADDRESS BOOK WITH COMPUSERVE

Here's how to use the WinCIM Address Book:

1. To list a name to the address book, click Address Book from the Mail pull-down menu, and click Add.

2. In the Address Entry box that appears on your screen, type the addressee's name, then tab to *Address:* and type in the person's CompuServe user ID. Click OK. You can also enter the person's fax number, telex number, MCI Mail address, or postal address and any comments that may help you identify the person later. Click OK to save the entry. There's also an easier way to save a name. Click the word, *From:* on any e-mail or forum message you receive. WinCIM will display the sender's name and address in the Address Entry box and prompt you to save it.

3. To retrieve an address from your book, click Create Mail from the Mail pull-down menu. Highlight a name from the list of names in your Address Book.

4. Click Copy, then OK. The name and address you choose will automatically appear at the top of the message blank that appears on your screen. If you're replying to another message, you can also click Copy Original to put everyone who received the original message (except you) into the list of recipients.

5. Editing the Address Book is simple, too. To delete an address, just click Address Book from the Mail menu and click Delete. You can also select Add to insert a new entry, Change to review or edit a listing, OK to save your changes, or Cancel to exit the Address Book without changing your listing. WinCIM also includes an Add Group command, which lets you group several addresses under a single heading. This is helpful if you frequently send messages to the same group of people.

Figure 6.4 shows an address being retrieved from the Address Book.

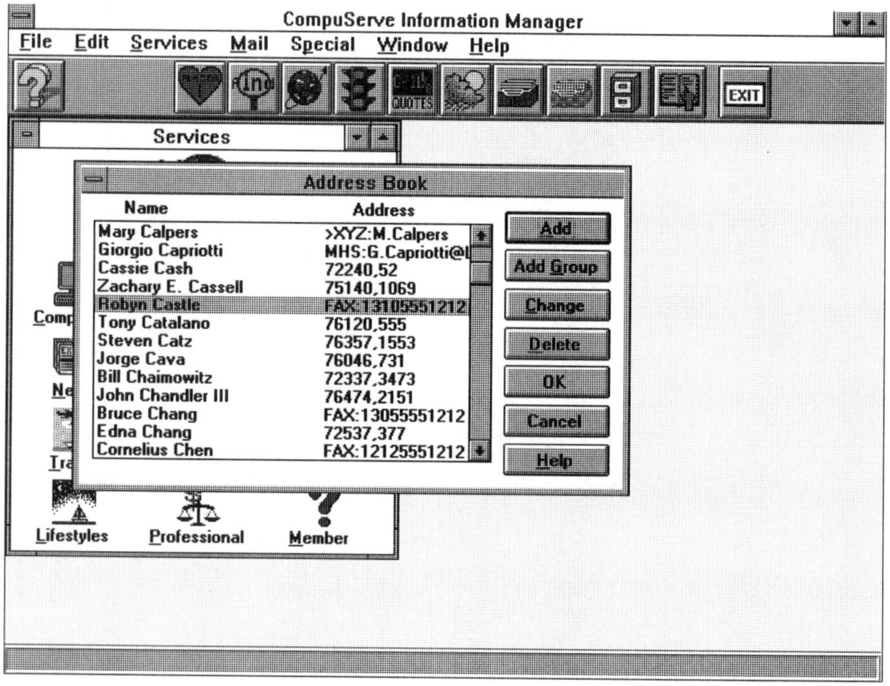

FIGURE 6.4: Retrieving an address from WinCIM's Address Book

CREATING AN ADDRESS BOOK WITH PRODIGY

Here's how to use the address book available on Prodigy:

1. Log onto Prodigy and select New Mail at the upper right-hand corner of your screen. Press ↵. Or, if you're already online, select Read Your Mail from the Jump box. (Note: Unlike CompuServe Information Manager's address book, the Prodigy address book can only be accessed after you've already logged onto the service.)

2. Select the number next to the message you want to read, and press ↵.

3. Select Option from the bottom of your screen. Press ↵.

4. Choose the Add button, then press ↵ to add the message-writer's Prodigy ID number to the address book.

5. Then type the person's name or nickname, and press ↵.

You can also add a name and address to the address book by choosing the Jump command from the bottom of your screen and typing **address book** in the Jumpwindow. Then choose Add, and type the person's name and Prodigy ID number.

To address a message to a person you've listed in your address book, simply type his or her name in the space next to *To:* on the message header. Your message will be sent to that person's Prodigy mailbox automatically. Remember: The name you type must be the same one you entered when you originally listed the person in your address book. (With Prodigy, unlike WinCIM, you can't just click *Address:* and press ↵ to get a list of names and ID numbers.)

Prodigy also lets you create a Mailing List that lets you send the same message to a group of people. You can save this list to be used again. You are limited, however, to two lists of up to 10 people each. Before you compile your list, you must first enter the recipients' names and ID numbers in your address book.

Online Networking: Private and Public Messages

Now that you know how to use e-mail, let's explore its potential. Besides speeding along your notes, letters, and computer files to colleagues, customers, and contacts, e-mail is also a great way to tap into the growing world of online networking.

Unlike off-line, or face-to-face, networking, which usually involves handing out business cards and wading through small talk at social functions, online networking is refreshingly direct and surprisingly accessible. Even the greenest entrepreneur can dial up an online service, pick out a bulletin board of interest and dive into a group discussion without risk of embarrassment. CompuServe, for example, offers dozens of "special interest groups" or "forums" for journalists, public relations people, computer consultants, international entrepreneurs, people who work from home, and other business owners and professionals.

The best way to get started, online veterans say, is simply to browse through a "message thread," or online discussion, on a bulletin board that interests you and reply to one of the many notes posted there. Notes like these are commonly referred to as *public messages*—as opposed to the *private messages* we've discussed so far, which are intended to be read by a specific online member. Posting a public message, which can be read by anyone who logs on, can be a good way to gain exposure for your business or seek advice from the widest possible circle of contacts. A private note, by contrast, may be preferable once you've already made an online contact, especially if it involves a promising business deal or job offer that you don't want the rest of the world to know about.

Figure 6.5 shows a typical public message on Prodigy.

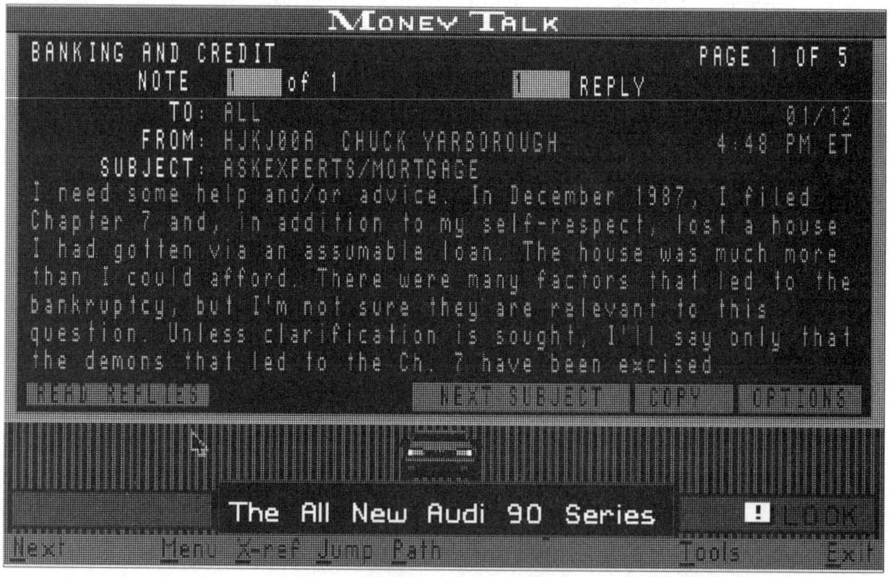

FIGURE 6.5:
Creating a public message on Prodigy

You can also get your name out by uploading, or posting, a how-to file that lets other forum members benefit from your professional or business expertise. Many forums also offer real-time conferences open to all bulletin board members. Once you log on, you can usually join a specialized forum at no extra charge.

To learn how to post a public message on Prodigy and CompuServe, see the detailed instructions in Chapter 8. You'll also learn more about networking in Chapter 13.

E-Mail Lingo and "Etiquette"

Although the possibilities of online communications are virtually endless, there are some (mostly unwritten) rules and rituals, too. For starters, there's the mesmerizing world of online lingo with its colons, dots, and dashes, which can often leave novices in the dark. Then there's the sticky wicket of online "etiquette"—everything from when to use (and not use) capital letters to when a public note jumps the line from a legitimate business announcement to improper customer solicitation.

One of the most important online commandments is, "Thou shalt not advertise"—unless you pay to place an ad. Prodigy, in particular, is very strict about this rule. As a Prodigy member, you can swap business and investment advice all day long, but the moment you start hawking your goods and services, a Prodigy representative will yank your message off the system. On the other hand, Prodigy is more than happy to sell you an ad on its TPI Online Classifieds.

Another important, though unwritten, rule is, "Thou shalt give something back to the other members." Veterans of online bulletin boards, such as CompuServe's Working from Home Forum, say it's considered rude to keep logging on and asking for free advice and contacts without offering anything in return. Uploading, or posting, a how-to file about your area of expertise is considered a gracious thank-you gesture. (And there's nothing wrong with attaching your name, phone number, address, and CompuServe ID to give your business a boost.)

"It's a give-and-take situation," says Sue DeFiore, who, together with her husband, Chuck, runs a home-based consulting business in Rancho Cordova, California, that advises small and home-based businesses. "Even a new person can participate."

But participating means gaining at least a passing knowledge of online lingo. Unlike the face-to-face meetings that take place in the off-line world, in which speakers express themselves through gestures, expressions, and sounds as well as words, online repartee—with only typed characters at your disposal—can occasionally result in misunderstandings. That's why many people choose to spice up their online notes with "emoticons" or "smileys" to express their true intentions.

These little symbols—usually placed strategically at the end of a sentence—may look like hieroglyphics at first, but, when you tilt your head to the left, they resemble little faces with a colon for eyes and a hyphen for a nose. A message that ends :-), for example, means "just kidding." One that ends :-(means "I'm sorry (to be the bearer of bad news)."

According to a recent article in *The Wall Street Journal*, one smiley dictionary making the rounds on computer bulletin boards lists 664 distinct variations, including:

:-D	I'm laughing
B-)	I'm cool
:*)	I'm drunk
:-':	I have a cold
{(:-)	I have a toupee

One popular emoticon on CompuServe is <g>, or <grin>, which means, "just kidding" or "only joking."

Acronyms are also popular in the world of online messages and bulletin boards. There's BTW ("by the way"), PITA ("pain in the a__"), OTOH ("on the other hand"), FWIW ("for what it's worth"), FYI ("for your information"), and many more.

AWTTW ("A word to the wise"): Don't use smiley symbols or acronyms unless you're sure you know what you're saying. Otherwise, you could end up with a ;-) (raised eyebrow) or two.

Summary

In this chapter, you learned the basics of getting started with electronic mail. With e-mail, as it's commonly known, you can send instant messages to colleagues, friends, and online acquaintances in a variety of formats, including fax, teletype, and postal mail. You also learned how to compile an online address book and explored the possibilities of online networking, complete with its own peculiar rules and rituals.

In the next chapter, you'll learn another important skill that will make your online experience even more rewarding—uploading (sending) and downloading (receiving) files.

CHAPTER 7

Uploading and Downloading

In Chapter 6, you mastered a key element of online communications—how to send, retrieve and store electronic mail. You also learned about compiling an online address book and got a taste of networking online.

In this chapter, you'll learn another vital communications skill—uploading (sending) and downloading (receiving) files—that will make your online experience even more rewarding. Once you get the hang of it, you'll be able to send and receive text, program, and graphics files in a matter of keystrokes, speeding computer files to their destinations with a single phone call and filling your hard drive with free software. You'll also learn how to print out hard-copy versions of the text you see on your screen and convert the compressed computer files you download from Prodigy, CompuServe, and other online services into programs that can run on your computer.

Making Your Files Fly

Now that you know how easy it is to send notes and messages online, you'll soon find yourself wanting to do more. If your business requires you to ship spreadsheets, reports, and other lengthy documents to off-site locations, using an online service as your communications link can save you time and money.

By uploading a file to your recipient's online mail box, you eliminate the need to print out and fax paper copies of your work or to copy the file onto a diskette and ship it by overnight mail—saving you and your clients the high cost of express delivery and retyping. On most online services, uploading a file is free except for the time it takes to send the file from your computer to your recipient's online mail box. It's a process that, depending on the size of the file and the speed of your modem, often takes no more than a few minutes.

UPLOADING A TEXT FILE

While you don't need to subscribe to an online service to upload a file—almost any communications software program will let you do the same thing—an online service with a front-end program like CompuServe Information Manager makes things a whole lot easier. That's because programs like CIM guide you step-by-step through what can be a confusingly technical process, and they don't require someone to sit at the computer terminal on the other end to "capture" your file as it comes in. (Prodigy, as noted earlier, does not yet offer uploading capabilities.)

Here's how to upload a text file using WinCIM:

1. Create a text file off-line using a word processor or text editor.

2. Save the document as an ASCII, or text-only, file. (The advantage to doing this is that an ASCII file can be read by virtually any computer, even one that uses a different word

processor or computing environment from yours. The disadvantage is that an ASCII file contains no formatting—any italics, boldface or page breaks that you inserted into your original text are automatically erased. If you want to send your text file the way you originally prepared it, you'll have to send it as a binary file as described below.)

3. Click Send File from the Mail pull-down menu.

4. Fill in the on-screen Recipient List with the recipient's name and e-mail address. You can do this by either typing the information into the box that appears on your screen or by copying a name and address from your WinCIM address book.

5. Type the subject of the file at the Subject: prompt.

6. At the File Name: prompt, type the full name of the file, specifying the disk drive, the path, the file name and the extension. A sample file name might look like this: **c:\winword\test.txt**

7. Click the circle next to Text. (If the size of your file exceeds 50,000 characters, or roughly 20 pages of typed text, click the circle next to Binary. WinCIM can't send large ASCII files.)

8. Once you've completed the envelope, click the Send Now button at the bottom of the box to log onto CompuServe and send the file immediately. Or, if you prefer, click Out Basket to send the file later. You'll save time and money with the Out Basket if you have several files to send.

Figure 7.1 shows a text file being uploaded onto CompuServe.

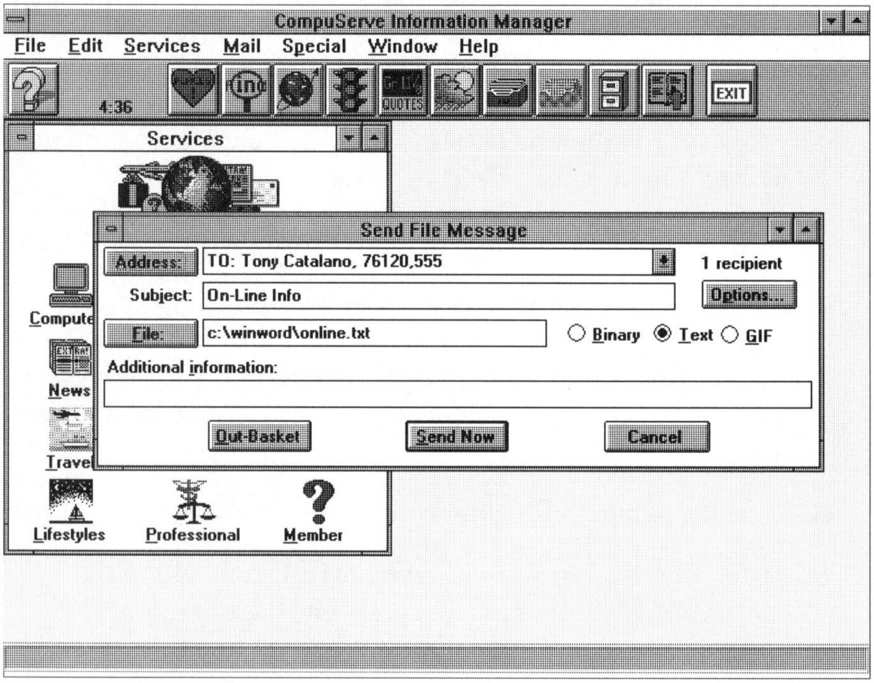

FIGURE 7.1: Uploading a text file on CompuServe

UPLOADING PROGRAM AND GRAPHICS FILES

To upload a program or graphics file with WinCIM, follow the instructions above except for one small variation. Instead of choosing Text, click Binary. This way, all your formatting will remain intact when your file gets to your recipient's online mail box. This is especially important for sending spreadsheets, where it's essential that the original columns and rows be preserved. Binary transfers are also essential for uploading program files, which consist of binary data and must arrive bug-free in order to work. (Binary data consists of eight-bit numbers, but an ASCII character contains only seven bits. Throw away that eighth bit, and you're left with garbage—a program that won't run.)

Bringing Your Files Home

While uploading files is an important online skill, many computer users find downloading even more vital. That's because mass-market online services like CompuServe and Prodigy offer users thousands of free and low-cost programs—provided you can figure out how to get them.

Knowing how to download is also crucial for retrieving text files—online bulletin boards are chock full of how-to files offering helpful business and technical advice, and online databases are filled to the brim with newspaper and magazine articles on almost every imaginable topic.

DOWNLOADING A TEXT FILE

Once you know how to upload a text file, figuring out how to download one is only slightly trickier. In fact, downloading a text file on a front-end program like WinCIM is almost automatic. Downloading a file without the aid of a front-end program is somewhat trickier and requires you to make more choices, such as which file-transfer *protocol* to use (see below).

Downloading On CompuServe

Let's look at two types of text-file downloads—retrieving a forum file from CompuServe's Working from Home Forum, a bulletin board for home-based business people, and retrieving a magazine article from CompuServe's Computer Database Plus, an online library that contains thousands of articles from a wide variety of computer publications.

Here's how to use WinCIM to download a forum file:

1. Before logging on, click the GO icon and type **work**. Click OK. WinCIM will automatically log you on and take you to the Working from Home Forum.

2. Once you're in the forum, click the Browse Library icon from the icon palette along the right side of your screen. The Browse command lets you review descriptions of the file's many forums and allows you to retrieve the files you choose.

3. Double-click the Library section you want to open.

4. Double-click the file you wish to see. A box will appear at the bottom of your screen that offers six options, including Next (to display summary information about the next file listed), View (to read the file online), Retrieve (to download a copy of the file to your computer) and Mark (to mark the file for later retrieval).

5. To download the file, click Retrieve.

6. In the box that appears on your screen, type the name that you would like the file to be called once you've downloaded it to your own computer. You can also select a new drive and directory—for example, the directory in which your word processor is located—or use the default settings that appear in the box to copy the file into the CompuServe directory. Then click OK. (If you don't specify a drive or directory, WinCIM will automatically deposit the file into a subdirectory called cserve\download on the drive onto which you loaded your program.)

7. Once you click OK, the downloading process begins. A small box appears on your screen that tells you the total size of the file (in bytes) and estimates how much time the entire copying process will take. A bar graph at the bottom of the box tells you when the operation is complete.

8. If you find several files that interest you, you may find it more economical to "mark" them than to retrieve them individually. To mark the files you want to download, click the box to the left of the box describing each file. After you've selected the files you want, click Retrieve Marked

from the Library pull-down menu. Then click Retrieve All from the left side of the box that appears and click the box next to the words, Disconnect when done. This tells WinCIM to download all the files you've selected and log you off.

Figure 7.2 shows a forum file being selected for downloading.

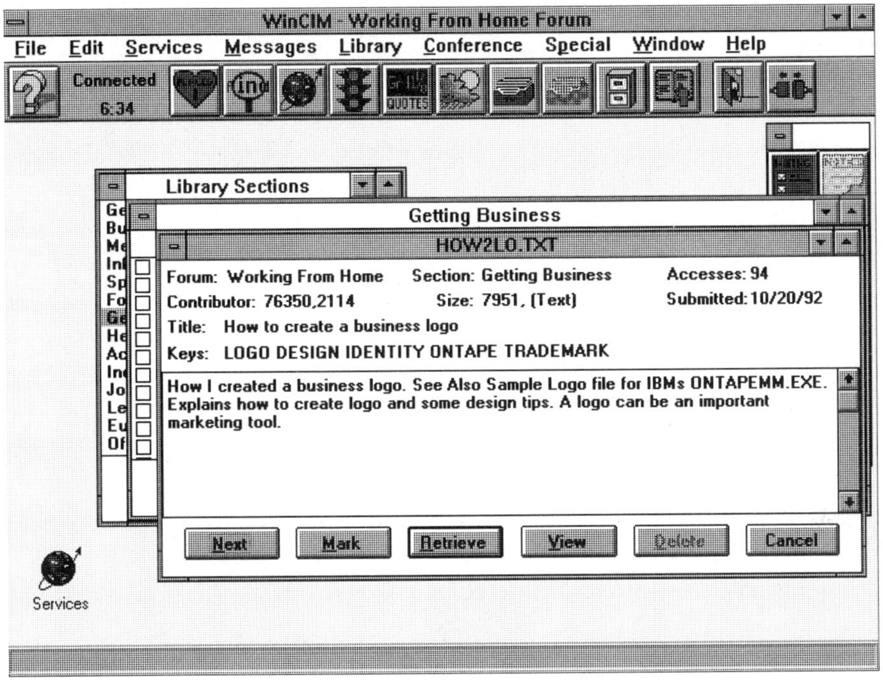

FIGURE 7.2: Downloading a text file from CompuServe's Working From Home Forum

Another way to download a text file is to "capture" it as it appears on your screen. When using WinCIM to search a database, for example, your screen will typically go blank and enter what is known as terminal emulation mode. This means that your computer will act as a dumb terminal that simply receives the information that CompuServe's host computer is sending. To store this data as a computer file, create a capture buffer by clicking Record in File from the Special pull-down menu at the top of your screen. While the capture buffer is turned on, you can print out the text inside by clicking Print from the File pull-down menu or you can save it as a file by clicking Save from the File menu and assigning it a name and a directory location.

Here's how to use WinCIM to download a magazine article from Computer Database Plus:

1. Log onto Computer Database Plus by clicking the GO icon from the toolbar at the top of your screen and typing **COMPDB** at the prompt.
2. Once you access the database, select Search for Articles. Press ↵.
3. Choose Key Words from the on-screen menu. Press ↵.
4. At the prompt, type **modem**. Press ↵.
5. Choose Display Menu of Article Citations. Press ↵.
6. Select 1 to view the first article on the list. Press ↵.
7. Click Special, then Record in File to create the capture buffer.
8. Name the file you wish to create, or accept the WinCIM default settings to download the file into the cserve\download subdirectory. Click OK.
9. To stop capturing text, click Special, then Record in File.

Figure 7.3 shows the article in the capture buffer.

Here's a tip: WinCIM's capture buffer is set to hold only 100 lines of text at a time. This can cause problems if you're downloading a long file—when the buffer is full, new lines replace the old ones starting at the top. To remedy this, click Special, then Preferences, then Terminal Emulation. Then, in the dialog box that appears on your screen, change the setting to your best estimate of the length of the file, say 300 or 500 lines.

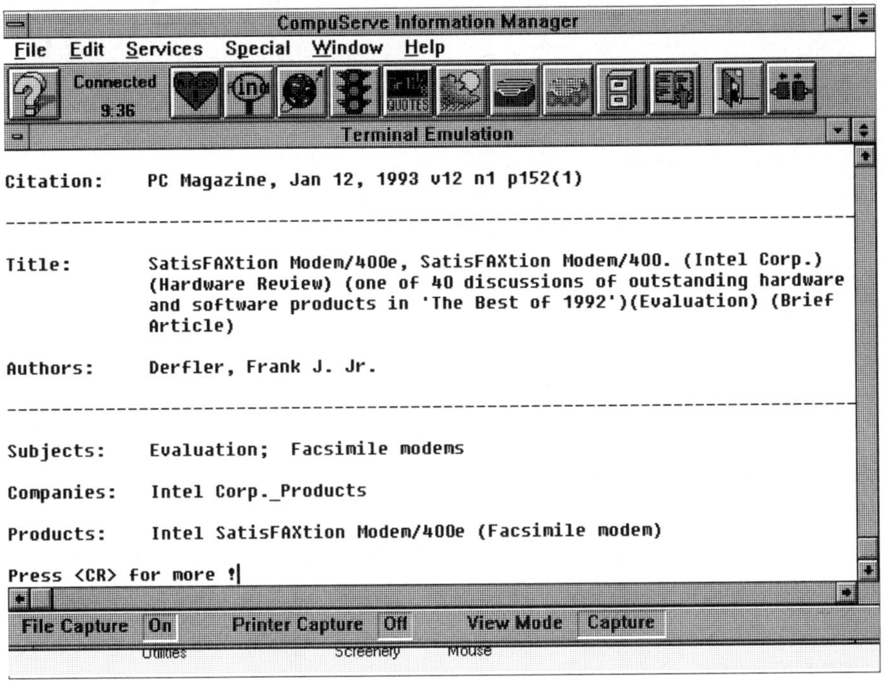

FIGURE 7.3: Capturing a magazine article from Computer Database Plus

Downloading On Prodigy

While Prodigy does not yet offer uploading, the service does let you download text and program files. In contrast to CompuServe, however, Prodigy's downloading process—for text files, at least—is cumbersome and time-consuming. If you're a novice user and the file is fairly short, you may find it easier just to print out the file on your computer printer.

Here's how to download a text file using Prodigy:

1. Log onto Prodigy and select the text you wish to copy to a file.
2. Choose TOOLS from the bottom of your screen. Press ↵.
3. Choose Copy Options from the TOOLS box. Press ↵.
4. Choose the Send to File option. Press ↵.

5. Pick a name for the file, and type it at the *File:* prompt. Press ↵.

6. This returns you to to the Copy Options box. Press ↵ to confirm that you want to send the document to a file rather than to a printer.

7. Choose ESC from the TOOLS menu at the bottom of your screen. Press ↵.

8. Choose COPY from the bottom of the box or screen. Press ↵. This will copy the text to the Prodigy directory under the file name you've specified.

Note: Prodigy assumes you want to download files into its own directory. At step 5 you can specify a different directory path, such as **c:\winword\prodigy.txt**; but you are limited to a total length of 30 characters, including the file name. (If your directory structure is more complex than that, you probably know how to move the file using DOS or Windows.)

Figure 7.4 shows a text file being downloaded from Prodigy.

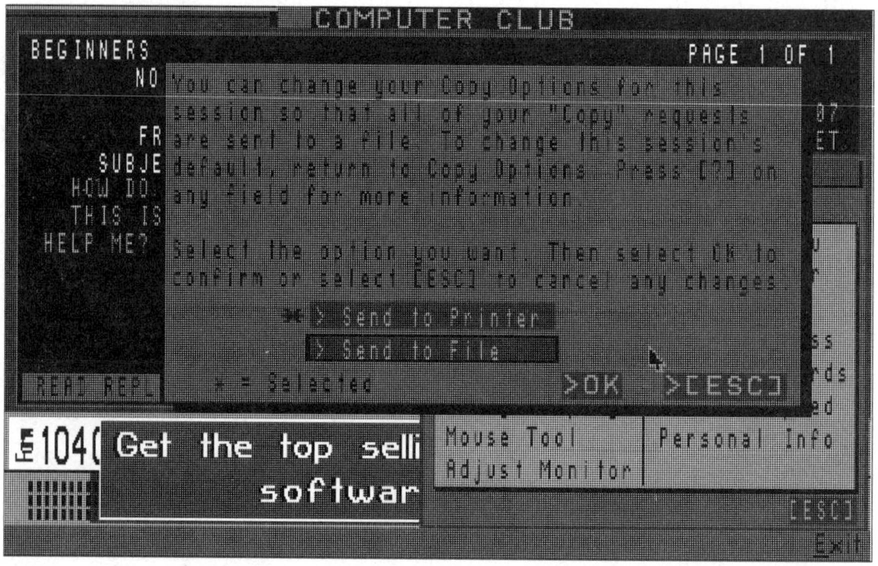

FIGURE 7.4:
Downloading a text file on Prodigy

DOWNLOADING PROGRAM AND GRAPHICS FILES

On most online services, retrieving a program or graphics file (often called a "binary" file) is no different from downloading a text file and not much tougher. (With CIM, simply select Binary, rather than Text.) The chief difficulty lies not in copying the file but in turning it into usable software once you get hold of it. That's because, while most text files arrive in ASCII format and can be read by virtually any computer, binary files and some text files are often compressed to save space. If they are program files, this means that they must be decompressed before you can run them—a process not so different from adding hot water to freeze-dried coffee to whip up a quick brew.

While some program files are self-extracting, which means they automatically balloon to full size once you execute them, other files require a special software program to decompress them. One of the most popular decompression programs is PKUNZIP, a shareware program that is available for downloading from any number of online services and bulletin boards. It's a companion to the PKZIP program, which compresses files. To get a copy of these programs on CompuServe, log onto the IBM Communications Forum and download a file called PK204C.EXE from the forum library. The file contains all the instructions you need to run it.

Prodigy also lets you download software—but only if you agree to pay an extra $14.95 a month for a Custom Choice called Ziffnet for Prodigy. Ziffnet, which is also available on CompuServe, offers access to thousands of free and low-cost software programs in addition to buying advice, technical tips, news and commentary, and a library containing demonstration versions of hundreds of leading commercial software packages.

Here's how to download the Ziffnet Download Manager using Ziffnet for Prodigy:

1. JUMP to Ziffnet for Prodigy. Press ↵.
2. Enroll in the Custom Choice option, if you haven't already done so.
3. Select the Contents option, then choose Software from the Ziffnet Contents menu that appears on your screen. Press ↵.
4. Select the For Beginners button at the bottom of the box. Press ↵.
5. Choose the Programs button at the bottom of the box. Press ↵.
6. Select Ziffnet Download Manager from the list of programs. Press ↵.
7. Choose the Download button at the bottom of the box. Press ↵.
8. Select the Begin Download option. Press ↵. This will make a copy of the program in your Prodigy directory, as illustrated in Figure 7.5.
9. When you're finished downloading, exit Prodigy and type **ZDM** at the DOS prompt. This will decompress the file so that you can use it to decompress other Ziffnet software.

Figure 7.5 shows the Ziffnet Download Manager being downloaded from Prodigy.

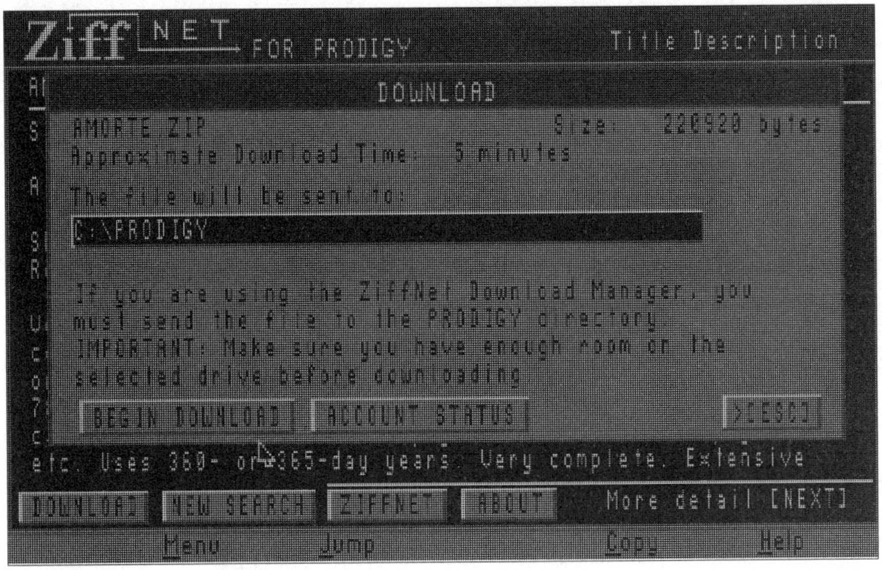

FIGURE 7.5: Downloading a program from Prodigy's Ziffnet database

Choosing a File Transfer Protocol

Before you transfer a file, you have to choose a *protocol*, or set of rules, that tells the modem in your PC how to communicate with the modem at the online service on the other end. While this sounds a little technical, the concept is actually not so different from what happens when you pick up the phone and call a friend or business associate. You dial the number and wait for the person on the other end to pick up his phone and say, "Hello." Then you state your name, and the conversation begins. It's the same way with computer modems, but, since modems can't "talk" the way we can, communications instructions must be spelled out even more precisely.

Hence, the need for protocols.

The good news is that you don't need to be an expert on file transfer protocols if you want to upload or download a file. Typically, your communications software does all the heavy lifting for you—all you do is select which protocol you want (see below) and make sure the computer on the other end is using the same one. In fact, if you stick with a front-end program like WinCIM, you'll never even need to make that choice. That's because the WinCIM system automatically defaults to the built-in CompuServe B+ protocol, which checks for transmission errors in 512K-block units of text. CompuServe insists that this proprietary protocol is faster than any others for use within the CompuServe environment.

On other online services, you'll be confronted with a dizzying array of choices depending on the communications software you use. Procomm Plus, for example, offers one of the widest arrays of protocols, including exotics like Kermit, Sealink and Modem7. Procomm's menu of protocols is illustrated in Figure 7.6.

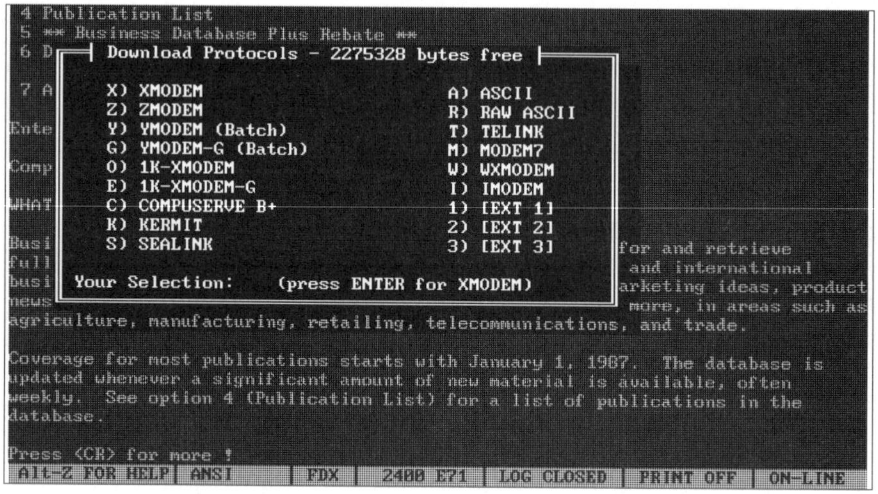

FIGURE 7.6:
Selecting a protocol from the Procomm Plus menu

Here's a sampling of some of the more popular protocols and what they do:

- XMODEM—Still the mainstay of the online world, XMODEM is supported by virtually every communications software program. It checks for errors in 128-byte data blocks and resends the block if there's a problem. It's slow but reliable. When in doubt, use it.
- YMODEM—Going XMODEM one better, YMODEM checks for errors in larger, 1024-byte (1K) blocks, speeding up the file transfer process. YMODEM is also capable of transferring multiple, or "batch" files, as opposed to XMODEM, which can only handle one file at a time.
- ZMODEM—The state-of-the-art file transfer method, ZMODEM is an efficient multiple-file protocol popular on many bulletin boards. It features automatic downloading and sends the file name, file size and creation date information along with each file. What's more, ZMODEM is flexible enough to vary the size of each data block to allow for noisy telephone lines and can even restart an interrupted transmission.
- ASCII—Not a true protocol, ASCII (American Standard Code for Information Interchange) has no error-checking and only a minimal "handshaking" capability to alert the remote computer to the file transmission. ASCII transfers are often quicker than XMODEM transfers but should only be used for shipping text files since some of the data may come through garbled.

Printing Text from the Screen

If the file you want to copy is short, you may not want to go to the trouble of downloading it and saving it on your hard disk. It may be faster and easier just to make a copy on your computer printer. WinCIM makes this simple. It's just like printing out a copy of an e-mail message; you click Print from the File pull-down menu.

Summary

In this chapter, you learned how to upload and download text, program, and graphics files—skills that can save you time and money by enabling you to speed computer files thousands of miles with a single phone call and pack your hard drive with free and low-cost software. You also learned how to print out hard copy versions of the text you see on your screen and convert the "freeze-dried" files you download from Prodigy, CompuServe, and other online services into quality software that can run on your computer.

In the next chapter, you'll learn how to tap into hundreds of online forums and bulletin boards to enhance your computing skills and help you pursue your business and professional interests.

CHAPTER 8

Forums and Bulletin Boards

In Chapter 7, you mastered one of the most valuable online communications skills—uploading (sending) and downloading (receiving) files. You learned how to send and retrieve text, program, and graphics files in a matter of keystrokes, and also how to print out hard-copy versions of the text you see on your screen and convert the compressed program files you download into software that can run on your computer.

Now that you know the basics—swapping files, sending e-mail, navigating online menus—you're ready to begin exploring what the online world has to offer. In this chapter, you'll learn how to tap into hundreds of online forums and bulletin boards to bolster your computing skills and advance your business and professional interests. You'll also learn how to swap ideas and experiences with an international community of contacts and colleagues, explore forum libraries, and "go live" with real-time chat sessions with other members. You'll also hear what veteran onliners have to say about making the most of the bulletin board experience—and get valuable pointers on turning the time you spend online into rewarding and profitable opportunities.

Hanging Out at the Online Bulletin Board

As anybody who's worked in an office knows, one of the most popular employee hang-outs is the company bulletin board. That's where you can learn about who's on the way up, who's on the way down, even who's on the way out. It's also the place where the boss posts the directions to the company picnic and where your co-workers tack up ads for everything from new roommates to used cars.

It shouldn't surprise you, then, that bulletin boards are just as popular in the online world, if not more so. As in the off-line world where people meet face to face, electronic bulletin boards serve not only as way stations for the latest news and notices, they also bring members together to chat, gossip, and swap advice and contacts.

Online bulletin boards are nothing new. Back in the late Seventies, they soared in popularity as early personal computer enthusiasts sought a forum to debate issues, send e-mail, and trade software. Soon, organized groups of computer users got into the act, too, as did businesses and government agencies in search of a fast, reliable way of storing and retrieving large amounts of information.

Today, there are over 20,000 electronic bulletin board systems (or BBSs) nationwide operated by individuals, businesses, nonprofit organizations, and government agencies. Many are free except for the cost of dialing in with your modem; and, like just about everything else online, they're open 24 hours a day, seven days a week.

The real value of online bulletin boards is their specialized focus. Unlike the community bulletin board at your local supermarket, online bulletin boards typically appeal to a niche audience—for example, people who use IBM-compatible, Macintosh, or Amiga computers, or people with a particular interest such as home-based business, desktop publishing, or horse breeding.

Some online bulletin boards are strictly local, targeting computer users in a particular city or town; others are national, offered through major online services like CompuServe, Prodigy, GEnie, Delphi, and America Online. Some boards attract members with free and low-cost software to download into their computers; others offer real-time discussions and a core of knowledgeable members eager to share tips and advice. For more information about specific bulletin boards and which online services offer them, see Chapter 13.

With so many online bulletin boards out there, it's virtually impossible to sample every one. To find out what's available locally, consult your local computing newspaper or user group. Computer dealers are another source of online information. And national online services such as CompuServe and Prodigy provide lists of bulletin boards—also known as "forums" and "roundtables"—in their online indexes and off-line instruction manuals.

Putting Online Bulletin Boards to Work for You

Despite the growing popularity of online bulletin boards, they can be somewhat intimidating for new users. That's because, unless you choose a board supported by a front-end program like those offered by CompuServe, Prodigy, or America Online, you'll have to wrestle with a perplexing array of technical issues such as setting up your communications software to dial the number and mastering a new set of navigational commands for each board you log onto. What's more, some bulletin boards restrict the amount of time you can spend online to as little as half an hour each day—forcing you, the novice user, to play "beat the clock" while you learn the system.

That's why, until you get comfortable with online communications, it's a good idea to stick with bulletin boards offered by major online services featuring pull-down menus, dialog boxes and mouse support. While services like these usually cost more than their local counterparts, they're also usually easier to access and navigate. And if, like many business users, you're more interested in making contacts than downloading free software, the "big boards" provide the added advantage of connecting you to a national and international network of customers and colleagues—a feature that the local BBS usually can't offer. CompuServe has one of the biggest and broadest selections of online bulletin boards—more than 350 at last count—with Prodigy coming up strong.

Professionals who access online bulletin boards on a regular basis say that logging on can pay big dividends in the form of profitable contacts. Andrew Rosenbaum and his wife, Laura Colby, both freelance journalists in Paris, say they have gotten job leads and article assignments through their participation in CompuServe's Journalism Forum. Linda Stern, a freelancer in Takoma Park, Maryland, says she got a regular fact-checking assignment from a monthly magazine through her activity on CompuServe's Investor's Forum. A contact on CompuServe's Working From Home Forum recently helped her land a book contract.

And, while even enthusiasts admit that online networking lacks the some of the immediacy of face-to-face schmoozing at a cocktail party or a trade show, a growing number of entrepreneurs insist it's the next best thing to being there—and far less costly. Chuck and Sue DeFiore, who run a home-based consulting firm in California that advises other small and home-based businesses, have parlayed their subscription to CompuServe into a global network of client contacts. For every $100 they spend online, the DeFiores say, they reap roughly $300 in business.

"The biggest thing online networking does is increase your market base," Chuck DeFiore says. "My goal is to move 50 percent of our business out of the local economy. That makes us free agents."

THE MESSAGE BOARD

Online bulletin boards are generally divided into three parts—the message board, the library, and the conference room. The message board, just like the off-line variety, is the place where members tack up notices—news, advice, announcements, requests for help. The library is the place where the files are kept—text files, program files, and graphics files available for reading and downloading. The conference room is where bulletin board members meet for one-on-one chats and real-time conferences about topics of interest.

Posting a Message

The fastest way to get an online conversation rolling is to tack up your own message on the electronic bulletin board of your choice.

Now that you know about some of the things that online bulletin boards can do, it's time to learn the basic skills you need to use them. While each bulletin board works slightly differently, I've chosen examples from CompuServe to illustrate the various techniques involved in sending and retrieving messages, searching for library files, joining in real-time conferences, and the like. While Prodigy offers bulletin boards, too, the Prodigy boards limit you to sending and retrieving messages; they do not offer the other standard bulletin board features.

Here's how to post a message using WinCIM:

1. Log onto CompuServe.

2. Select a bulletin board that interests you and access it by clicking the GO icon on the toolbar at the top of your screen and typing the board's keyword at the prompt. (If you don't know the keyword, choose GO INDEX and search by subject matter.)

3. Join the bulletin board by clicking Join.

4. Click the Create Message icon from the icon palette at the right side on your screen. A message box, similar to the one you used to create an e-mail message in Chapter 6, will appear on your screen.

5. Fill in the message topic and the recipient's CompuServe address at the *Subj:* and *To:* prompts at the top of the box. To give your message the maximum possible exposure, type **All** after the *To:* prompt. If your question is for the bulletin board operator (or sysop, as they're commonly known), type **Sysop** at the prompt. (You can post your message in a different forum by clicking the arrow next to the *Forum:* prompt; you can also post a message in a different section of the same forum by clicking the arrow next to the *Section:* prompt.)

6. Tab to the text portion of the message box, and compose your message.

7. Click the Send button from the bottom of the box. This posts your message on the forum for everyone to read.

Figure 8.1 shows a message about to be sent to everyone on the WordStar Forum.

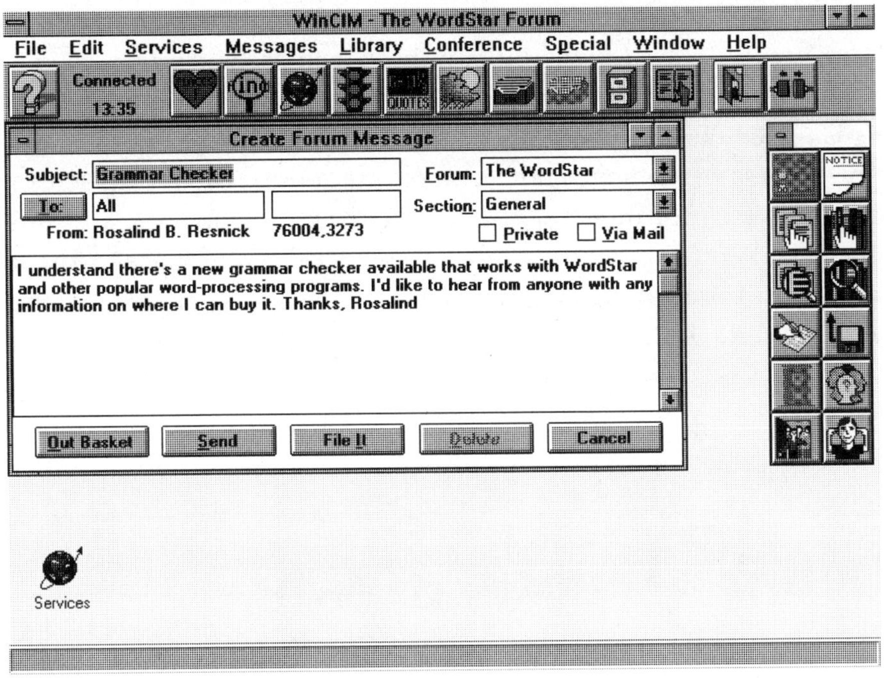

FIGURE 8.1:

Creating a message on CompuServe's WordStar Forum

Responding to a Message

Another way to spark an on-line discussion is to reply to a message that's been left by somebody else. It doesn't even have to be addressed to you! To respond to an on-line message using WinCIM, click Reply from the bottom of the message box that appears on your screen. A new message box will appear on your screen with the subject and the recipient's address already filled in. Simply type in your reply, and click Send.

You can also follow the same steps to reply to any messages that have been sent to you in response to the initial note you posted. If you want to keep your conversation private, put an X in the brackets beside the *Via Mail* box. This way, your reply will appear only in the recipient's CompuServe mail box and no one else will see it.

Reading a Message

There are two ways to read bulletin board messages—browsing and searching. Just like window-shopping at a department store, browsing is preferable if you're not sure what you're looking for. Click the Browse Messages icon from the icon palette at the right of your screen to display a list of message board selections. Double-click a forum topic, and WinCIM will list all the messages posted in that section of the forum. For example, Figure 8.2 shows the list of messages in the DOS & Windows DTP section of the Desktop Publishing Forum. To read a message, simply double-click it.

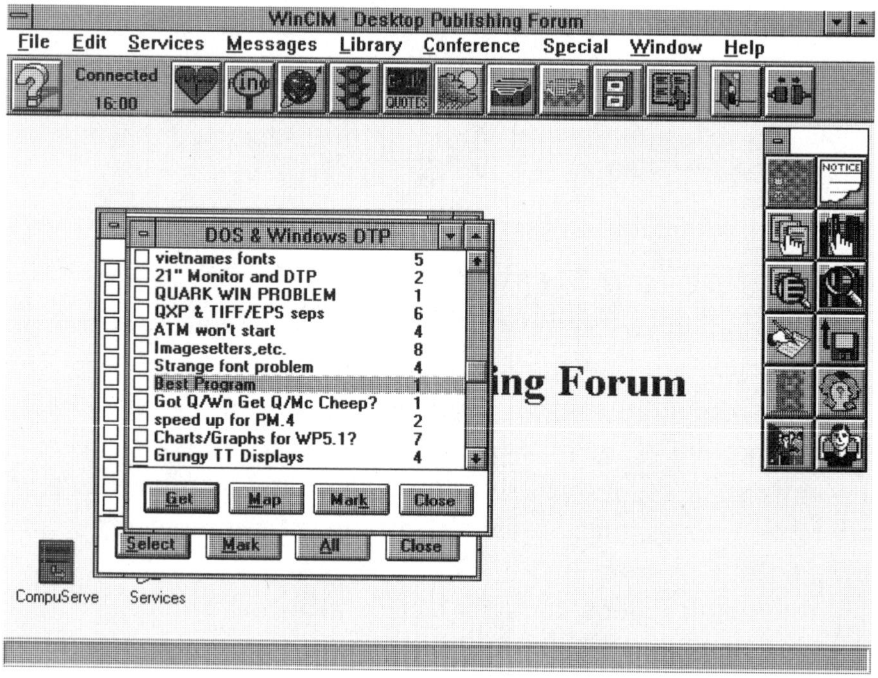

FIGURE 8.2:

Browsing through messages on CompuServe's Desktop Publishing Forum

To search for a message about a specific topic, click the Search Messages icon from the icon palette. The on-screen box that appears lets you search for messages by topic, sender, or recipient. To narrow your search, click None; to broaden it, choose All. You can also narrow or expand your search by changing the starting date of the messages you want to see. You can also click Mark Results so that you can download the files later.

THE LIBRARY

Like your local public library, the libraries housed on electronic bulletin boards contain the electronic equivalent of articles, reports, even books. While the message board contains a series of brief notes, the forum library stores lengthier files uploaded by forum members. These files include not only electronic versions of the kind of documents found in off-line libraries but also software, transcripts of online conferences, and sequences of messages (called "message threads") saved by the sysop.

Like the message boards, CompuServe's forum libraries are organized into sections, each one dedicated to a particular aspect of the forum's general area of interest. For example, Figure 8.3 shows the files in the Stocks/the Market section of CompuServe's Investor's Forum library. To use WinCIM browse through the files—the equivalent of meandering through the aisles of an off-line library—simply click the Browse Library icon at the right of your screen. Then double-click a section from the menu that appears, and select a file from the section's menu. You can also search for a specific file the same way you looked for a forum message—by file name, user ID, message number, or keywords. (It sure beats the old Dewey Decimal System!)

WinCIM then gives you the choice of reading a short summary, or abstract, of the file; viewing the entire file; retrieving (downloading) the file; marking the file to be downloaded later; skipping to the next file; or returning to the main menu. For step-by-step instructions on downloading forum files, see Chapter 7.

Online bulletin boards also give you, the user, the chance to contribute files of your own to their electronic libraries. Unlike off-line libraries that just lend you materials, online libraries encourage you

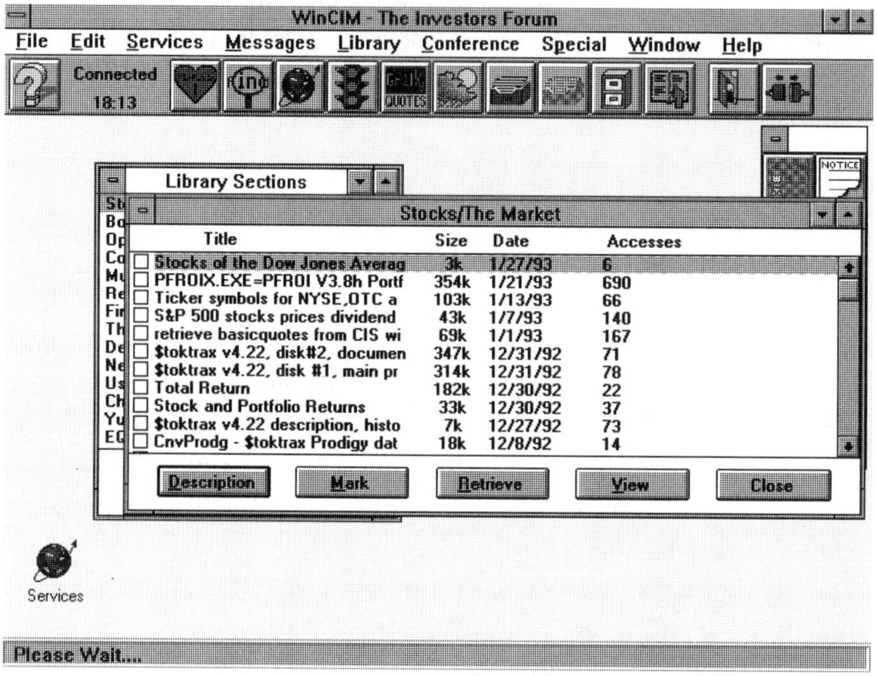

FIGURE 8.3:
The Library of CompuServe's Investor's Forum

to make it a two-way street—sometimes rewarding you with free connect time for every file you donate. To upload a file using WinCIM, click the Contribute icon at the right side of the screen and type in the file name, title, keywords, and a short description of the file at the appropriate prompts. Click OK, and WinCIM will automatically upload the file to the Library section where you want it placed.

THE CONFERENCE ROOM

Another popular feature of online bulletin boards is the conference room. Like conference rooms offered by hotels and convention centers, online conference rooms provide places where forum members can hold "live" conversations—everything from private conversations and casual chats to scheduled meetings and guest lectures.

And, unlike their counterparts in the off-line world, there's no special fee to rent the room—only the board's ordinary connect-time charges, if any.

Here's how to participate in an online conference on CompuServe:

1. Click Enter Room from WinCIM's Conference pull-down menu to display a list of available conference rooms. The menu also lets you choose options to find out who else is in the room (Who's Here), change your real name to a nickname (Set Nickname), listen in on a conversation in another conference room (Listen), even squelch conversation from anyone you'd rather not hear from (Ignore).

2. Once you choose a room, a conferencing "window" appears on your screen. To join in the chatter, just start typing. Your words will appear in the Input Box at the bottom of your screen. But don't worry about making a typo or accidentally typing something you didn't mean. Nothing will be sent until you reach the right margin of the Input Box of press ↵.

3. To hold a private discussion on-line, click Invite to ask one or more people to join in. Simply click the box next to the person's name in the dialog box that appears on your screen. When you have marked the name of everyone you want to invite, click Invite. Invitations are then sent to everyone whose names you have chosen.

Tip: For faster access to CompuServe's conferencing features, WinCIM lets you click icons similar to the ones that let you access messages and library files. Conferencing icons include Who's Here, Ignore and Invite.

Figure 8.4 shows the beginning of a conference on the Microsoft Word Forum in CompuServe.

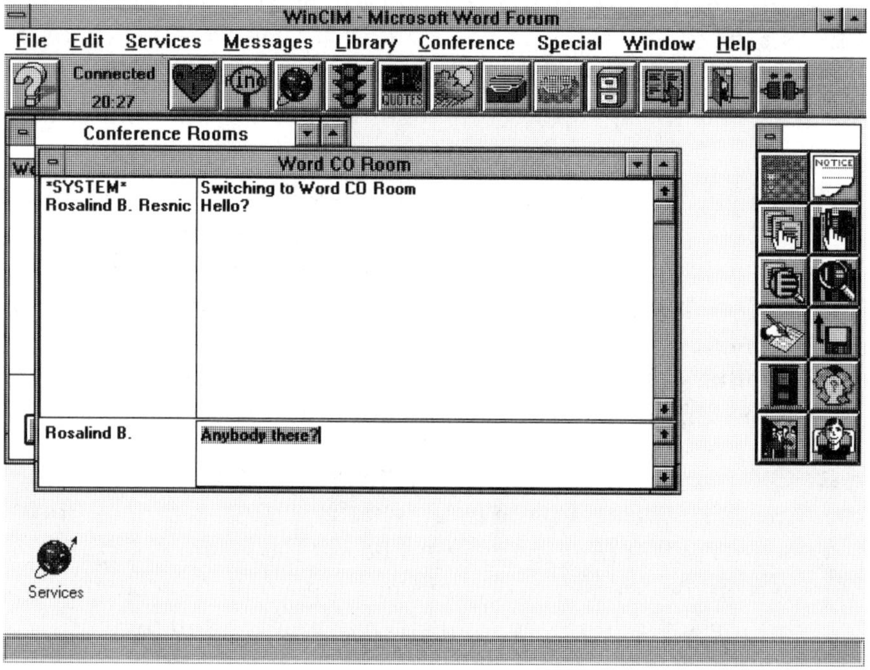

FIGURE 8.4: Starting an online conference on CompuServe's Microsoft Word Forum

Finding Kindred Spirits

Another benefit of online bulletin boards is the opportunity to meet colleagues, contacts, and clients with similar interests and goals. Because online networking is such a vital feature of most boards, many of the major online services allow you to search for members by name, interests, and other keywords. However, some services, such as Prodigy, permit you to search the membership database only by name and geographic location and do not let you limit your search to members on individual bulletin boards.

Here's how to search a forum membership directory using WinCIM:

1. Select Search Membership from the Special pull-down menu at the top of your screen.

2. The *Search for Member* box that appears on your screen lets you search by user name, user ID, and interests. If you are searching for a particular name but aren't sure how it's spelled, try typing in the first few letters. To search by interest, enter the first part of the word. Typing **comput**, for example, will locate all forum members who have listed interests that include computers and computing.

3. Once the member's name appears on your screen, you can add it to your online address book by clicking Get, then Name, then OK from the dialog boxes that appear on your screen. Click Next to view the next entry in the forum's membership directory. Click Cancel to return to the list of entries or the search criteria prompt.

4. To change your own entry, click Change Member Entry from the Special pull-down menu and type in your interests. Since CompuServe automatically records your name and user ID number when you join the forum, it's not necessary to retype them.

Figure 8.5 shows a membership search underway in WinCIM.

Tuning In to Online Chat Boards

Not every online bulletin board features message threads and libraries; some are pure talk. America Online, for example, offers a wide variety of real-time chat boards that let members meet, mingle, and share thoughts, secrets, even fantasies. Because the service allows you to pick a "screen name" that's different from your own, you can type whatever you like without risk of embarrassment. While chat boards like these may not spark too many business deals or employment offers (of the mainstream kind, that is), they can and occasionally do lead to off-line romance and even marriage. They're also a fun way to unwind at the end of a busy day.

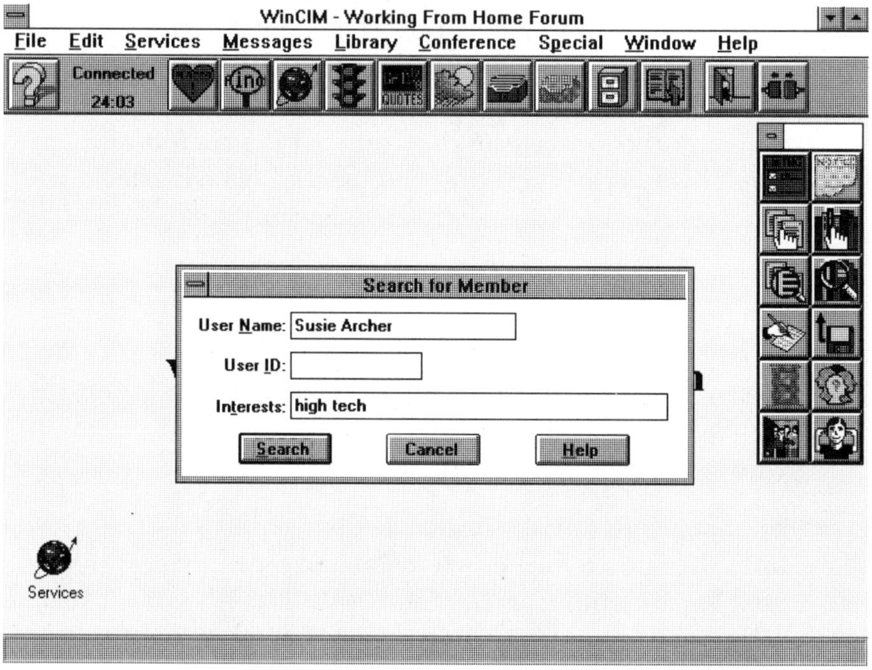

FIGURE 8.5: Searching the membership directory on CompuServe's Working From Home Forum

COMPUSERVE'S CB SIMULATOR

One of the most popular online chat boards is CompuServe's CB Simulator. Similar to the Citizens Band radios popular among long-distance truckers, CB Simulator is an electronic party line that lets members tune in for anonymous chats with anybody else who happens to be on the dial.

CompuServe offers two CB "bands"—the CB General Band and the CB Adult Band. The General Band offers G-rated channels such as the Breakfast Club, Heart to Heart, and Habla Espanol. The Adult Band offers R-rated fare like Gender Alternatives and Lesbian Lifestyles that are closed to CompuServe members under 18. However, both bands share a set of common rules: No "handle" can be used that the average person would find abusive, profane, or sexually offensive. The same goes for messages transmitted over an open channel. Disruptive behavior and business advertising are also taboo. Break the rules and you risk getting booted off the service for good.

Here's how to tune in a chat session on CompuServe's CB simulator:

1. Click the GO icon from the toolbar at the top of your screen. Type **CB**. Click OK.
2. Double-click Access CB General Band or Access CB Adult Band from the menu that appears on your screen.
3. CompuServe then prompts you to choose a "handle," or nickname, just like you would on CB radio. Your handle can contain up to 19 characters but can't include asterisks (*), pound signs (#) or braces ({ }). You can reserve your handle for future sessions by clicking Preferences from the Special pull-down menu and clicking CB Simulator. From there, you simply type your nickname at the *Handle:* prompt and click OK.
4. To choose a CB channel, click one of the numbers (1 through 40) that appears on WinCIM's Channel Selector grid. The channel's name will appear in the upper-left corner of the Channel Selector box. Select the Tune button at the bottom of the box to tune in a particular channel. There's also a Monitor button lets you listen in on another channel, a Who button that lists the other CBers on-line, and a Status button that shows the number of people tuned into each channel.
5. To jump into the conversation, just start typing. Your words will appear in the main conversation window as well as the Input Box at the bottom of your screen. As with the forum conferences described above, nothing you type will be sent to the main window until you reach the right margin of the Input Box or press ↵.

6. To keep track of the people you meet on CB simulator, click Friends from the People pull-down menu. The Friends List box that appears lets you record their handles and CompuServe ID numbers for future reference. The Open, Add and Delete buttons at the right allow you to insert and delete listings and edit them to add information.

7. To exit CB Simulator, click the Leave icon from the toolbar at the top of your screen.

Tip: For faster access to CompuServe's CB Simulator, WinCIM also gives you the option of clicking a palette of icons similar to the ones available in the CompuServe forums. CB icons include Channel Selector, Who's Here, and Change Handle.

Figure 8.6 shows a CB Simulator conversation underway.

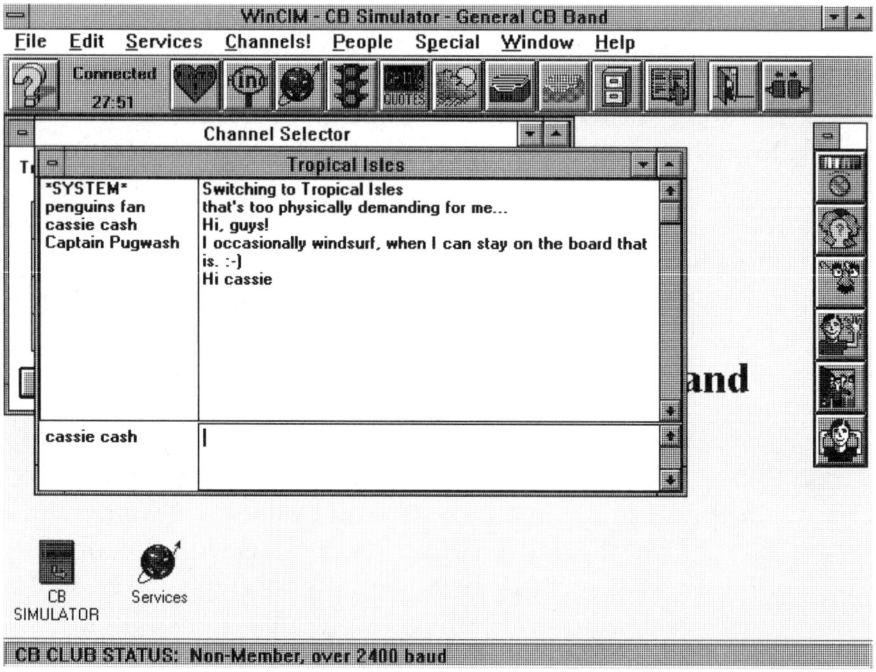

FIGURE 8.6: A conversation underway on COmpuServe's CB Simulator

Summary

In this chapter, you began to scratch the surface of what the online world has to offer. You learned how to tap into hundreds of online forums and bulletin boards to bolster your computing skills and pursue your business and professional goals and interests. You also learned how to swap ideas and experiences with an international community of like-minded colleagues, explore forum libraries and "go live" with real-time chat sessions with other members.

In the next chapter, you'll learn how to tap into online databases, those vast storehouses of online articles, market information and financial statistics that can give your business a competitive edge.

CHAPTER 9

Tapping into Databases

In Chapter 8, you began to scratch the surface of the online world's many riches. You learned how to tap into hundreds of online forums and bulletin boards to enhance your computing skills and advance your business and professional interests, how to swap ideas and experiences with an international community of contacts and colleagues, explore bulletin board libraries, and how to "go live" with real-time chat sessions with other members. Now, you're ready to mine the mother lode.

In this chapter, you'll learn about tapping into online databases, those vast repositories of online news articles, market information and financial statistics that can give your business a competitive edge. You'll get a brief overview of some of the online databases now available and learn how to access online encyclopedias, demographic reports, full-text databases, even online telephone directories. Along the way, you'll find out how to save time and money with proven search techniques and shortcuts.

Online Access versus Online Overload

One of the best things about online services is the access they give you to electronic databases. Whether you need to know the number of Big Macs sold in Omaha last year or the market for satellite dishes in Uzbekistan, you can be sure there's an online database out there somewhere that has exactly what you're looking for. At last count, there were more than 5500 databases available online, housing millions of articles, abstracts, reports and statistics from newspapers, newsletters, magazines, trade journals, and government publications from Harrisburg to Helsinki.

Market intelligence—the stock-in-trade of companies large and small—is especially plentiful online. Dialog Information Services, the online powerhouse owned by the Knight-Ridder publishing company, offers access to Standard & Poor's Register, PTS Marketing and Advertising Reference Service, and Trademarkscan. Data-Star, a service of Switzerland's Radio-Suisse, carries Tradstat, a database containing official government import/export information on more than 60,000 commodities from Europe, Japan, Canada, Taiwan, South America and the United States. And CompuServe, along with several other online services, offers access to D&B Dun's Market Identifiers, which provides names, addresses, sales figures and other vital statistics on millions of US companies.

With online databases like these, it's easy to ferret out answers to such baffling questions as "Which part of the country buys the most chocolate truffles?," helping you and your company crack new markets and boost business with clients you already have. With online databases, you also get fast, accurate information about target markets, trademark availability, credit information—even your competition's marketing plan.

The trouble is, with all the information out there, it's easy to get overloaded. And, unless you're a research professional, it's hard to know where to start. That's why many of the nation's top corporations employ full-time librarians just to sift through this mountain of electronic data to get to the good stuff. And the good stuff doesn't come cheap: Some databases cost hundreds of dollars an hour to access, and it's not uncommon for big companies to rack up hundreds of thousands of dollars a year in online charges.

Even so, electronic sleuthing doesn't have to be ruinously expensive—or the exclusive province of trained librarians. If you know what to do and where to go, you can scout out free and low-cost information that doesn't bust your budget. And, since many of the more popular business databases are offered by more than one online service, you can log on through the service you already subscribe to, using commands and menus you already know. By shopping around for the most cost-effective source of information you can find—and using off-line alternatives whenever possible, even the smallest business can afford to compete with the big guys.

Take Michael Miora, a computer consultant from Playa del Rey, California. Miora says he relies on CompuServe's Commerce Business Daily database to keep tabs on companies that have just won government contracts—companies he hopes he can turn into clients.

"All I have to do is pick up the phone and tell them that, while they're hiring, we'll gladly provide them with temporary consulting services," Miora says.

While *Commerce Business Daily* is available in a print version as well, the off-line publication is lengthy and poorly organized, Miora says. So, instead of spending hours each day paging through it manually, Miora simply plugs in a couple of keywords and phrases to search the online version for topics of interest to his business. While it's a little more expensive to do it this way, it's still pretty cheap—only

$2 a search and $2 for each article retrieved—and frees up Miora's valuable time.

Miora says he does tap into pricier databases on occasion—usually to do research for a client. But that doesn't hurt his bottom line, since he passes on the cost. Once he shows his clients how cost-effective online databases really are, he says, he rarely gets a complaint.

"The way I've explained it is, 'You could pay for my time while I go to the library and research it manually,'" Miora says, "'but why not let my computer do the work for you?'"

Doing Your Homework with Online Bulletin Boards and Encyclopedias

If you're new to online databases and aren't sure where to begin, it's usually best to start from the general and work toward the specific, casting as wide a net as you possibly can. One of the best ways to do this is by posting a note on the appropriate online bulletin board—public relations, desktop publishing, computer consulting, or the like—and ask for advice from forum members who may have already discovered the same information you're looking for. Not only will you save time by not reinventing the wheel, but, with online services like CompuServe, all you'll pay for is the time you're connected to the service. Unlike many databases, bulletin boards rarely have surcharges.

Another low-cost way to start your search is by logging onto an online encyclopedia. Both Prodigy and CompuServe provide access to Grolier's Academic American Encyclopedia under their basic services plans, making this one database that you can take your time searching without fear of running up big bills. Grolier's online encyclopedia contains more than 33,000 articles and is updated four times a year, giving it an edge over the off-line kind that gathers dust in your bookcase and goes out of date before you've finished paying for it. Grolier's online encyclopedia also contains time-saving features like article outlines, statistics-packed fact boxes, cross-referencing tools and bibliographies to direct you to off-line sources of information.

TARGETING YOUR MARKET

Just how can an online encyclopedia help you scout out new markets? As an example, let's say that your company sells spare parts for drilling rigs to US oil companies. Now you hear that Venezuela, one of the world's leading petroleum producers, is staging an economic recovery and might be a lucrative export market. But is it politically stable?

Here's how you would use Prodigy to access the Grolier's online encyclopedia and research this question:

1. Log onto Prodigy and select the JUMP button at the bottom of your screen.
2. Type **encyclopedia** in the box that appears. Press ↵.
3. Type **Venezuela** at the *Article Name:* prompt. Press ↵.
4. Choose Venezuela from the list of article titles, and press ↵.
5. Select an entry from the Table of Contents box. To see more entries, choose the Next button from the bottom of the Table of Contents box. Economic Activity, one of the selections on the new screen that appears, recounts Venezuela's economic troubles in the 1980s when its oil-based economy collapsed under the weight of falling oil prices and too much foreign debt. The entry also tells you that the country's recent austerity program has sparked riots and a general strike.
6. To learn more about Venezuela, you would choose Cross-References from the bottom of your screen and type in any

word that appears in all capitals in the Venezuela article. This would automatically take you to articles about Caracas, Venezuela's capital city, the Andes mountain chain, and other topics of interest.

7. To print out an encyclopedia entry, you would type **C** and press ↵. To save it as a file on your hard disk, follow the downloading instructions in Chapter 7.

Figure 9.1 illustrates this search in progress.

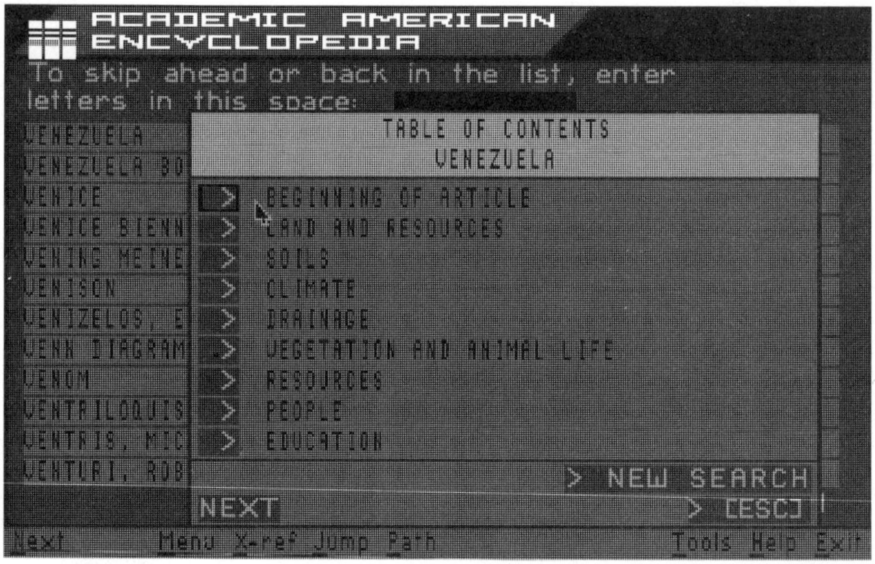

FIGURE 9.1:
Using Prodigy to search Grolier's online encyclopedia for information about Venezuela

Search Tips—Grolier's Encyclopedia

If you decide to use Grolier's online encyclopedia, make sure the search word you type is:

- Singular (for example, **widget**, not **widgets**)
- Spelled correctly (enter only as much of the word as you know)

- At least three letters long

It's also helpful if your search string is not too specific (for example, try **computer**, not **diskette**).

Mining Your Modem for Money

While online encyclopedias are cheap, comprehensive, and easy to search, they're not very useful when it comes to hunting for specific business information, such as sales leads, company contacts, demographic profiles, industry trends, and import/export data about specific products. For information like this, you've got to go a step farther and tap into those databases that offer up-to-the-minute market intelligence. A good place to start is with full-text databases that offer access to recent articles from trade journals, newspapers and magazines. You can usually search databases such as these by topic, title, publication date, even the name of the periodical an article appeared in, just by typing in a couple of keywords (see below for step-by-step instructions). They also tend to be less expensive than highly specialized databases about a single esoteric subject.

FULL-TEXT DATABASES: BLACK AND WHITE AND READ ALL OVER

One excellent source of full-text databases is CompuServe. Its Business Database Plus, for example, contains articles from over 450 regional, national and international business publications. Magazine Database Plus has articles from more than 90 of North America's leading magazines, from *The Atlantic* to *US News & World Report*. CompuServe's Newspaper Library provides access to 48 major US dailies, putting articles online as soon as two days after publication. There's also Computer Database Plus, which contains summaries and full-text articles from more than 130 computer-oriented magazines, newspapers, and trade journals.

Typically, databases like these allow you to enter one or more search words to hunt for a topic. After you type in a couple of key descriptive words or phrases, a list of article titles appears on your screen. Then you simply scan the titles (or glance at the abstracts, if they're available) and download any articles of interest.

Searching CompuServe's Computer Database Plus

For example, here's how to use CompuServe's Computer Database Plus to find articles about laser printers and scanners:

1. Using WinCIM, click the GO icon from the toolbar at the top of your screen. Type **COMPDB** at the prompt. Click OK.
2. Double-click Access Computer Database Plus.
3. Choose Search for Articles. Press ↵. Select Quick Reference instead, if you want a summary of basic operations and search methods.
4. Choose one of the nine options that appears on the Search Methods menu. To search for articles about laser printers and scanners, your best bet may be Key Words (words occurring in article titles, subject headings, company names or product names), Words in Article Text (words that appears anywhere in the article) or Subject Headings (phrases that describe article topics). You can also search under Product Name if you're looking for information about a particular make or model or under Article Types if you're looking for a product review.
5. After you make your choice, type in several words that define your search—say, **SCANNER OR LASER AND PRINTER**. Press ↵. By using the connecting words *or* and *and*, you tell Computer Database Plus to search for articles

containing the word *scanner*, plus articles containing both *laser* and *printer*. (For more about online search methods, see below.)

6. Once Computer Database Plus performs its search, it displays the results on a Search Summary menu. This lets you choose from seven options, including Display a Menu of Matching Articles, Narrow the Search, Replace (Erase) an Existing Search Method, and Start Over. Make a selection, and press ↵.
7. From the list of article titles that appears, select the ones you want to see and print them out or download them into a text file. Some articles offer the full text, others only an abstract. (For step-by-step downloading instructions, see Chapter 7.)
8. When you've finished your search, type **EXIT** at the prompt to leave the database and review your charges. Computer Database Plus carries a $15 an hour surcharge plus another $2.50 for every article retrieved ($1.50 if no abstracts are available). There's a $1 charge for each abstract.

Figure 9.2 shows this search in progress.

Search Tips—Online Databases

No matter which online database you work with, here are some quick tips to make your database search easier:

- Define your search off-line. Before you log on, jot down a couple of words that describe what you're looking for. The more time you spend with an ordinary piece of paper, the less time and money you'll spend online.
- Use AND to reduce the number of matching articles you retrieve. For example, **SPREADSHEET AND SOFTWARE AND WINDOWS**.

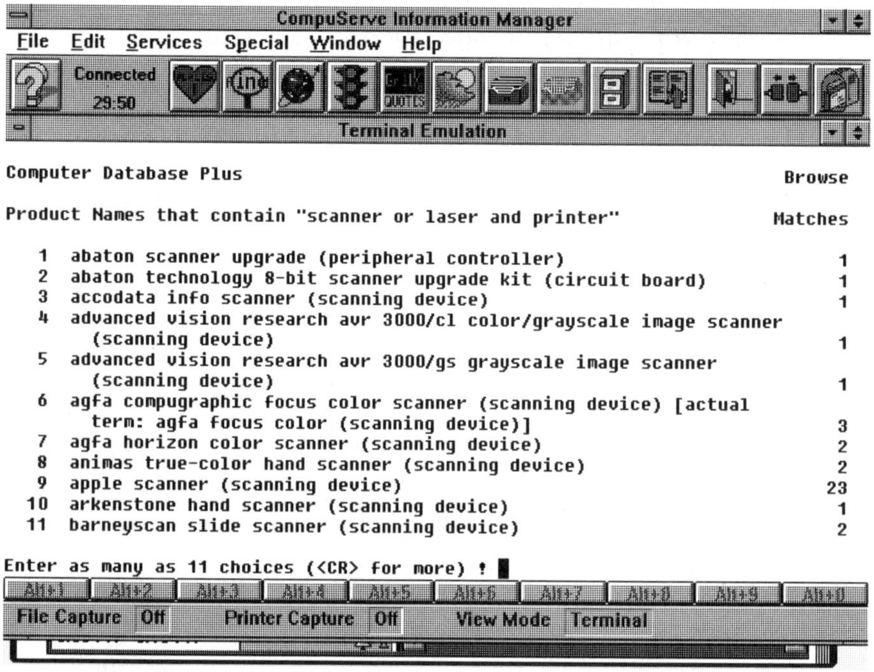

FIGURE 9.2: Searching Computer Database Plus for articles about laser printers and scanners

- Use OR to increase the number of matching articles. For example, **MOUSE OR TRACKBALL** finds articles that contain one or both of these items.

- Use NOT to exclude articles containing a specific term. For example, **PUBLISHING NOT DESKTOP** searches for all articles on publishing except for desktop publishing.

- Use "wildcards" to broaden your search. For example, in Computer Database Plus, **COMPUT*** finds all articles about computers, computing, computerization and so on. Other databases use the forward slash (/) as a wildcard, as in **COMPUT/**.

- Omit common words, such as OF, THE, AT and IN.

Keeping these rules in mind, it's important to remember that which search term goes where is not as important as crafting a search phrase that makes common sense. Miora, the computer consultant, advises novice online users to "think before you type."

"Construct your search parameters in the way you think about the subject," Miora says. "Pretend you're talking to the librarian at the research desk."

At the same time, because talk is cheap and online services are not, Miora advises making your initial search as specific as possible, then broadening it as you go. That's because most online databases charge only for what they find, billing you little or nothing for searches that don't turn up any matches, or "hits."

IQUEST

If you're not sure which database to search and want a little online hand-holding, don't be shy about asking for help.

One valuable search tool is IQuest, a joint effort of CompuServe, Telebase Systems, Inc. and Western Union Corp. Comprehensive and easy to use, IQuest acts as a gateway to more than 850 publications, databases, and indexes spanning the worlds of business, government, research, news, entertainment, and sports. IQuest's detailed menus prompt you for details about your information needs, then scan high-powered online services such as Dialog, BRS, NewsNet and Vu/Text for all relevant full-text articles and bibliographic citations.

If you're still floundering, type **SOS** at any prompt and a trained researcher will come online and help point you in the right direction. Better yet, log off and call CompuServe or the database vendor directly—you'll save on connect-time charges.

Of course, convenience like this doesn't come cheap. Each I-Quest search costs $9, and a few of its databases carry surcharges as high as $75. And, if your search turns up more than 10 matches, you'll need to fork over another $9 just to see the next group of 10 article titles. To see an abstract, or article summary, costs another $3.

That's why, if you already know which database you want, you can save time and money by accessing IQuest-II, which lets you specify the name of the database you want and bypass the IQuest menus. You can save even more money by logging onto an IQuest database, such as D&B-Dun's Market Identifiers, directly through CompuServe. This way, you'll pay only $2 to $4 per search, rather than the $9 IQuest charges. Just click Go from the WinCIM toolbar at the top of the screen and enter a keyword, such as **DUNS**.

Figure 9.3 shows an IQuest search in progress.

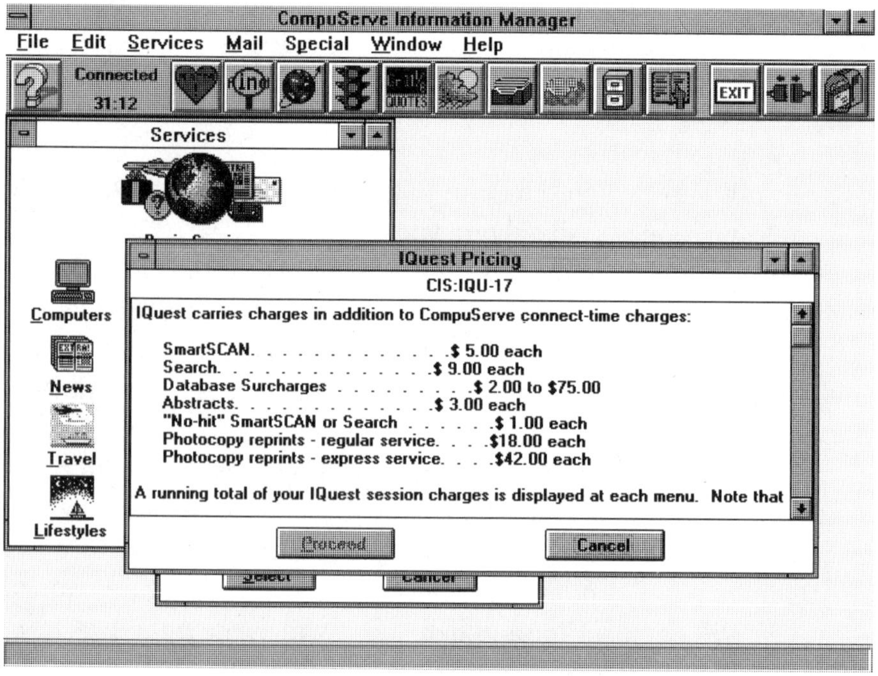

FIGURE 9.3:

CompuServe's IQuest database

TRACKING PEOPLE TRENDS

Apart from its collection of newspaper and magazine databases, CompuServe also offers a wide array of demographic databases to fit every pocketbook, from the surcharge-free CENDATA database published by the US Census Bureau to SUPERSITE, a surcharged database that generates detailed reports based on income, housing, education, employment, five-year forecasts, and sales potential.

Unlike full-text databases that use keywords to search libraries of newspapers and magazines, demographic databases can be searched by ZIP code, census tract, even Arbitron ratings. While databases like these don't come cheap—the least expensive SUPERSITE report, for example, costs $20—they're ideal for any company involved in direct-mail marketing.

Searching CompuServe's SUPERSITE database

To understand how demographic databases work, let's take a look at how SUPERSITE can help find the information you need:

1. Click Go from the toolbar at the top of the screen and type **Supersite**. Press ↵.
2. The menu that appears on your screen lets you choose from several options, including How to Use SUPERSITE, Review of SUPERSITE surcharges, View Sample Reports, and ACORN User's Guide.
3. After reading the instructions, choose SUPERSITE (E$) from the menu and press ↵. Supersite's main menu then prompts you to choose the type of geographic area you want to search—by ZIP code, country, state, Standard Metropolitan Statistical Area (SMSA), ADI (Arbitron TV Markets), DMA (Nielsen TV Markets), or other options.
4. Once you specify the area type, SUPERSITE asks you for more information. Although the steps may vary depending on what you're looking for, you usually specify the geographic area and then the type of report—demographic, sales potential, or ACORN target marketing. ACORN, which stands for A Classification of Residential Neighborhoods, divides the nation's neighborhoods into 44 market segments by demographic, socioeconomic, and housing characteristics.

5. Before generating the report, SUPERSITE gives you a chance to view sample reports. You can also cancel the report if you change your mind.

PAGING THROUGH BUSINESS DIRECTORIES

Once you've identified your trends and target markets, you need to zero in on your potential customers. One way to do this is to tap into an online business directory—the electronic equivalent of those giant compendiums that gather dust on the shelves of America's corporate libraries. While both the online and the off-line versions offer the same information, online directories are far easier to search, and you can download the search results into a file on disk, eliminating the necessity of rekeying the data.

Some of the more popular business directories available on CompuServe include D&B Dun's Market Identifiers for the United States, Canada, and the rest of the world; Dun's Electronic Business Directory, which lists more than 8.5 million US business professionals and companies; S&P Online, which provides information on 4700 companies; and Thomas Register Online, which contains information on nearly 150,000 US and Canadian manufacturers and service providers.

*Let Your Keyboard Do the Walking: CompuServe's Phone*File*

In addition to its business-to-business directories, CompuServe also offers access to Phone*File, an online directory that contains the names, addresses and phone numbers of over 80 million households throughout the United States. In most cases, you can locate a listing with as little information as a telephone number or a last name and geographical area. And, by database standards, it's cheap, too—25 cents a minute, no more than you'd pay for directory assistance from your local phone company. (An even bigger bargain is AT&T's toll-free 800 directory, which is free on CompuServe.)

To use Phone*File, select Go from the WinCIM toolbar at the top of the screen and type **PHONEFILE**. Then double-click Access Phone*File from the menu to log onto the database. Phone*File's main menu lets you search by name and address, surname and geographical area, and phone number. To start your search, simply choose Name and Address, and Phone*File will prompt you to enter the person's name, street address, city, state, and ZIP code. Phone*File then generates a report complete with phone number and details such as spouse's name and length of residence. To start a new search, press ↵.

A sample Phone*File report (with fictitious data) appears in Figure 9.4.

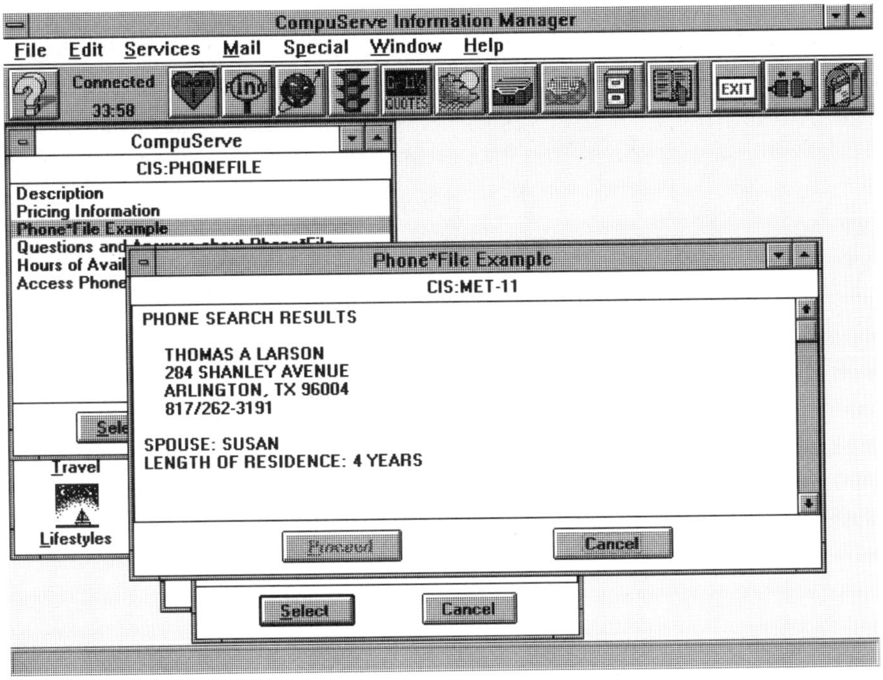

FIGURE 9.4:
A sample Phone*File report

CompuServe also offers a similar database, called Biz*File, that acts as an electronic Yellow Pages, giving you online access to over 10 million business establishments in the United States and Canada. Each listing includes the company's name, address, telephone number and length of time it has been listed in the directory. And, unlike the off-line Yellow Phones put out by your local phone company, this "phone book" can be searched by company name, geographical location, telephone number or type of business. Like Phone*File, it costs 25 cents a minute.

Summary

In this chapter, you learned about tapping into online databases and mining the riches of those vast storehouses of online news articles, market information and financial statistics that can give your business a competitive edge. You got a brief overview of the over 5500 databases now available online and learned how to access online encyclopedias, full-text databases, demographic reports, even online telephone directories. Along the way, you discovered how to save time and money with user-tested search techniques and shortcuts.

In the next chapter, you'll explore the pleasures and pitfalls of logging on overseas. By boning up before you go, you'll learn how to turn your laptop and modem into your office away from the office, mastering tips and tricks to help you log on from hard-wired phone jacks in foreign hotel rooms.

CHAPTER 10

Logging On Overseas

In Chapter 9, you learned how to mine your modem for money, mastering the skills required to tap into the online world's vast storehouse of news articles, market intelligence, demographic data, and business information.

Now you know virtually everything you need to go online—how to log on, zip from menu to menu, send and receive e-mail, upload, download, access bulletin boards and search electronic databases. So, as long as you and your computer never leave the country, using online services should be a snap. But, if you're like many business people these days, your marketplace has become increasingly global—and that means travel. It can also mean trouble if you blithely assume that logging on in a foreign country will be as simple as it is here.

That's why, in this chapter, you'll master the ultimate telecommunications skill—logging on overseas. By boning up before you go, you'll learn how to turn your laptop and modem into your office away from the office, mastering tips and tricks to help you access online services from hard-wired phone jacks in overseas hotel rooms. You'll also get the low-down on how to assemble a portable communications tool kit complete with screwdrivers, alligator clips, surge protectors, and AC converters. And last, but not least, you'll learn how to pinch pesos on overseas access charges and how to get help in Helsinki even if you don't speak the lingo.

Know Before You Go: Disasters That Await You

Though the world may be a smaller place these days thanks to satellite hookups, cellular phones, long-distance calling cards and the like, it's still a Tower of Babel when it comes to online communications. That's because, while the international community has united behind a handful of basic standards for computer hardware and software, telephone and electrical systems still vary widely from place to place. This means that if you tote your laptop to Germany, for example, you'll need a special adapter to plug it into the wall and you may have to hack apart the phone plug if you want to connect your modem to the jack.

But logging on overseas takes more than just the right equipment. It also requires a working knowledge of the rules of the road—and a healthy appreciation for the potential disasters that await you. This I know from personal experience. Several years ago, my husband, daughter and I decided to rent an apartment in Verona for a month, and I brought along my laptop, figuring I'd write a few travel articles while I was there. Shortly after we'd moved in, we were doing some laundry and I thought I'd recharge my laptop battery while waiting for our clothes to dry. No sooner did the washer-dryer kick into its "dry" cycle than all our power shut off and my computer's voltage converter and surge protector were fried beyond repair. (Thankfully, my laptop and modem were spared.)

Now, I wish I could say that what happened to me in Italy was just a fluke, but a half-dozen CompuServe members I contacted before I left on my trip recounted horror stories of their own. Stephen Sanders, a member of CompuServe's IBM European Users Forum, told me his modem got zapped in a lightning storm while he was visiting Rome a few years ago. He now swears by in-line surge protectors.

"If you need to ship your modem back to the States for repair and want it within a month," Sanders warns, "you'll need to spend well over $100 for UPS or Fedex."

BRAVING THE RISKS

That's not to say, of course, that you should leave your laptop and modem behind when you go abroad. Despite the risks, for a growing number of international business executives, portable computers and modems have become as indispensable as a fresh shirt and a toothbrush. That's because, for about $2000, you can buy a lightweight computer system that doubles as a full-service traveling office, enabling you to send and receive electronic messages, type reports, crunch numbers, make customer presentations, search online databases for news and developments, and even send faxes.

One such intrepid traveler is Jonathan Scott, president of Traveling Software, Inc., the Bothell, Washington, company that publishes the popular Laplink program. On his way home from a business trip in Tokyo not long ago, Scott thought he'd drop in on a contact in California. Before boarding the plane to Los Angeles, he decided to do a little homework. Switching on his portable computer, he plugged his modem into a nearby phone jack and, within minutes, had logged onto Dow Jones News/Retrieval and downloaded the latest financial information about the company he was about to visit.

When he arrived at the company's headquarters the next day, Scott congratulated the company on its just-released quarterly earnings, astonishing executives who knew that he had spent the previous week in Japan.

"You can't go on a trip overseas for five or 10 days and not know what's going on," Scott says. "Otherwise, the competition is going to kill you."

But, despite the advantages, even veteran travelers say that getting your computer equipment to work overseas often takes much more experience and technical savvy than the computer ads suggest. Even people who swear by international telecommunications say they always pack screwdrivers, pliers, and other tools in their briefcases and that, even after much tinkering, they can't always get their computer or modem to work.

"Sometimes you use the 'F' word and go back to Plan B," says Joseph Klock, Jr., managing partner of the Miami law firm of Steel Hector & Davis and a frequent business traveler to the Dominican Republic and other Caribbean islands. Mr. Klock says he will not stay in a hotel without a fax machine that he can use as a backup if he encounters computer trouble.

Preparing for Pitfalls

Despite the horror stories, logging onto an online service overseas doesn't have to be precarious—so long as you take the proper precautions.

Here are seven road-tested tips guaranteed to make overseas communications a little less bumpy:

1. **Know before you go:** Before you board the plane, log onto an online service like CompuServe and chat with other members who have traveled to the place you're planning to go. You can do this by posting a note on a travel-related bulletin board such as CompuServe's IBM European Users Forum, Travel Forum, TAPCIS Forum, or Foreign Language Education Forum.

   Check out the forum libraries for files containing advice about logging on overseas and getting your equipment up and running. For example, the TRAVEL.KIT file in the IBM European Users Forum, illustrated in Figure 10.1, offers

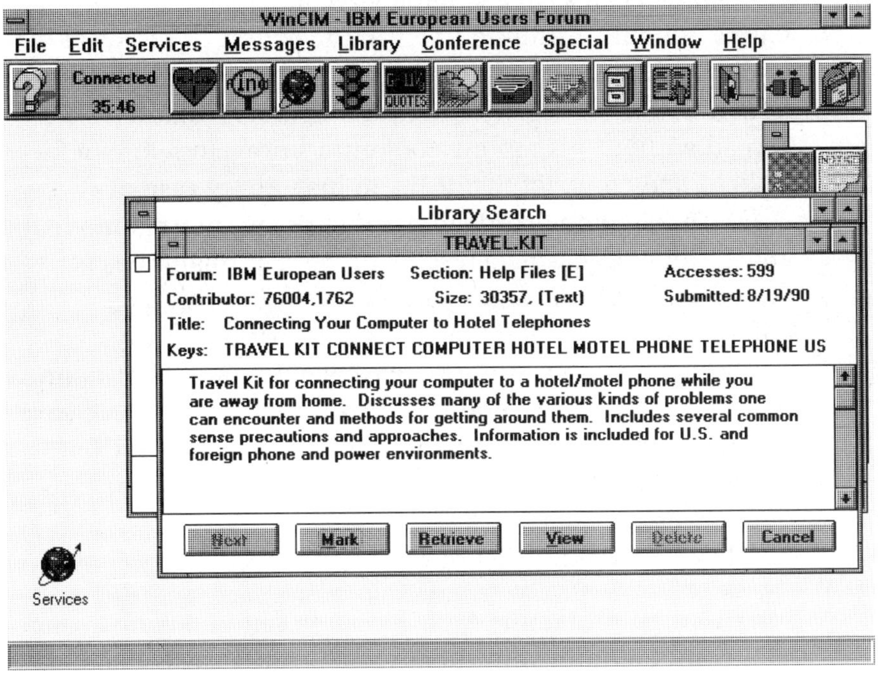

FIGURE 10.1:
CompuServe's TRAVEL.KIT file (IBM European Users Forum)

step-by-step instructions on overseas power safety and phone-line installation. A must-read for travelers to Italy is the Italy.Acc file, which tells you everything from how to play "let's hack the phone plug" to how to shave lire off your Italian phone bill.

2. **Come prepared:** Pack surge protectors, voltage converters, plug adapters and the like. Unlike the United States, Europe runs on 220 volts/50 watts power and its electrical outlets have two round holes instead of twin slots. You may also need a phone cord with a "spade" end or alligator clips that can be connected to a foreign phone jack—modular plugs are still a rarity in Europe and other places. Better yet, skip all that and take along a portable modem with an acoustic coupler, which connects your modem to the phone's handset via rubber cups that fit over the mouth and ear pieces.

Thom Hartmann, a CompuServe member who has logged roughly 2 million miles in the course of his speaking engagements, business travel, and volunteer work for an international relief organization, says he never ventures abroad without his mobile communications tool kit—a kit so light and compact that it fits in his toiletry case.

With his phone cord, alligator clips, an internal modem and 1"-long, thick-bladed screwdriver, Hartmann has accessed CompuServe from around the globe with nary a glitch. It sure beats lugging a portable printer, he says.

"I just keep the appropriate cable with me," Hartmann says. "Even hotels without printers have faxes, so I can save my file as an ASCII document, send it to myself via CompuServe Mail, and then get the equivalent of a 200-dpi printout delivered to me."

Here's a complete list of what you'll need:

- **A surge protector**: A power surge can knock out your computer and your modem in a matter of seconds. Shipping your machine back to the United States for repairs can be time-consuming and costly.
- **A voltage converter and conversion plug**: Unlike the United States, much of Europe runs on 220 volts/50 watts power, and electrical outlets there have two round holes instead of twin slots. Read the label to make sure the plug and converter will work in the country you intend to travel to.
- **Two long phone cords**: You'll need one with a modular end that connects into US-style jacks, and another with a "spade" end or alligator clips that can be connected to a foreign phone jack. This is important if you plan to send or receive electronic messages with your modem.
- **Three screwdrivers (1/8" flat-blade, 1/4" flat-blade and #1 Phillips) and a utility knife**: In some countries, especially if you stay in a hotel, the phone cord is hardwired into the wall, making a jack connection

impossible. You'll need screwdrivers and a knife to pry open the cover and wire your phone cord manually.

- **An acoustic coupler:** If hacking foreign phone plugs is not for you, consider an acoustic coupler that connects your modem to the phone's handset using rubber cups that fit over the mouth and ear pieces. Konexx Koupler Model 203 ($149) by Unlimited Systems in San Diego is smaller than a standard telephone handset, making it ideal for portable use. And, unlike early couplers, it is capable of handling high-speed data transmission of 2,400 to 9,600 bps. Contact the company at (619) 277-3300.
- **Instructions:** Be sure to pack the manuals for both your laptop and modem. In Italy, for example, phones use pulse dialing, not tone dialing as in the United States, which means you'll have to reprogram your communications software to get your modem to dial out. If you're a member of CompuServe, you should also print out a copy of TRAVEL.KIT in the IBM European Users Forum. This electronic guide provides excellent step-by-step instructions on power safety and overseas phone line installation.

Pack these items in your briefcase, and you'll be able to log on anywhere from Paris to Pago Pago. You can get everything you need, except the acoustic couplers, at your local Radio Shack for less than $50, though it's also a good idea to bring spares. Outside the major cities, many of these items are rarities.

3. **Reprogram your modem:** While few people in the United States use pulse-dial phones any more, in Europe and other places, pulse-dialing is often the only kind of phone service available. This means you'll have to dig out the manual that came with your communications software and change the T (tone) to a P (pulse) to get your modem to dial the number. If you're using a Hayes-compatible modem, the four letters

that appear before your modem dials the number should be ATDP instead of ATDT.

You may also have to rewrite your modem initialization string and change your dialing command suffix to ^M. Otherwise, you may get an error message telling you that there is no dial tone on the line. For tips on how to do this, call the publisher of your communications software or post a note on an online bulletin board asking for help.

Figure 10.2 shows the screen that Procomm Plus uses for changing modem command options—in this case, to the settings for logging onto CompuServe in Italy.

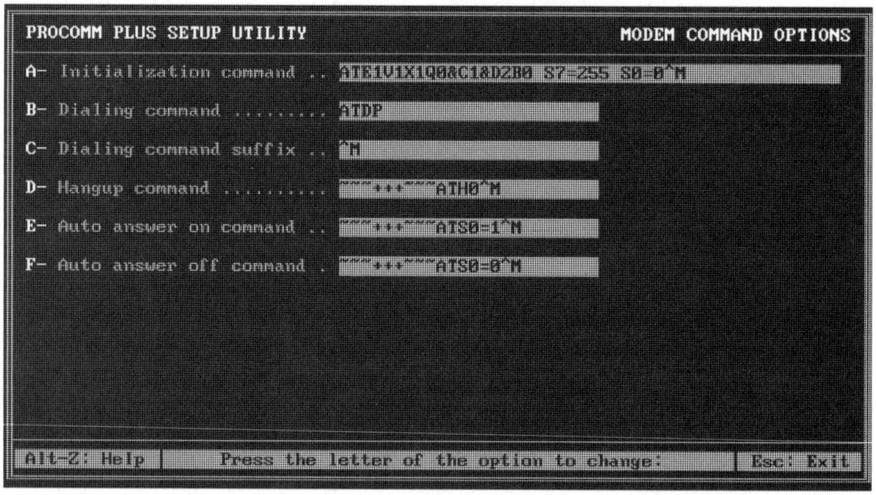

FIGURE 10.2: Using Procomm Plus to log onto CompuServe in Italy

4. Load in a script-reading program: Programs like TAPCIS, AutoSIG, OzCIS and CISOP that automatically log you on and off CompuServe, pick up your e-mail and let you write messages off-line are a cost-effective way to log on overseas. Other online services offer similar programs.

Fernando Gelbard, who lives in California but manufactures aluminum and tires in Argentina, has used TAPCIS to access CompuServe everywhere from Poland to Australia. Not long ago, he logged on from a cruise ship in the Indian Ocean, making his connection via satellite.

"My office is where I am," Gelbard says. "From on board that cruise ship, for instance, I sent a string of CompuServe messages to my daughter's fax in Los Angeles. TAPCIS let me transmit a few pages in about two minutes, so I saved lots of money."

The bottom line: $6 a page versus $15 a page on the shipboard fax machine. The convenience, he adds, was worth even more.

5. **Have local access phone numbers ready**: When logging onto an online service overseas, it doesn't make sense to dial in through the same local access number you call at home—unless you want to make your long-distance phone company rich, that is. Some online services offer local access numbers in major foreign cities and countries. Others can be accessed through foreign telephone networks such as Europe's Infonet and Canada's DataPac. Though these networks do tack on surcharges, the connections are often better and the lines less crowded than the local foreign phone company.

   The best idea is to compile a list of overseas phone numbers before you get to your destination. On CompuServe, select Go from the Services pull-down menu and type **phones**, following the submenus until you find the country you're looking for; it's easy to do and free of connect-time charges.

   Figure 10.3 shows the Milan phone numbers for accessing CompuServe through Infonet.

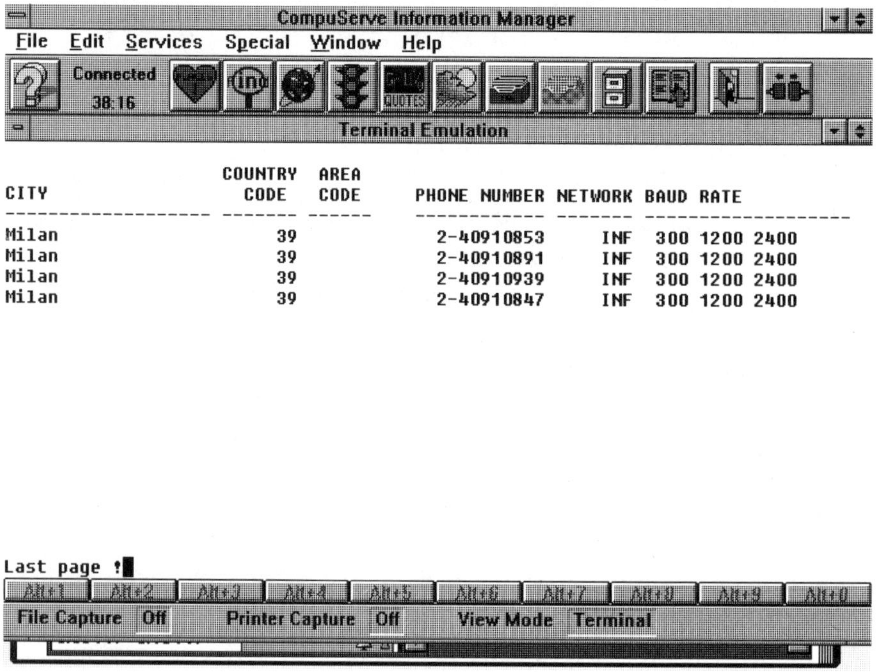

FIGURE 10.3: Infonet access numbers for CompuServe in Milan

6. **Get help before you need it:** Before you go, it's a good idea to call the companies that manufactured your laptop and your modem and ask them for their local technical support number in the city or country where you're headed. It may be difficult to track down those numbers once you get there.

   Online service members who live in the country you're traveling to and speak the language may also be able to help. Online bulletin boards like CompuServe's are good places to make contacts.

7. **Have a backup plan:** If possible, check into a hotel that has computers, printers and fax machines available. That way, if you can't get your modem to work, you can copy your file onto a floppy disk, stick it in the hotel computer, print out a copy on the hotel printer and fax the document to your office in the States. It's a costly and time-consuming process, but it's better than dictating your report over the phone.

Pinching Pesos on Phone Calls and Access Charges

No matter how you slice it, logging on overseas will cost you serious money. That's because many foreign phone companies still have monopolies over local phone service and often use their power to jack up the rates. Also, most US-based online services such as Prodigy and CompuServe have few local access phone numbers outside the United States, if any. This means you'll have to log on through an international telecommunications network, paying a hefty fee to the middleman.

In Moscow, for example, TYMNET charges $45.70 an hour to log onto CompuServe; in Venezuela, you'd pay $49.70 an hour. Throughout Europe, Infonet charges $11 an hour to access CompuServe, while other networks charge $18 to log on in South Africa and up to $35 an hour to log on in Japan. These prices do not include the cost of the local or international phone call you have to make to dial in or the CompuServe connect-time charges you pay once you're online.

Even so, there are some ways to avoid this kind of "sticker shock." One is to log on during off-peak times such as nights and weekends when some networks charge lower rates. Another is to dial the nearest local access number even if it means making a long-distance or international call—it may be cheaper than dialing in through a network.

And, finally, if you're planning to stay in a certain country for a while or travel there frequently, it pays to contact the local phone company to see what deals it offers. In Italy, for instance, you can save some money by signing up for an account with ITAPAC, Italy's country-wide data transmission network. It's cheaper than the alternatives, even with a monthly fee of about $10. On the other hand, ITAPAC can only accommodate relatively slow modem speeds, and it may be months before your service is connected.

Figure 10.4 shows the first screenful of information that CompuServe Information Manager provides about rates for accessing CompuServe from different networks in various European countries. To get this information from WinCIM, click the GO icon from the toolbar at the top of the screen and type **rates**. Then follow the submenus until you find the country you're looking for.

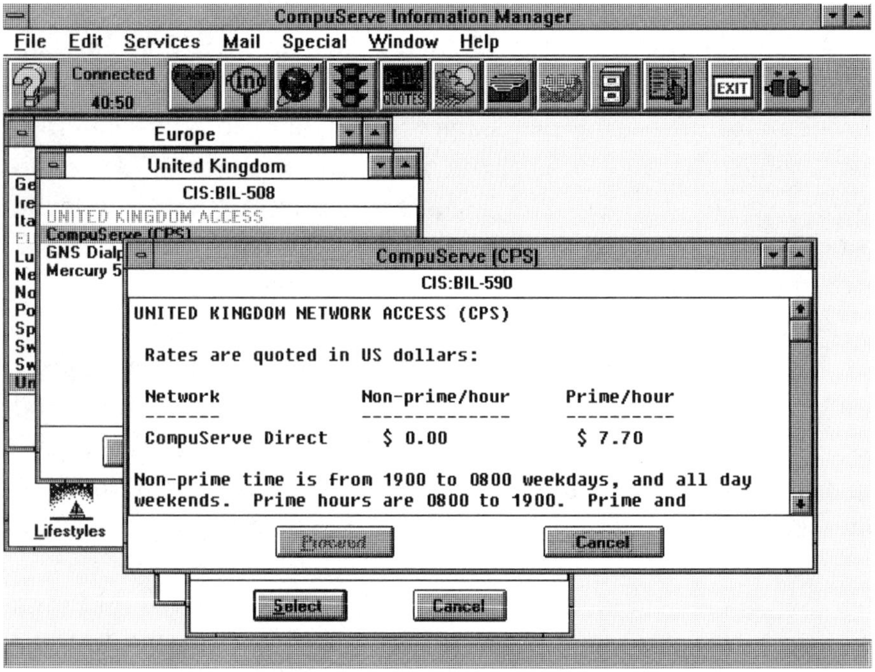

FIGURE 10.4: Network rates to access CompuServe in Europe

Logging onto CompuServe in Europe

Now that you know how to get your modem up and running—and how to get the best deal on your overseas connections—let's take a look at how the log-on process really works. Hint: Don't assume you can simply type in your user ID and password the way you can in the United States.

While the log-on process varies somewhat from country to country and network to network, going online overseas really isn't much trickier than logging on from your home or office in the United States. As an example, here's how to access CompuServe through the Infonet network in Milan. For information on logging on in other foreign cities and countries, select Go from the pull-down menu and type **phones**.

1. Using WinCIM, click Sessions Settings from the Special pull-down menu at the top of your screen.
2. Click the ↓ next to the *Session:* prompt, and type **Milan**.
3. Click the ↓ next to *Primary Network*, and scroll down until you get to InfoNet-Euro. Click it so that it appears in the Primary Network box.
4. Click OK to save your settings.
5. Log onto CompuServe as you normally do—by clicking Get New Mail or Browse or the GO command—and WinCIM will do the rest.
6. To log on again when you return to the United States, click the ↓ next to the Session: prompt and click Primary Connection from the list.

Summary

In this chapter, you mastered the ultimate telecommunications skill—logging on overseas. You now know how to access online services even from hard-wired phone jacks in overseas hotel rooms, and you can turn your laptop and modem into your office away from the office. You also got step-by-step instructions on assembling a portable communications tool kit complete with screwdrivers, alligator clips, surge protectors and AC converters. And last, but not least, you learned how to pinch pesos on overseas access charges and how to get help in Helsinki even if you don't speak the lingo.

Now that you've completed the first part of this book, you're ready to move on to Part 2—The Online World—which gives you a Cook's tour of the riches that await you and how much to expect to pay.

PART 2

The Online World

Part 1 introduced you to the ins and outs of working with online services—everything from logging on to extracting information from databases to avoiding the pitfalls of working overseas. Now you're ready for a tour of the different kinds of information available in the online world.

Chapter 11 compares Prodigy and CompuServe—two very different kinds of online services. Chapters 12 through 16 fill you in on everything from ferreting out investment information to shopping, networking, getting technical help, and making travel reservations online. As a Conclusion, you'll get a brief look at the future of electronic information retrieval.

CHAPTER 11

The Big Guns

With so many online services out there—Prodigy, CompuServe, GEnie, America Online, and Delphi, just to name the top five—which one do you choose?

The answer, of course, depends on what you need an online service for. If you're a small business owner who's new to computers, you'll probably want an online service that's easy to use, offers fax and e-mail capabilities, and features bulletin boards that can help you make contacts and manage your business—all for one low price. If you like to play the stock market, on the other hand, you may prefer an online service that gives you access to a wide range of financial databases, offers online brokerage and banking, and lets you download stock prices directly into your computer spreadsheet.

While all five of the online services just mentioned offer e-mail, bulletin boards, databases, and other standard features, Prodigy and CompuServe—the big guns of the online world—offer the best value for most computer users. With their wide array of services, attractive pricing and relative ease of use, it's no surprise that Prodigy and CompuServe now boast more members than the other three services combined. As this book goes to print, Prodigy has more than 2 million members, with CompuServe in second place with over 1.1 million.

Even so, Prodigy and CompuServe are not interchangeable. They are two very different kinds of online services with distinct missions, target markets, strengths, weaknesses, and pricing structures. In this chapter, you'll get an inside look at the pros and cons of logging onto each of these services to help you decide whether to sign up for Prodigy or CompuServe—or both. Though much of this information has been presented earlier in the book, this chapter will present a point-by-point comparison that will assist you in making an informed choice. After all, with CompuServe charging 22 cents a minute for 2400 bps pay-as-you-go access (or 13 cents a minute with the $8.95 flat-fee plan) and Prodigy charging $14.95 a month, subscribing to both services can get expensive—fast.

Of course, you may conclude that neither of the "big guns" is right for you. In that case, you can always flip to the back of the book and check out the appendix on GEnie, Delphi, and America Online.

The Evolution of Prodigy and CompuServe

Though Prodigy and CompuServe are the nation's most popular online services, they were not the first. Dialog, one of the country's leading purveyors of online databases, started out as an in-house research project at the Lockheed Missiles and Space Co. in 1963, becoming available to the public in 1972. Back then, the idea was to develop a system that would allow users to pose questions to a huge mainframe computer and receive responses in seconds instead of days.

Mass-market online services didn't get started until much later—not surprising if you consider that the IBM PC and the revolution it sparked have been around for less than 15 years. CompuServe, one of the first companies to offer information services to the general public, didn't adopt its current form until 1979, and Prodigy, now the nation's largest online service, didn't get up and running until nearly a decade later.

THE COMPUSERVE CONNECTION

An information powerhouse that doubles as one of the online world's leading communications hubs, CompuServe Information Service offers access to more than 1700 databases, including text libraries and financial data, and a wide range of services such as fax delivery, brokerage, shopping, and travel reservations. Owned by H&R Block, the giant tax-preparation company, CompuServe is accessible throughout the United States and from more than 100 countries worldwide, often by a local phone call.

Though CompuServe offers the standard online staples of news, weather, sports and games, the service is especially useful for small business owners. That's because it also offers hundreds of forums on topics ranging from desktop publishing and computer consulting to public relations and working from home. CompuServe's forums also provide technical support for most major hardware and software vendors, and the service's extensive e-mail system makes it easy to upload and download files and to communicate with the service's 1.1 million members.

But CompuServe does have its drawbacks compared to Prodigy—it's harder to use, and it tends to be more expensive. For novice users, the service's extensive command structure can be difficult to navigate without a front-end program like CompuServe Information Manager (CIM), a graphical interface, available in DOS, Windows, and Macintosh versions, that lets you click pull-down boxes and other on-screen options with your mouse. Also, CompuServe is expensive—22 cents a minute at 1200 or 2400 bps—if you choose the pay-as-you go option. Recently, CompuServe has tried to take away the sting with an $8.95 all-you-can-eat plan that offers unlimited access to basic services such as news wire services and lots of free e-mail. Unfortunately, CompuServe's forums are not included in this plan, so you're still stuck paying 13 cents a minute to log onto the bulletin boards.

The bottom line: You can get almost anything you want on CompuServe, whenever you want, but it isn't always easy or cheap. And, despite CompuServe's recent efforts to make its system more user-friendly, you've still got to know something about computers before you can start to feel at home.

CompuServe's main menu is shown in Figure 11.1.

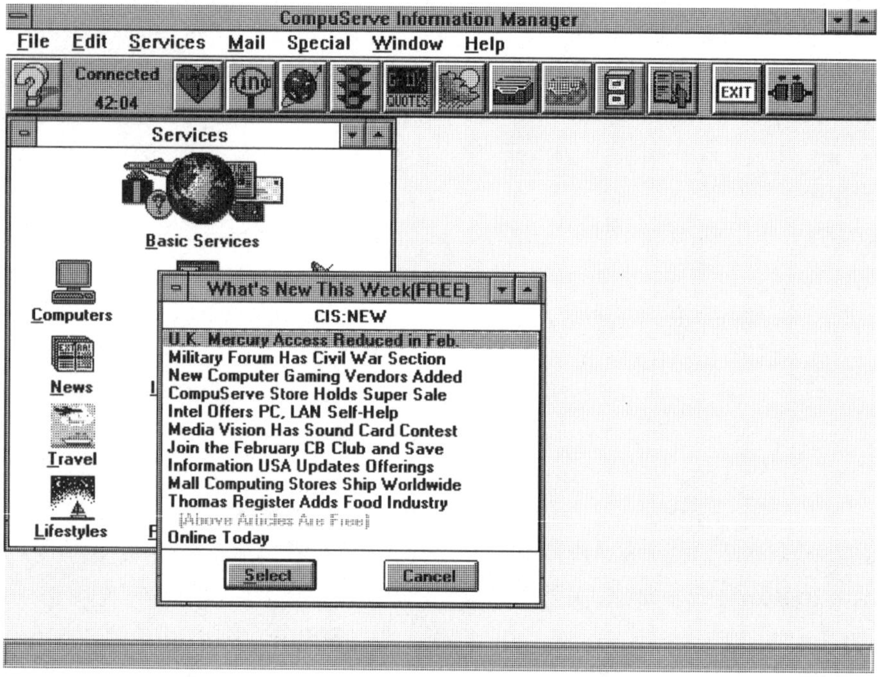

FIGURE 11.1: CompuServe's Main Menu

PRODIGY IS BORN

Designed with the novice user in mind, Prodigy Interactive Personal Service revolutionized the online world when it burst on the scene in 1988. The brainchild of IBM and Sears, Prodigy is part user-friendly videotext service, part Home Shopping Network, reflecting both sides of its unusual lineage. Even if you've never used a computer before, Prodigy's colorful, cartoon-like interface and simple on-screen commands make the service easy to master without so much as a glance at a user's manual. Another plus is Prodigy's extensive shopping service, which lets users browse the wares of hundreds of online vendors hawking everything from PCs to flowers.

But Prodigy is more than CompuServe with a human face. Unlike other online services that charge by the minute or tack on extra fees for specialized databases, Prodigy offers unlimited access to virtually its entire array of business and consumer information for one flat monthly fee. And, while the price has risen from $9.95 a month when the service first started to $14.95 now, Prodigy's basic package is still one of the biggest bargains online. That's because the service's on-screen ads help defray the costs that, on services like CompuServe, are picked up largely by the subscriber.

Even so, Prodigy does have its drawbacks compared to CompuServe—its limited set of features and relatively slow speed. Though the service has recently added hundreds of new features such as an online encyclopedia and bulletin boards for popular hardware and software applications, Prodigy still lacks the breadth and depth of CompuServe. Prodigy also suffers from limited e-mail and file-transfer capabilities, a problem the service has promised to remedy for an additional fee. Speed, too, is a problem. Even at 2400 bps, Prodigy can really drag, especially when it comes to transmitting a page full of graphics to your screen; then there are all those ads that crawl across the bottom. Prodigy recently introduced 9600 bps access in major cities for an additional $2 monthly fee, though you may need a fairly powerful computer, such as an IBM-compatible 25 MHz 386, to take maximum advantage of the higher speed.

The bottom line: Prodigy may not have everything you want—after all, it's designed for consumers, not business use. On the other hand, it's fun and easy to use and you won't spend a fortune trying to find your way around it. The question is, as Prodigy evolves into a full-featured online service with all the bells and whistles, will it still be such a bargain?

Prodigy's Main menu is shown in Figure 11.2.

FIGURE 11.2: Prodigy's Main menu

How the Big Two Stack Up

Now that you know a little about the Big Two and the differences between them, let's take a closer look at how Prodigy and CompuServe compare in features, pricing, speed, and accessibility. One thing you'll discover is that, while the two competitors are still very different, they're growing more and more alike all the time. CompuServe, for example, has recently unveiled its $8.95-a-month, all-you-can-eat flat-fee plan, while Prodigy, for its part, is in the midst of expanding its bulletin boards and e-mail system. In 1992, both services began offering access to Ziff-Davis' Ziffnet database, which offers buying advice and downloadable software.

FEATURES AND OPTIONS

When you're in the market for an online service, it pays to look at what the service offers—e-mail, databases, bulletin boards, shopping, custom add-ons—before you consider the sticker price. After all, what's the use of signing up for a service that lets you linger as long as you like if it doesn't give you what you want while you're there?

E-mail

When it comes to e-mail, CompuServe is head and shoulders above Prodigy—for now. Not only does CompuServe let you send electronic messages and exchange computer files with other members, the service also offers links to AT&T Mail, AT&T Easylink, MCI Mail and the Internet, a global electronic mail system with links to millions of users. CompuServe also offers telex services, fax delivery, and postal mail; the service can even be used to exchange messages on a local area network.

CompuServe Information Manager, the service's easy-to-use front-end program, offers off-line editing capabilities and a handy address book.

Prodigy, on the other hand, limits you to exchanging short messages with other Prodigy members. Until now, Prodigy has not allowed its members to send messages typed off-line or to upload files; downloading, for the most part, has been time-consuming and difficult. As this book goes to press, however, Prodigy has vowed to add an optional off-line editor, uploading capabilities, fax delivery, postal mail, and an Internet link by the end of 1993. Prodigy members will be charged extra for these services, though Prodigy has yet to say how much.

Databases

Apart from its superior e-mail capabilities, CompuServe also offers access to a wider range of databases—though some of Prodigy's homegrown offerings are pretty impressive.

CompuServe's 1700 databases range from weather maps and newspaper and magazine libraries (the first screenful of available newspapers is illustrated in Figure 11.3) to credit reports, travel guides and financial analyses. For example, CompuServe's SCREEN and COSCREEN allow investors to select stocks, bonds, options and futures that meet specific performance criteria. For detailed information on publicly-traded companies, you can tap into the Disclosure II database, Standard & Poor's, TRW Credit Reports(R) and Value Line. Other databases provide access to financial news services, economic trends and forecasts, mutual fund prospectuses, banks and information about insurance and Social Security.

If you need to research a topic for business, school or just for fun, CompuServe offers access to more than 850 bibliographic and full-text databases through a gateway called IQuest (see Chapter 9 for details). And, if you're shopping for computer hardware or software, there's Computer Database Plus, a vast collection of computer-related

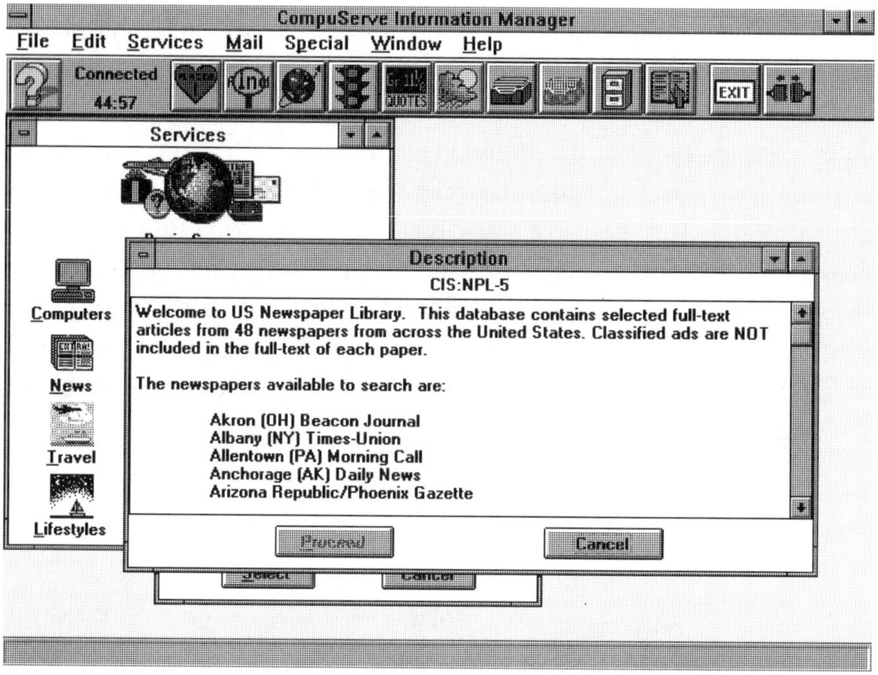

FIGURE 11.3:
CompuServe's Newspaper Library Database

summaries and full-text articles from more than 130 leading publications in the computer industry.

Prodigy, for its part, offers roughly 1000 databases and other features, though it doesn't offer the searchable text libraries and wealth of financial data that CompuServe does. On the other hand, Prodigy does have some innovative offerings of its own—BillPay USA, which lets you pay your bills online through virtually any bank or financial institution in the country; Strategic Investor, a searchable database of 5000 stocks and 3500 mutual funds that includes financial information and company charts from Investors Business Daily (illustrated in Figure 11.4); and an in-house writing team that recaps the top stories from a variety of news sources. During the recent Presidential election, Prodigy's Political Profile database helped members keep tabs on the nation's quadrennial horse race and the PAC money that paid for it.

Even so, choosing between CompuServe and Prodigy doesn't necessarily mean a choice between two completely different sets of databases—there is some overlap. Besides Ziffnet, databases available on both services include Grolier's Academic American Encyclopedia,

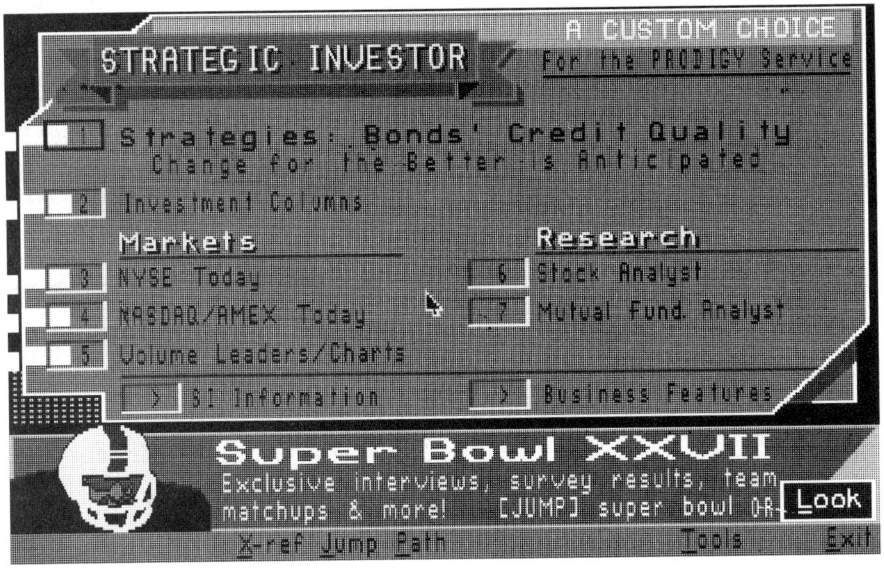

FIGURE 11.4:
Prodigy's Strategic Investor Custom Choice

American Airlines' Eaasy Sabre reservations system, and product reports and evaluations from Consumer Reports magazine.

Bulletin Boards

Both Prodigy and CompuServe offer hundreds of bulletin boards on topics as diverse as brewing beer, vintage cars, and grandparenting. As this book goes to print, CompuServe has roughly 350 bulletin boards. Prodigy now claims a total of 400 boards; but unlike CompuServe, it counts each topic available as a separate bulletin board.

CompuServe's forums are geared primarily toward professionals, computer users, and avid hobbyists, while Prodigy bulletin boards tend to be more oriented toward consumers. Both sets of bulletin boards allow members to swap notes with one another, though CompuServe's boards also let you attend real-time conferences and download software and text files from online libraries.

CompuServe's forums range from the Investor's Forum for armchair and professional investors and the Desktop Publishing Forum for electronic publishers to the Legal Forum for attorneys, paralegals, and lay people interested in the law; the AMIA Medical Forum for doctors and other members of the medical community; the Computer Consultant's Forum, and the International Entrepreneurs' Network for business owners interested in chatting about business-related problems, ideas, and techniques. CompuServe also provides computer hardware and software support forums staffed by big-name vendors such as Borland, Lotus, Microsoft, and IBM.

When it comes to bulletin boards, Prodigy is catching up fast, though many of its new boards are targeted more toward consumers than investors or business users. Currently, the most valuable bulletin board for the online business crowd is Money Talk, which brings investors together to argue, debate and share tips and ideas. In recent months, however, Prodigy has introduced a number of new business-related boards, including Careers (accounting, architecture, engineering, journalism, legal and sales), Environment (biosphere, endangered species, hazardous waste, recycling), Science & Technology (aerospace, astronomy, genetics, oceanography) and Service Clubs (Elks, Jaycees, Kiwanis, Moose, Rotary).

Shopping

When it comes to shopping, both Prodigy and CompuServe offer a wealth of online vendors, letting you avoid the lines at the mall without sacrificing price or selection. Both services allow you to order merchandise at the touch of a keystroke—any time of night or day.

Prodigy has 35 merchants online, ranging from Land's End to Hammacher Schlemmer. CompuServe's Electronic Mall has more than 100 vendors, including Brooks Brothers, Walden Computer Books, and the Museum of Fine Arts in Boston. (Unlike Prodigy, however, CompuServe includes some companies, such as car manufacturers, that provide product information but not retail sales through the Mall.)

As for price, Prodigy's shopping service is included in the basic monthly fee. CompuServe's Mall is free of connect time, but you still pay the network charge of 30 cents an hour.

Custom Add-Ons

Both services offer custom add-ons that can be purchased for an additional fee on top of the regular monthly fee or connect-time charges.

Prodigy's Custom Choices, for example, have grown to include everything from an online version of Sesame Street ($9.95 a month for five hours' use) to Prodigy Network Golf Tour ($8.95 for each monthly tournament). Prodigy's Strategic Investor, shown earlier, costs $14.95 a month. So does Ziffnet for Prodigy (though you pay more if you use it more than three hours a month).

CompuServe, for its part, offers the Executive Service Option, which provides access to in-depth financial databases, a news-article clipping service, discounts on CompuServe merchandise, and other amenities. To access this option, you must spend at least $10 a month on CompuServe in connect-time or other charges.

PRICING

Now that you know what both services have to offer, how much does it all cost?

The answer is tougher to calculate than it used to be.

Prodigy charges $14.95 a month for its basic service, but if you want access to Strategic Investor or any other Custom Choice, you have to pay more—often doubling your monthly bill. Plus, you may end up paying extra for e-mail, fax, and uploading options once they become available. And don't forget Prodigy's special front-end software (you can't log on without it), which lists for $49.95, though it's often discounted at computer superstores.

CompuServe, on the other hand, charges 22 cents a minute, or $12.80 an hour, for 1200 or 2400 bps access, though you can save money with the $8.95-a-month flat fee plan that includes access to basic services and lets you send the equivalent of 60 three-page messages. By signing up for the flat-fee plan, you also get a break on CompuServe's hourly connect-time rates. Under the plan, 300 bps access costs $6 an hour (compared to $6.30 an hour for the as-you-go plan), 1200 bps and 2400 bps access cost $8 an hour (compared to $12.80 an hour), and 9600 bps access costs $16 an hour (compared to $22.90 an hour).

But beware: Bulletin boards are not included in the flat-fee plan, and you may incur steep surcharges to access special databases and other features. Like Prodigy's front-end software, CompuServe Information Manager costs $49.95, though it, too, is often discounted at retail.

EASE OF USE

Prodigy's plain-English commands and menus make it easier than CompuServe for novice computer users to navigate. Laid out like a general-interest newspaper or magazine, Prodigy presents its menus as a series of "covers"—The Front Page, Money, Arts and Sports—and lets users flip through them by typing in Jump words or choosing numbers next to features listed on the screen. Some users have complained, however, that the rapid growth in the number of Prodigy features has made this menu structure difficult to follow (see "Looking Ahead" below).

CompuServe, for its part, lets you choose from a table of contents—Basic Services, Computer & Software Support, and Reference Library, for example—with a series of submenus that let you access specific topics and databases. If you already know what you're looking for, CompuServe's Go command lets you skip to a database or bulletin board by typing a single keyword. For novices, though, CompuServe's menus and command structure are much easier to use with a front-end program like CompuServe Information Manager—that's why the step-by-step instructions in this book have assumed that you're using WinCIM.

SPEED

When it comes to speed, CompuServe is definitely faster than Prodigy. First, it's a text-based service, so there are no fancy graphics or online ads that crawl across your screen. Second, CompuServe allows for 9600 bps access in 170 major US cities plus London, Frankfurt, Munich, Zurich, and Paris.

Until recently, Prodigy supported modem speeds only as fast as 2400 bps, though the service introduced 9600 bps access in major cities in late 1992 for an additional $2 monthly fee.

ACCESSIBILITY

CompuServe can be accessed from all over the world—and frequently is, by business travelers, foreign residents, and vacationers. To accommodate its global reach, CompuServe offers more than 2000 local access numbers, with local direct-dial access available from 350 US cities. As discussed in Chapter 10, there's also gateway access through networks from 120 other European locations.

Prodigy, for its part, boasts 526 local access numbers, but only in the United States. Accessing Prodigy from another country requires an international call.

"We want to make the service a complete success in the United States before we go overseas," says Prodigy spokesman Steve Hein.

And the Winner Is . . .

So which service should you sign up for? The answer, of course, is whichever service best suits your needs.

At this point, CompuServe is clearly the better business tool, especially for small business owners looking to make contacts and get their fledgling companies up and running. But it's harder to use than Prodigy and not as much fun.

On the other hand, if your goal is to follow the stock market and monitor your investments, you can get a pretty good deal by signing up for Prodigy's Strategic Investor and accessing Prodigy's other financial features that come standard. And Prodigy's Money Talk bulletin board is beginning to attract some very knowledgeable investors who aren't afraid to speak their minds. Recently, a pack of Prodigy subscribers leaped on financial guru William Donoghue when he attacked a Vanguard mutual fund in error.

Looking Ahead: The Future of Prodigy and CompuServe

Needless to say, neither service is resting on its laurels.

Prodigy, as mentioned above, has already introduced 9600 bps access and is planning to offer better e-mail capabilities, an off-line text editor and hundreds more bulletin boards some time in 1993. Prodigy has also taken steps to improve its navigational structure, which, even the service itself admits, can be difficult for members to follow.

"As we've added content, members have told us they're increasingly unaware of all that the Prodigy service offers, and unsure of how to find what they're looking for," Steven Shaber, Prodigy's Director of Service Development, told members in an online letter in November. "We've redone the infrastructure to address these access problems."

Translation: Prodigy now is organized a bit more like CompuServe and some of the other online services. For example, JUMP, Prodigy's basic access command, has been redesigned. While you can still go directly to specific features by typing the Jump words assigned to them, such as **company news** and **eaasy sabre**, now JUMP can also be used to find content quickly by subject. There's also a CONTENTS window similar to CompuServe's main menu that lets you access 10 broad categories, including business and finance, entertainment and arts, sports, travel and computers. A new cross-reference command, called X-REF, displays a list of all the categories that contain the feature you're using at the time. Prodigy's new look is illustrated in Figure 11.5.

CompuServe, for its part, is not planning any structural changes to its system, though the service does intend to continue expanding internationally and adding new forums and databases, according to CompuServe spokesman Dave Kishler.

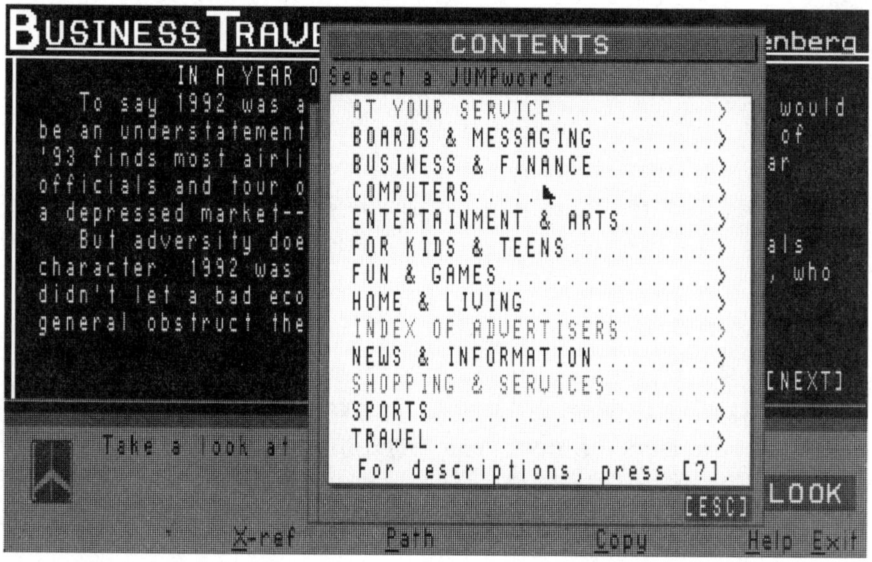

FIGURE 11.5: Prodigy's new look

Summary

In this chapter, you weighed the pros and cons of the online's world's "big guns"—Prodigy and CompuServe. Along the way, you learned how the two services stacked up in terms of features, pricing, speed, and accessibility—and how to decide which one, if either, is right for you. You also caught a glimpse of how the two services are changing and discovered that, while still very different, Prodigy and CompuServe are growing more alike all the time.

In the next chapter, you'll take a look at the lucrative world of online finance. You'll tour the wealth of financial information that's available online and learn how to download it into the kind of electronic spreadsheets you use every day.

CHAPTER 12

Dollars and Sense

In the last chapter, you considered the pros and cons of two of the online's world's "big guns"—Prodigy and CompuServe. You learned how the two services stacked up in terms of features, pricing, speed, and accessibility—allowing you to make the right choice for yourself and your business.

In this chapter, you'll tour the lucrative world of online finance, exploring the wealth of financial data that's available online. Both Prodigy and CompuServe offer a wide range of financial information, but, as you'll see, there are more specialized services for investors who need them. You'll learn how to download this information into the kind of electronic spreadsheets you use every day. You'll also learn how to save money with online brokerage services and weigh the pros and cons of using them to trade stocks, bonds, and mutual funds. Finally, you'll hear the stories of investors who participate in online bulletin boards and stock-trading clubs, hoping, one day, to strike it rich.

A Wealth of Financial Data Just a Phone Call Away

Not long ago, Mark Morgenstern, a 42-year-old armchair stock market enthusiast, got a tip about gold mining stocks and decided to take a flyer. After doing some research of his own, Morgenstern plunked down $8000 on several different issues and, in a few short weeks, pocketed a $1500 profit.

Morgenstern, a pharmacist by profession, doesn't have an inside line into Wall Street's trading rooms. What he does have is a subscription to Prodigy. Although this service is geared more to home users than to business people, it offers everything from investor bulletin boards and advice columns to stock quotes, industry news, and detailed financial data about publicly traded companies.

And, as you've seen throughout this book, online services can give you answers in minutes to questions that might take hours to research off-line in printed form—without having to trudge to the local library, newsstand, or bookstore. That kind of speed and convenience is especially important when you want to spot a hot stock, plan for your retirement, or even just see how your money's doing.

The downside, of course, is price. Depending on which online service and which database you choose, you can end up paying a pretty penny for such rapid access. For example, Dow Jones News/Retrieval, the best-stocked source of online financial information in the world, can run you close to $200 an hour after adding in access fees and surcharges. On the other hand, DJN/R is the only online service with up-to-the-minute stock quotes—and that may be just what you need. If, on the other hand, you can afford to wait 15 minutes, you can get delayed stock quotes on Prodigy, CompuServe and other online services as part of your monthly fee.

Tapping into Financial Databases via the Big Two

Apart from timely stock quotes, online financial databases offer everything from business news and corporate balance sheets to earnings predictions by Wall Street analysts and reports on insider trades made by a company's officers and directors. Many online services also offer interactive databases that let you pay bills, trade stocks and mutual funds, and bank your extra cash—all without leaving your computer. Others offer searchable databases of business-related newspaper and magazine articles.

GETTING FINANCIAL INFORMATION WITH PRODIGY

Prodigy's Money section, for example, offers advice on financial planning and home business, electronic bill-paying, home banking, an online brokerage service, stock quotes, business news, and the Money Talk bulletin board. Prodigy's Business & Industry News offers a quick review of general business developments and reports on specific industries, while Company News from Dow Jones offers late-breaking news on any publicly traded company as soon as 90 seconds after it appears on Dow Jones News/Retrieval service. (Tip: If you don't need the information right away, it's cheaper to get it through Prodigy than by logging onto DJN/R directly.)

Prodigy's QuoteCheck service, meanwhile, supplies 15-minute delayed quotes on stocks, mutual funds and bonds, while Quote Track automatically updates the stock prices of your personal investment portfolio of up to 50 different securities. If you're willing to pay an extra $14.95 a month, you can log onto Prodigy's Strategic Investor, a giant database with reports on more than 4500 stocks and 3000 mutual funds plus market news, charts, and columns from *Investor's Business Daily*.

Strategic Investor lets you compare stocks by name, industry, price/earnings ratio, dividend yield, earnings, financial strength, and other key statistics. The database also ranks mutual funds from best to worst in terms of short-term and long-term performance and provides comparative data on investment objectives, expenses, assets, capital distributions, and dividend yield. What's more, you can access companies' earnings and balance sheet information and download this information for use with popular spreadsheet software such as Lotus 1-2-3, Excel, and Managing Your Money.

A typical Strategic Investor screen is shown in Figure 12.1.

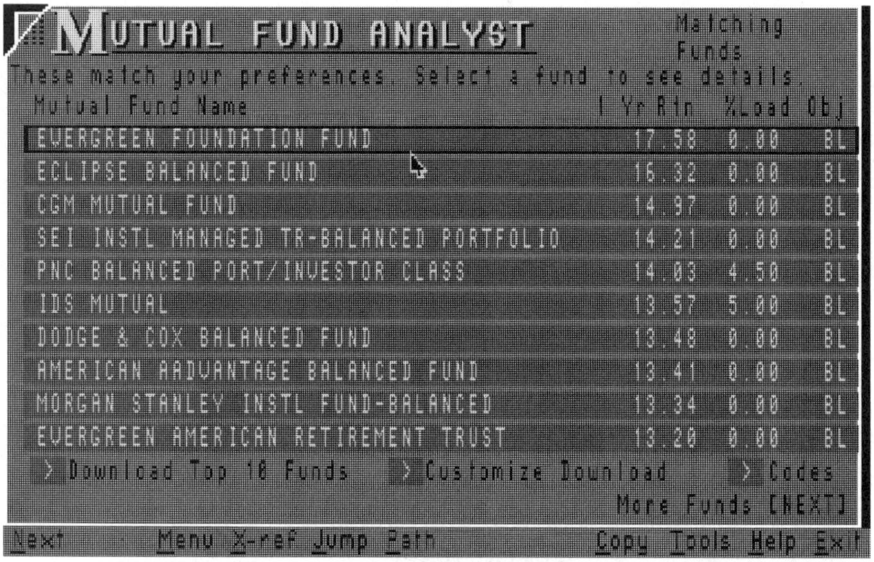

FIGURE 12.1: Searching for Mutual Funds with Prodigy's Strategic Investor

GETTING FINANCIAL INFORMATION WITH COMPUSERVE

CompuServe, too, contains a wide array of financial databases, including the powerful Company Analyzer, a one-stop shopping service that offers in-depth reports on individual stocks. The Analyzer menu lets you choose from 16 options, including return on $1000 invested, earnings and growth forecasts, a management discussion, and the stock price history going back to 1978. Just enter a company name, ticker symbol, or CUSIP number, and the Analyzer will search the various financial services to determine which ones contain information about the company you have requested. Figure 12.2 shows a screenful of information from Company Analyzer.

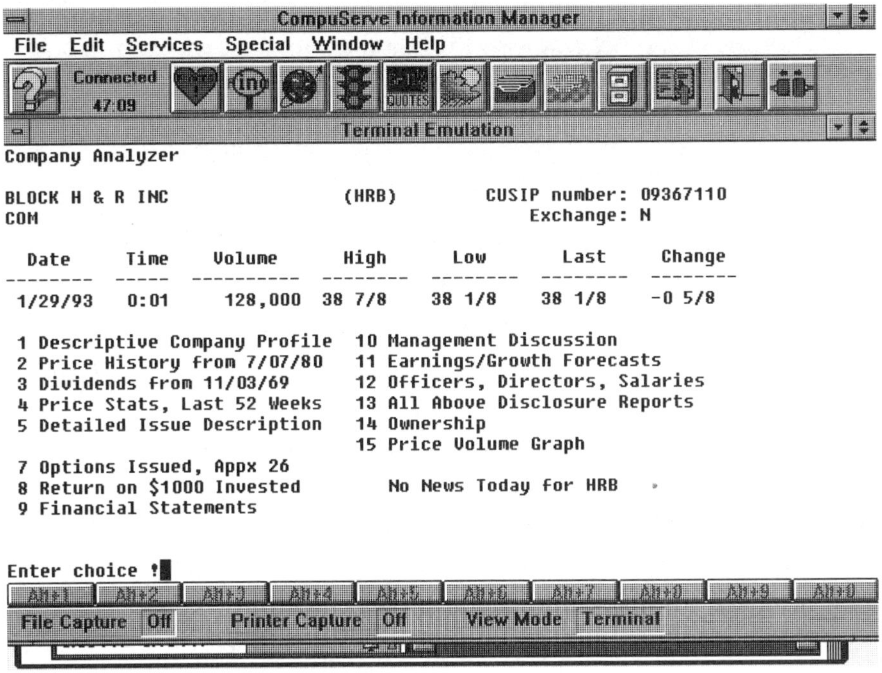

FIGURE 12.2: Shopping for stocks with CompuServe's Company Analyzer

CompuServe's financial offerings also include online advice from MMS International's team of stock, bond, and currency market analysts; online brokerage services, and Business Database Plus, a searchable database of business articles from 115 regional newspapers and magazines. CompuServe also provides delayed stock quotes for 9000 stocks traded on the nation's major exchanges; pricing history on 46,000 stocks, bonds, warrants and mutual funds from 1974 to the present; Value Line forecasts of roughly 1800 companies; and access to corporate reports and financial statements from Standard & Poor's and Disclosure.

But, while CompuServe offers a lot, you'll have to pay a high price to get it. Unless you sign up for CompuServe's $8.95 flat-fee plan, you'll pay 22 cents a minute just to stay connected plus the additional surcharges tacked on by the databases you access. (**Tip**: If you like to log on every couple of hours to check how your stocks are doing, it pays to sign up for the flat-fee plan. That's because the plan lets you retrieve as many delayed quotes on stocks, options, indexes, exchange rates and mutual funds as you like for no additional charge.)

Using More Specialized Financial Services

As useful as Prodigy and CompuServe can be to individual investors, there may come a time when you need to ferret out information not readily available through online services geared toward the end user. What you need to know may be so highly specialized that you'll have to call in the experts—sophisticated databases containing articles from obscure newsletters and trade publications, import/export data from faraway countries, even foreign-language newspapers and magazines. To tap into databases like these, you may need to dial up the same online services employed by corporate librarians, Wall Street brokerage houses, and academic researchers.

The pros and cons of logging onto a specialized online service are clear-cut. On the plus side, such services give you access to the kind of information that would be difficult, if not impossible, to find elsewhere. Depending on which database you search, you can quickly and easily identify industry trends, forecast performance for a product still in development, even size up a marketing opportunity half-way around the world. Also, because some specialized online services such as Dialog and DJN/R make certain databases available through mass-market services like CompuServe and GEnie, it may be cheaper to log on directly than to pay a middleman.

On the minus side, many of these specialized online services cost an arm and a leg. Not only are their databases expensive, so is accessing the system. For example, I/Plus Direct, a powerful investment research service, charges $95 an hour—and that's just for logging on! Adding to the cost is the fact that many of these services, such as Dialog and NewsNet, do not operate their own telecommunications networks and must be accessed through Tymnet or SprintNet, piling network surcharges onto your bill. Another drawback is that services like these can be tricky to use—after all, their sophisticated command structures were designed with professional librarians in mind, not the average computer user.

The good news is that specialized online services like Dialog, DJN/R, and the others are making a big push these days to attract the same kind of people who log onto CompuServe and Prodigy. To encourage more people to log on, these high-end services have redesigned their systems to make them less costly and easier to use, with simplified commands and user-friendly menus.

"With the proliferation of computers, growth in research has been incredible," says Robert Becker, president of Thomson and Thomson, the leading producer of online trademark databases. "To continue this expansion, simpler access to online is needed. Our growth depends on a growing base of users. To attract new searchers, online should be as easy as picking a book off the shelf or thumbing through a magazine."

All in all, the key to using sophisticated services like Dialog, DJN/R, and the others is to know what you're looking for—and how much you want to spend—before you log on. That's why it pays to shop around. For example, if you're a CompuServe member and you only plan to access a Dialog database every once in a while, it may be a good idea to conduct your search through CompuServe's IQuest system. Though you may end up paying a little more, you'll have an easier time searching and you won't have to pay Dialog's $40 annual fee. Likewise, if you intend to use a certain specialized database a great deal, it may pay to sign up for a flat-fee plan that offers unlimited usage for one monthly price, such as the ones offered by DJN/R.

Below are brief descriptions of six online services that offer access to a vast array of sophisticated financial information—at a price. To find out more and to get log-on instructions, contact the companies at the addresses and phone numbers listed after the summary. Local access numbers for Tymnet and SprintNet are available through many of the mass-market online services. Using WinCIM, for example, click the GO icon from the toolbar at the top of your screen and type **phones**.

DIALOG

Whatever you're searching for, chances are you'll find it on Dialog.

Dialog Information Services, owned by the Knight-Ridder Publishing Co., offers more than 400 databases containing roughly 330 million records spanning business, science, and technology. These databases include information on more than 12 million domestic and 1 million international companies; references and abstracts of articles from more than 100,000 publications; and the complete text of over 2500 journals and newsletters. Dialog's many offerings range from *Microprocessor Report* to *Micronesian Investment Quarterly*. Figure 12.3 illustrates Dialog's menu system in action.

Launched in 1968 by Lockheed Missiles & Space Co.'s Information Services Laboratory after winning a NASA contract, Dialog in 1972 became the first service to offer online databases to the public. Today, more than 80 percent of the Fortune 500 companies subscribe to Dialog, as do government agencies, business consultants, libraries, universities, and research institutions around the globe. Dialog is also available on CD-ROM.

Though Dialog has the data to satisfy virtually all your information needs, it can also get pricey. Many of its databases charge more than $100 an hour for basic access (plus additional charges for each record retrieved), and a few charge more than $200 an hour. For access to Dialog at a discount, consider signing up for the Knowledge Index service, which offers you access to more than 120 Dialog databases during evenings and weekends at a reduced rate using a simplified command system or easy-to-use menus. Recently, Dialog transferred access to the Knowledge Index to CompuServe, which announced plans to change $24 per hour for access to the service, regardless of modem speed. All connect-time charges will be included.

For more information, contact Dialog Information Services, 3460 Hillview Ave., Palo Alto CA 94304, or call (415) 858-2700 or (800) 334-2564.

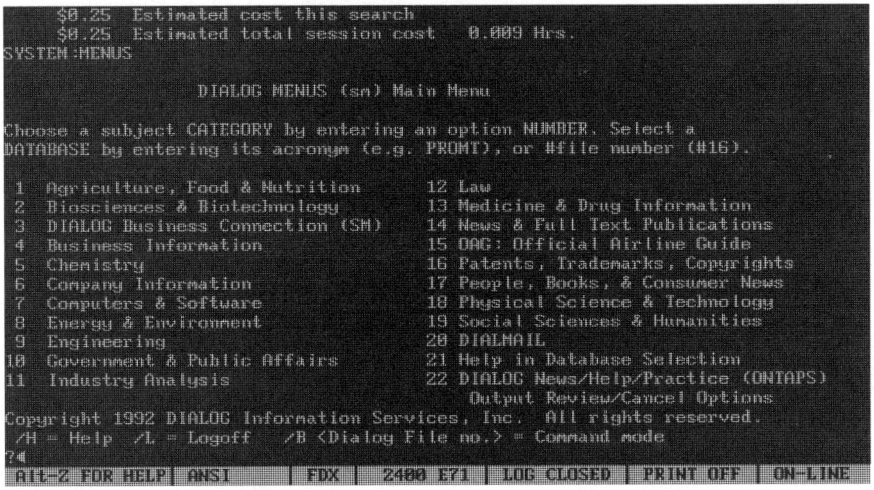

FIGURE 12.3:
Dialog's "menu" option makes the system easier to search

DOW JONES NEWS/RETRIEVAL

No serious investor should be without access to Dow Jones News/Retrieval.

Produced by the same company that puts out *The Wall Street Journal*, DJN/R houses over 60 databases containing articles from more than 1300 international, national and regional publications. It's also the only online service that offers the full text of the *Journal*, *Barron's*, *Business & Finance Report*, and *American Demographics* plus up-to-the-minute reports on Securities and Exchange Commission filings. DJN/R also offers a clipping feature that lets you create folders to track news about companies that interest you, plus access to online travel information through the Official Airline Guide Electronic Edition and MCI Mail, a top-flight electronic communications service.

DJN/R prices its services according to connect time and information unit charges, though recently the service has taken steps to base its charges more on the quantity of information received and less on the number of minutes spent online. During the day (prime time), connect charges can run as high as $1.95 a minute at 2400 bps and $1.89 cents per information unit (1000 characters) retrieved. After factoring in the various charges, it's possible to spend close to $200 an hour to use DJN/R. There's also an $18 annual fee. You can save money by logging on at night (non-prime time) when connect rates are as low as 15 cents a minute and information units are as low as 30 cents.

Recently, DJN/R has added a number of enhancements that make it easier and cheaper for individual investors to use. For example, the DowQuest menu system, which lets you search over 350 periodicals by typing in simple English keywords, lets you find what you're looking for in a matter of minutes—even if you've never logged on before. DowQuest is illustrated in Figure 12.4. DJN/R is also planning to unveil an easy-to-use Windows version in 1993.

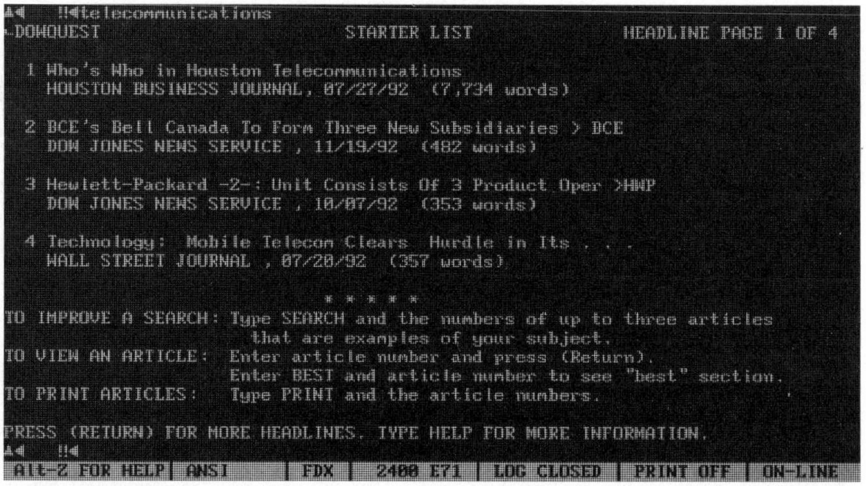

FIGURE 12.4: Dow Jones News/Retrieval's DowQuest feature lets you search by keyword

(For those who want a Windows interface now, there's a program called Cypress that retails for $179. To order, call 1-800-367-8729, or write to Trax Softworks, Inc., 5840 Uplander Way, Culver City, CA 90230.)

DJN/R has also introduced four flat-fee plans that give investors unlimited access to certain databases during nights and weekends for a fixed monthly charge. The plans are News & Quotes ($25), which includes current and historical stock quotes and stock market indexes; Forecasts & Analyses ($25), which includes reports on mutual funds, corporate ownership and corporate earnings estimates; and General Interest ($12.50), which includes an online encyclopedia, career-management advice, and book and movie reviews. Combination plans are available for $35 to $49.95 a month.

DJN/R is available through online gateways provided by GEnie, MCI Mail, and the Internet, a global communications network consisting of more than 6000 individual networks in 40 countries (see below).

For more information, contact Dow Jones News/Retrieval, P.O. Box 300, Princeton NJ 08543, or call 1-800-522-3567.

NEWSNET

If you're looking for business news on a timely basis, NewsNet is the place to go.

This online service's unique feature is its access to more than 600 business newsletters in dozens of industries. The service also lets you tap into 20 worldwide news wires from Associated Press, United Press International, Reuters, Agence France-Presse, PR Newswire, Business Wire, even Xinhua from Beijing and Jiji from Tokyo. Among NewsNet's offerings: Minority Markets Alert, Space Business News, Japan Computer Industry Scan, and Oil Spill Intelligence Report. There's also NewsFlash, an electronic clipping service that lets you monitor topics of interest and create your own personalized "newspaper" every day. A NewsNet report about camcorders is illustrated in Figure 12.5.

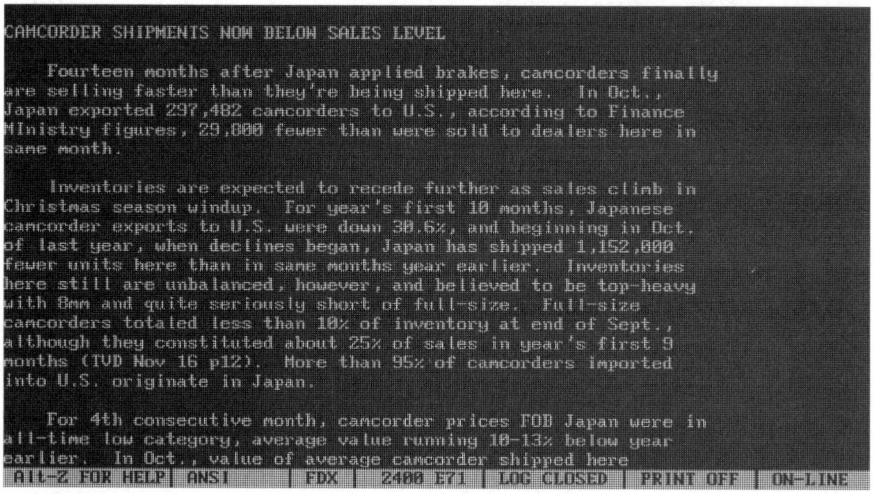

CAMCORDER SHIPMENTS NOW BELOW SALES LEVEL

Fourteen months after Japan applied brakes, camcorders finally are selling faster than they're being shipped here. In Oct., Japan exported 297,482 camcorders to U.S., according to Finance Ministry figures, 29,000 fewer than were sold to dealers here in same month.

Inventories are expected to recede further as sales climb in Christmas season windup. For year's first 10 months, Japanese camcorder exports to U.S. were down 30.6%, and beginning in Oct. of last year, when declines began, Japan has shipped 1,152,000 fewer units here than in same months year earlier. Inventories here still are unbalanced, however, and believed to be top-heavy with 8mm and quite seriously short of full-size. Full-size camcorders totaled less than 10% of inventory at end of Sept., although they constituted about 25% of sales in year's first 9 months (TVD Nov 16 p12). More than 95% of camcorders imported into U.S. originate in Japan.

For 4th consecutive month, camcorder prices FOB Japan were in all-time low category, average value running 10-13% below year earlier. In Oct., value of average camcorder shipped here

Alt-Z FOR HELP | ANSI | FDX | 2400 E71 | LOG CLOSED | PRINT OFF | ON-LINE

FIGURE 12.5: NewsNet's hundreds of newsletters can keep you abreast of market trends worldwide

NewsNet's basic access charge is $60 an hour at 1200 bps and $90 an hour at 2400 bps plus surcharges for databases searched and reports generated. There's also a $120-a-year subscription fee, or $15 a month. Volume discounts are available for subscribers who spend over $5000 a year on the service.

For more information, contact Newsnet, 945 Haverford Rd., Bryn Mawr PA 19010, or call 1-215-527-8030 or 1-800-345-1301.

DATA-STAR

If your business involves international trade—or even if you're just thinking about tapping into global markets—Data-Star can give you an edge.

Recently acquired by Knight-Ridder, parent company of Dialog, Data-Star features more than 300 databases offering worldwide information on business, medicine, science, pharmaceuticals and technology. Among its unique databases: Advertise (in German), Japan News Wire, Il Sole 24 Ore (in Italian) and Firmimport/Firmexport (in French). Data-Star offers plenty in English, too, though many of its offerings, such as Predicasts and D&B Dun's databases, are available elsewhere for less. One unique offering available in English is Data-Star's Tradstat database which contains official government import/export statistics on more than 60,000 commodities from Europe, Japan, Canada, Taiwan, South America, and the United States.

Data-Star's opening menu is shown in Figure 12.6.

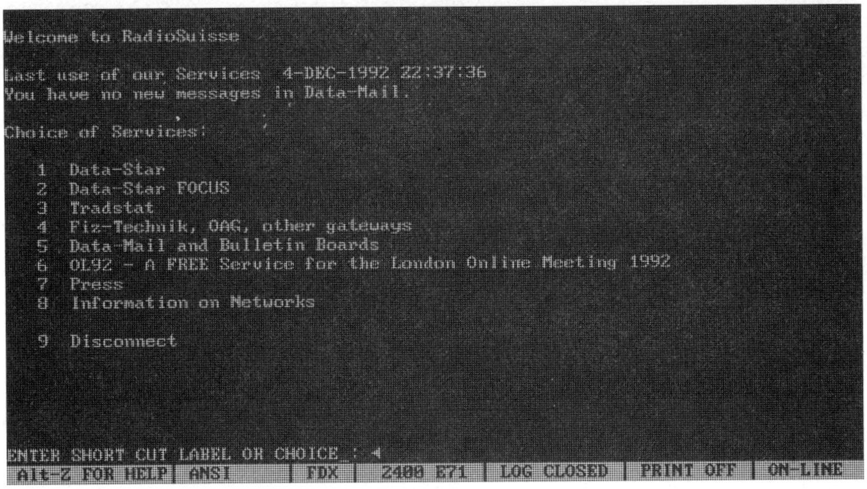

FIGURE 12.6:

Data-Star, a service of Radio-Suisse, can provide an international edge

Data-Star charges vary depending on the database searched, the amount of time spent searching and the number of records retrieved. The Drug News Daily database, for example, costs $116.70 an hour to access; Automotive Industry News costs $118.20 an hour. North American users get a $20-an-hour discount if they use the service between 1 P.M. and 1 A.M. Eastern standard time. The Tradstat database costs $60 an hour to access plus $7.40 to $25.50 for each report.

For more information, contact Data-Star, 485 Devon Park Dr., Wayne PA 19087, or call 1-215-687-6777 or 1-800-221-7754.

I/PLUS DIRECT

If you're wondering what Wall Street thinks about that hot stock your co-workers are buzzing about, I/Plus Direct can help you find out.

I/Plus Direct, a new online investment research service by Thomson Financial Networks, is an easy-to-use version of Thomson's Investext database available on CompuServe and other major online services. With the help of easy-to-use menus, I/Plus Direct lets you search over 400,000 full-text company, industry, geographic and topical reports authored by analysts at close to 300 of the world's leading investment banks, brokerage firms and consulting companies.

I/Plus Direct also offers exclusive access to three new Thomson Financial databases: MarkIntel Master, which features full-text major market studies from leading consulting firms such as Decision Resources and Forrester Research; MarkIntel, a companion market research file offering reports by international business consultants Frost & Sullivan; and BondText, a database of research about corporate, government, and municipal bonds. These and other I/Plus services are available through the menu shown in Figure 12.7.

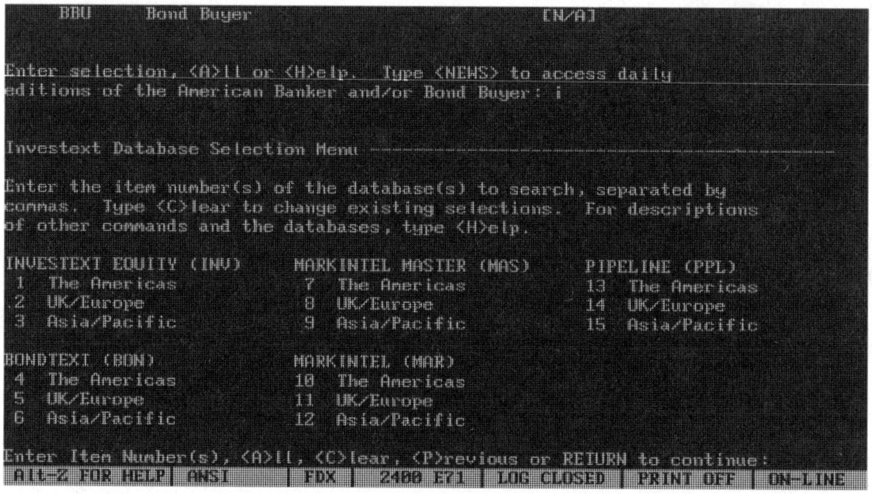

FIGURE 12.7:

I/Plus Direct offers exclusive access to three new financial databases

I/Plus isn't cheap. Connecting with the service costs $95 an hour, including telecommunications charges, plus a $75 one-time sign-up fee. There are also additional charges to display reports, graphs and charts. A single page of an Investext report, for example, costs $5.50 for online display and $5.95 for off-line delivery. A report abstract costs $1 a page, while a graph or chart sells for $9.95 a page.

For more information, contact I/Plus Direct, c/o Thomson Financial Services, 11 Farnsworth St., Boston MA 02210, or call 1-212-952-7060 or 1-800-662-7878.

THE INTERNET

Unlike the five online services described above, the Internet is not primarily geared toward business users, though its worldwide communications capabilities and unparalleled access to academic and government research make it an enormously powerful information tool. Described in a recent *New York Times* article as "the network of all networks," the Internet is a global computer hookup in which any other network can participate. Once the sole domain of U.S. government-sponsored research scientists, the Internet now embraces satellites, cable, fiber and telephone lines and can be accessed through CompuServe, America Online, Delphi, DJN/R, GEnie, and, soon, Prodigy. (Of the major commercial online services, however, only Delphi provides access to the Internet's full range of database and file-transfer capabilities, rather than just an E-mail link.) Figure 12.8 shows the CompuServe Information Manager screen for access to the Internet.

Why log onto the Internet? First, there's the service's enormous resources—access to 6000 individual networks in 40 countries around the globe, over 1,600 topical discussion groups covering everything from technology to science fiction, and millions of data files and downloadable software programs. The Internet also lets you send e-mail to millions of people worldwide, often for less than you'd pay to send messages on a regular online service.

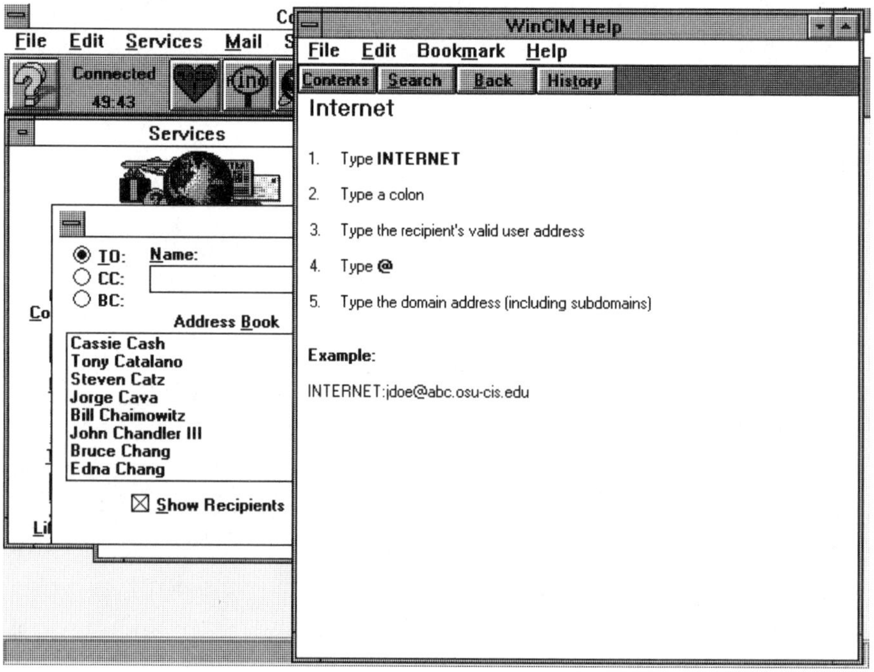

FIGURE 12.8: Personal computer users can long onto the Internet through CompuServe and other mass-market online services

"For business users, the Internet offers less expensive access and more effective access to online services such as Dialog," says Daniel Dern, author of *The Internet Guide for New Users*, scheduled for release by McGraw-Hill in mid-1993. "The Internet is also a popular way to use electronic mail."

These days, Dern says, anyone with a computer and a modem can log onto the Internet for as little as $10 to $20 a month plus long-distance phone charges. The trouble is, logging onto the Internet is not as simple as dialing an 800 number and ordering a start-up kit. Unlike most other online services, the Internet has no central headquarters, centrally offered services, or monthly pricing plan. And, though there are several off-line catalogs now available, there's no on-line index that tells you what information is available on the Internet and where to look for it.

To access the Internet directly, contact Digital Express Group at 1-301-220-2020, NetCom, Inc. at 1-408-554-8649, Panix at 1-718-832-1525 or The World/Software Tool & Die at 1-617-739-0202.

Cost-Cutting Tips

As you've seen, logging onto high-powered online services like the ones described above can get expensive. On the other hand, there's no sense in being "pound-wise and penny-foolish" when it comes to getting information that can save you time and make you money.

Here are some tips to cut your costs and make your searches more productive:

- **Search smart:** Before you start any search, you've got to know what you're looking for. For tips on how to find what you're looking for, while conserving your time and money, see Chapter 9.
- **Search simple:** Unless you really get a kick out of poring over a manual trying to memorize complex commands, it's a good idea to pay a little more to search the service using easy-to-use menus. Not only will you get the information faster, but you won't find yourself helplessly watching screen after screen of high-priced data scrolling down your screen while frantically searching for a way to log off.
- **Search late:** Log on at night while the corporate world is asleep, and you stand to reap big bargains online. Not only do services such as Dialog and DJN/R offer cut-rate after-hours plans, but several of the telecommunications networks do, too. Tymnet, for example, charges $11.70 an hour to access the network during the day but only $1.70 an hour for evening and weekend access.

- **Search professionally**: Don't be afraid to admit you're stuck. If you've searched and searched and come up empty-handed, it may be time to call in an information broker to search the databases for you in return for a fee. Information brokers typically charge $45 to $85 an hour—plus the cost of accessing the databases and retrieving the information, but hiring someone who knows what he's doing may turn out to be faster and cheaper than fumbling around in the dark on your own.

Downloading Data to Your Spreadsheet

With all the financial information available, you'd think that downloading it into your electronic spreadsheet would be a snap. Unfortunately, this isn't true. On many online services, it's still a chore—especially for novice users.

On CompuServe, for instance, getting stock quotes is as easy as typing in the company's ticker symbol, but you can't download the quotes into your Microsoft Excel or Lotus 1-2-3 spreadsheet until you've mastered a complex sequence of menus and commands. Downloading DJN/R's data requires a program called Spreadsheet Link 2.0 (for IBM and IBM-compatible computers only), which automatically collects data from 10 News/Retrieval databases and formats the information into Lotus 1-2-3, Quattro Pro, and Excel spreadsheets. The program costs $149, with a 20 percent discount for DJN/R subscribers.

For now, the easiest way to download stock quotes to your spreadsheet is to log onto Prodigy's Quote Track or Quote Check features. Unlike the other online services profiled, Prodigy lets you quickly and easily download stock quotes directly to Quattro Pro, Microsoft Excel, Lotus 1-2-3, and Quicken 5.0 and 6.0 spreadsheets. Quote track is illustrated in Figure 12.9.

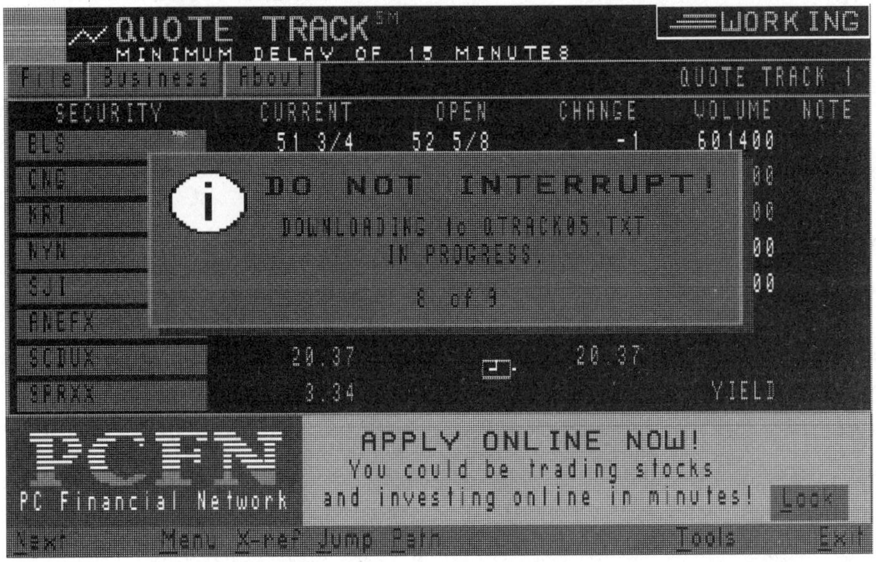

FIGURE 12.9: Downloading stock quotes from Prodigy's Quote Track service

Here's how to do it:

1. Log onto Prodigy. Select JUMP from the bottom of your screen and type **quote track** in the JUMPwindow that appears. Press ↵.
2. Follow the online instructions to create a Quote Track list containing the stocks and other securities in your portfolio. Each list may contain as many as 50 symbols.
3. Select FILE from the top of your screen, then choose REPORT SETUP. This opens a box that lets you choose whether to download the entire list of quotes or only those currently displayed on your screen. It also lets you decide whether to see the stocks' current or closing prices, and asks what kind of spreadsheet you'll be downloading the stock quotes to.

4. Select ENTER FILE NAME and type a name for the file, or accept the default setting (for example, QTRACK00.WKS).

5. Press ↵ or select OK to begin the downloading process. Once the quotes have been downloaded, you can retrieve them from your Prodigy directory.

Online Brokerages: Trading Stocks Where You Buy Your Socks

If you've ever played the market, you've probably experienced the exhilaration of spotting an undervalued stock, playing a hunch, and reaping a tidy profit—on paper, that is. But, if you're like most small investors, you've also experienced the disappointment of seeing your stock market winnings whittled down to size by the hefty fees and commissions charged by your full-service broker.

There is a better way—and it's as easy as logging on.

These days, anybody with the financial savvy to buy and sell securities without a broker's advice can trade stocks, bonds, options, certificates of deposit and mutual funds online, cutting out the middleman and saving big bucks. Either place your trade through an online service—Prodigy, CompuServe, GEnie, America Online, and Dow Jones News/Retrieval all offer online brokerage capabilities—or invest in an off-the-shelf program like Reality Technologies' Smart Investor or Meca Software's Fidelity Online Xpress that lets you log on directly. Both programs retail for under $100.

The savings can be substantial—as much as several hundred dollars on a single trade. For example, Personal Control Financial Network (PCFN), the online brokerage service offered on Prodigy, charges commissions as low as $45 for a trade of 200 shares priced at $25 a share. That's $81 less than you'd ordinarily pay a full-service broker (who might try to sell you stocks you don't want to buy). Plus, there's no monthly service charge and immediate online trade confirmation. In fact, some brokerage houses that also take orders over the phone—such as Fidelity and Charles Schwab—offer 10 percent off their already discounted rates to customers who trade by modem.

There is a catch, though. While online brokerages charge lower rates than many telephone brokers, most of them tack on some sort of access fee—either to dial up the brokerage service, to log onto the online service that offers it, or to download the financial data you'll need to make an intelligent trading decision in the first place. And, even though mistakes are less likely when you type your orders directly into your computer than when you place them verbally, foul-ups can happen online, too, some users warn.

"I've [earned] a Ph.D. Cum Laude in the School of Hard Knocks when it comes to [online] brokers," says Sandy Schupper, a CompuServe member from Venom, Pennsylvania, who now sticks to off-line brokerage firms. "When they make an error, you eat it. This has cost me thousands of dollars. In one case, I called in an order at 6:14 A.M. Pacific Time and they entered it at 6:39 A.M. Then they refused to make it good, saying this was a reasonable period of time [in which to execute the order]."

Clearly, online trading is not for everyone. Richard Brueckner, managing director of Donaldson Lufkin & Jenrette Securities Corp., the New York brokerage firm that manages Prodigy's PCFN service, says that only about 100,000 people trade stocks online—a tiny fraction of the roughly 20 million Americans who buy and sell securities each year. But, he says, the number of online traders is growing fast. PCFN has grown eight-fold over the last two years and now handles about 1000 trades a day, Brueckner says. Prodigy says that PCFN is now the nation's largest online broker, with some 70,000 accounts resulting in trades amounting to $1.5 billion in 1992.

Besides low prices, "there's also the element of convenience," Brueckner says. "This is the kind of service where you can make an investment decision after reading *Barron's* and *The New York Times* on Sunday afternoon and then forget about it."

MAKING A TRADE

Depending on which online brokerage you use, trading stocks online is almost as goof-proof as using the ATM machine at your local bank.

Here's how you would buy 100 shares of Apple Computer on Prodigy. (**Tip**: For novice users, it's a good idea to practice your skills using PCFN's demo program before you start trading for real.)

1. Log onto Prodigy. Choose JUMP from the bottom of your screen and type **PCFN** in the JUMPwindow. Press ↵.
2. Type in your PCFN account number, and choose STOCKS from the menu. Press ↵.
3. The menu that appears will then prompt you to enter the company's stock symbol or name (AAPL or Apple), the number of shares you wish to buy (100), the price at which you want to purchase them and other information. Or choose the TRADE ASSIST button at the top of the screen, and a series of pop-up windows will explain each choice and describe each step as you go along, as illustrated in Figure 12.10.

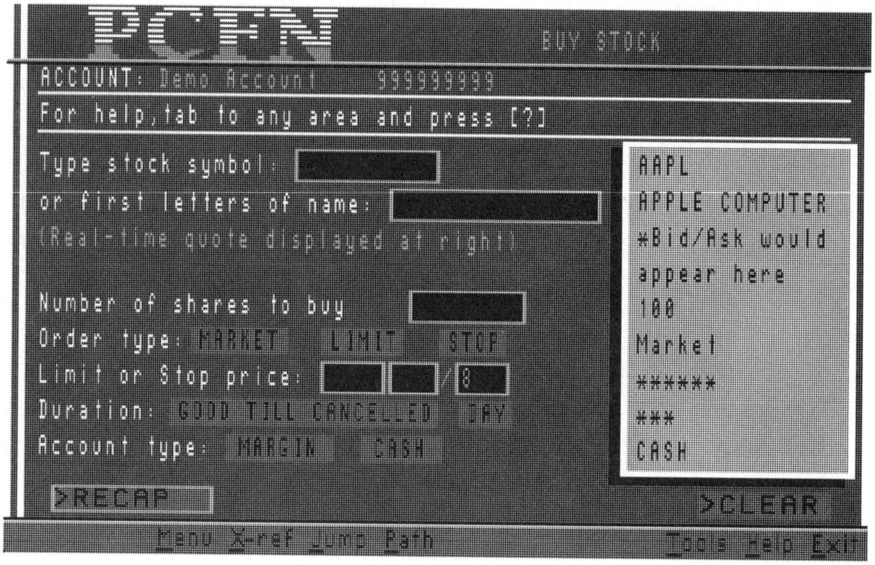

FIGURE 12.10:

Buying 100 shares of Apple Computer with Prodigy's PCFN brokerage service

4. If you want to change an instruction before submitting the order, simply move the cursor to the item and make the new selection.

5. When your order is ready, choose RECAP to open a window with a summary for your review, then select SEND TO PCFN to execute your trade. Once your trade is completed, an online execution report will show you the price you received, the number of shares traded, the commission cost, the total amount to be settled, the settlement date, and any funds that are due.

HOW THE ONLINE BROKERAGES STACK UP

Which online brokerage you choose will probably depend on how often you trade and how comfortable you are in making your own investment decisions. If you're market-savvy and already subscribe to a particular online service, it's probably a good idea to use the broker offered by that service rather than pay extra fees to save a few dollars elsewhere. Investors who want soup-to-nuts portfolio management may be better off with one of the programs mentioned above, while heavy traders who know their way around a computer ought to consider CompuServe's E-Trade Securities, a deep-discount brokerage.

Prodigy's PCFN brokerage is a good choice for online novices. For the same $14.95 a month you pay to subscribe to Prodigy, you can access online brokerage services, too. There's no additional monthly fee to trade stocks, bonds, options, mutual funds, or certificates of deposit through PCFN and no hourly connect-time charges, either. Plus, PCFN is simple to use, offers instant trade confirmation online, and keeps its rates low—$40 for a stock or option trade of under $2500 and $50 for most Treasury bonds. Heavy traders can even qualify for "frequent trader discounts" by racking up $1000 or more in PCFN brokerage commissions over a 12-month period.

CompuServe, for its part, offers three online trading options: Quick & Reilly, Spear & Rees, and E-Trade Securities. All are discount brokers, though E-Trade charges the lowest rates by far—$29 on any trade of 100 shares or less and no connect-time fees. The other two brokerage firms charge $14 an hour on trades made during the day and $4 an hour for trades made in the evening. (That's on top of the 22 cents a minute you pay to connect to CompuServe at 2400 bps.)

Another online option is Fidelity Investors Express, a brokerage service available through Dow Jones News/Retrieval. DJN/R charges a monthly fee of $12.95 but no per-minute access charges.

The Financial Meet Market

But the world of online financial information consists of more than just stock quotes, databases and brokerage services. There's the added bonus of being able to log onto investor clubs and bulletin boards to swap tips, trends, and theories with investors nationwide—without ever leaving your computer.

"It's a new way of networking," says Art Bechhoefer, who runs The Investor's Network forum for America Online. "You connect with people all over the country. You get access to information that you might not get access to otherwise."

INVESTOR BULLETIN BOARDS

Just like bulletin boards in other parts of the online world, financial bulletin boards act as watering holes where amateur and professional investors like to gather.

Prodigy offers the Money Talk bulletin board, where investors meet online to chat about hot stocks, market trends, and other topics of interest. CompuServe offers an online meeting place called the Investors Forum, which gives investors a chance to discuss market trends, download investment software and participate in real-time conferences with professional money managers and stock brokers.

CompuServe's Financial Forums let investors ask experts about investments and the economy plus technical topics such as running Lotus 1-2-3.

On the other hand, just because online investment advice is readily accessible doesn't mean you should swallow it whole. In fact, Prodigy's Money Talk board came under attack in a recent *Wall Street Journal* article that suggested that some of the tips posted there might have come from Prodigy members with an interest in seeing certain stocks go up or down.

Money Talk regulars, though, don't seem fazed by such criticism, saying that they don't believe everything they read on the bulletin board anyway.

"Why would people even make a comment if they didn't have some sort of interest?" says Hal Kirven, a Prodigy member from Columbus, Georgia, who trades stocks for a living.

The opening menu for Money Talk is shown in Figure 12.11.

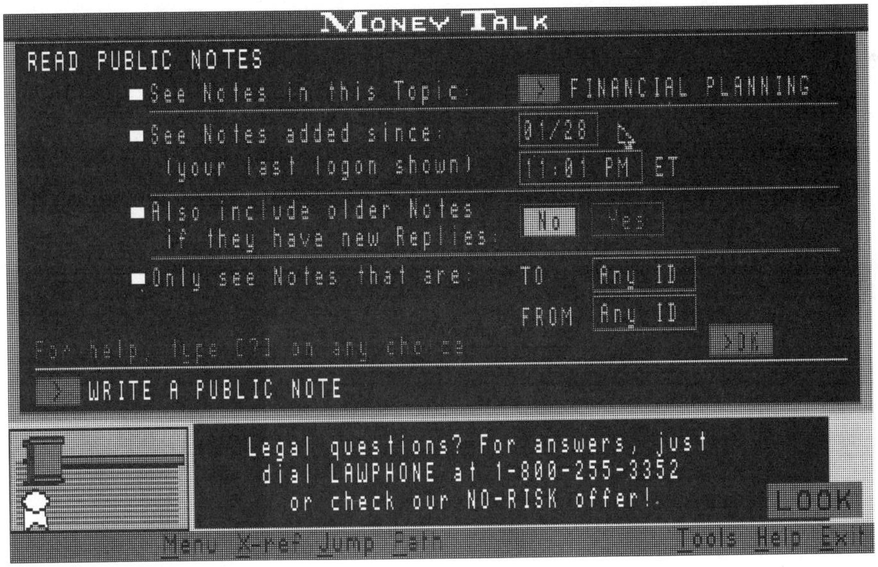

FIGURE 12.11:

Prodigy's Money Talk Bulletin Board

ONLINE INVESTMENT CLUBS

With investor bulletin boards such a popular feature, it's not surprising that online investment clubs are springing up, too.

The Pioneer Online Investment Club, formed in August 1991, was one of the first clubs in the United States to conduct business online, meeting not in someone's living room but in CompuServe's NAIC Forum. The National Association of Investors Corporation (NAIC) in Royal Oak, Michigan, is a 40-year-old educational organization that boasts approximately 7000 clubs with 105,000 members nationwide. (The NAIC Forum menu, with Pioneers Online selected, is shown in Figure 12.12.)

The club has already invested in McDonald's and other stocks, and its members have included a Washington lobbyist, a volunteer firefighter from Nashville, an English professor who teaches in Japan, and an engineer from Seattle.

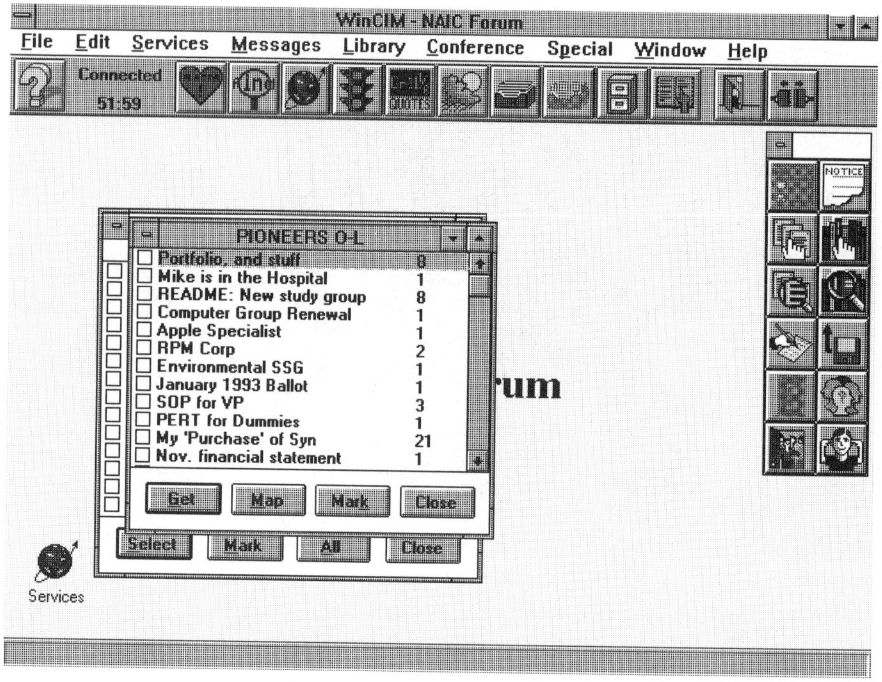

FIGURE 12.12:
CompuServe's NAIC Forum

"With most clubs, you meet on the third Thursday," says club member Sammye Baker, who runs a lighting manufacturing company in Indianapolis with her husband. "This one meets all the time."

Despite the club's advantages, though, members say that making an online club run smoothly takes lots of work—in part because of the nature of the online medium. Baker says the club's founders spent the summer of 1991 discussing logistics—how to set up the club, how to deal with tax issues, whom the members should send their checks to. Running club meetings online has also presented special challenges. Discussing which stock to buy, for example, can drag on for months. Though members can send each other messages almost instantaneously, some members may not log onto CompuServe for several days. This can slow communication to a crawl.

But the biggest disadvantage, says club member Bill Bentley, a Mountain Lakes, New Jersey, engineering executive, is cost.

"I never spent more than $10 a year on CompuServe before I joined this club," Bentley says. "Now, it's more like $10 a week."

Summary

In this chapter, you toured the fast-growing world of online finance. You explored the wealth of financial data that's available online—both from Prodigy and CompuServe and from more specialized services—and learned how to download it into the kind of electronic spreadsheets you use every day. You also found out how to save money with online brokerage services and weighed the pros and cons of using them to trade stocks, bonds and mutual funds. Finally, you heard the stories of investors who participate in online bulletin boards and stock-trading clubs, hoping, one day, to strike it rich.

In the next chapter, you'll learn about "working the room"—how to drum up business and meet professional colleagues by joining online business clubs and bulletin boards. You'll also find out how to get professional advice and locate doctors, lawyers, and tax experts online.

CHAPTER 13

Working the Room

In the last chapter, you toured the lucrative world of online finance. You explored the wealth of financial data that's available online and learned how to download it into the kind of electronic spreadsheets you use every day, as well as how to save money with online brokerage services.

In this chapter, you'll learn about "working the room"—how to drum up business and meet professional colleagues by joining online business clubs and bulletin boards. You'll also discover how to tap into a national network of professional support services to get fast, free, up-to-date advice about business and employment issues involving the law, accounting, and health care.

Online Networking for Fun and Profit

In the off-line world of face-to-face business lunches, conventions, and trade shows, meeting new people can be a daunting prospect.

Whether you're trying to lasso new customers or drum up more business from the ones you already have, in-person salesmanship can be difficult for all but the most thick-skinned. For many people, it's just as tough over the phone. After all, nobody likes rejection.

That's where online networking comes in. A cross between old-fashioned letter-writing and high-tech communication, online networking lets you "work the room" without actually being there. By logging onto an online service or bulletin board, you can use your computer and modem to send e-mail to that promising prospect in Seattle, display your expertise in a real-time chat session, or even log off if you're not sure how to answer somebody's question. Even if you're not among the painfully shy, modem-to-modem communication is a great way to find a job, start a business, get free advice, and hob-nob with terrific people you'd never meet in the company elevator. And, of course, there's no need to dress up, make small talk, or pass out business cards.

HELP FOR HOME BUSINESS OWNERS

Online networking can be especially useful for people who run their businesses from home. That's because most home business owners don't like to be away from their phones and computers for very long and can't afford to boost their visibility by placing big ads in the Yellow Pages or attending all the trade shows.

Fortunately, the online world offers plenty of opportunities to meet potential customers—all without spending a fortune or leaving your computer. CompuServe's Working From Home Forum, run by home business gurus Paul and Sarah Edwards, lets home-office professionals compare notes on everything from marketing tips to health insurance. CompuServe also offers a Computer Consultant's Forum, illustrated in Figure 13.1, that provides a place for computer

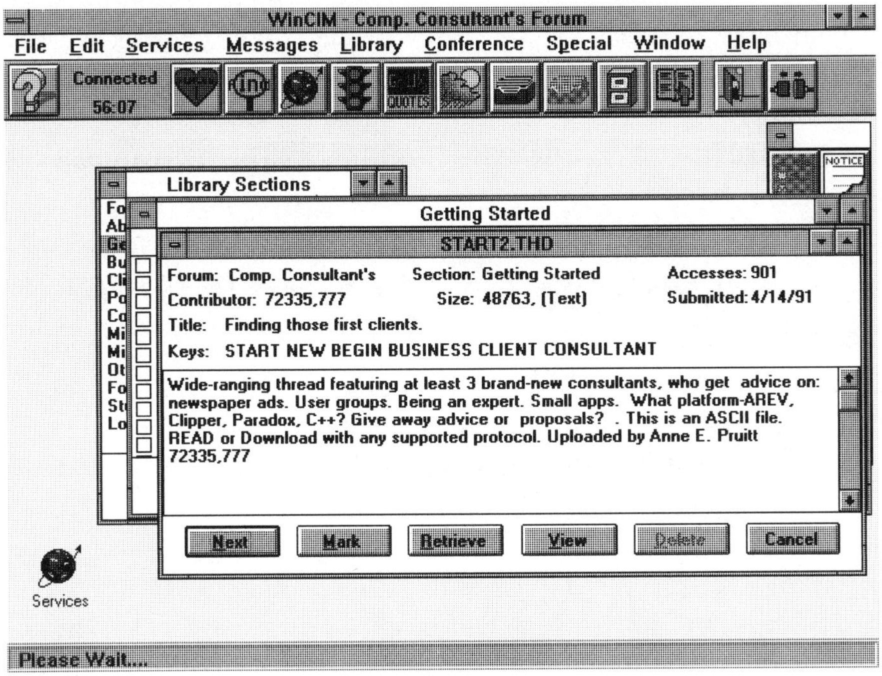

FIGURE 13.1: CompuServe's Computer Consultant's Forum

consultants to share business tips, technical information, and solutions to client problems. GEnie's Computer Press Association Roundtable features a bulletin board where editors can post help-wanted notices and freelance writers, many of whom work from home, can download business leads. America Online lets entrepreneurs get help from the Service Corps of Retired Executives at the Microsoft Small Business Center.

It's opportunities like this that enable Scott Michael Moore, a lawyer who specializes in international trade, to run a thriving practice out of the log cabin in rural Mohawk, Michigan, that he calls home. But though Moore lives in a hamlet 450 miles northeast of Minneapolis, that hasn't hurt his business. Moore's clients, few of whom he has ever met face to face, live as far away as Nigeria, Norway, Kuwait, and China.

The secret to Moore's success? A subscription to CompuServe that lets him network with clients and contacts worldwide. The cost: $50 a month to run an ad on the service and "chat" with other members online.

"It's extremely cost-effective for me in terms of international exposure," he says.

LOOKING FOR JOBS IN ALL THE RIGHT PLACES

Of course, not all online networking is done through word of mouth. These days, thousands of job seekers and employers are mixing and matching through the electronic equivalent of old-fashioned dating services. Though online bulletin boards have yet to replace the time-honored practice of scanning the newspaper classifieds, they are beginning to catch on. For job hunters, there's the opportunity to put their resumes in front of those employers who are actively looking to hire—instead of mailing out resumes blind. For employers, there's the advantage of using cost-efficient electronic tools to search for candidates who meet their precise job descriptions, eliminating headhunters who typically charge a hefty percentage of the new hire's first-year salary.

But that's not all. Besides those bulletin boards and databases geared toward job seekers and employers, mass-market services like CompuServe and Prodigy are offering online classifieds and special-interest forums where like-minded colleagues can get together to network and find jobs and freelance assignments. CompuServe, for example, offers access to the Adnet Online Employment Advertising Network, an electronic database of U.S. and international job openings. The service's Working from Home Forum recently beefed up its Jobs/Telecommuting Section, illustrated in Figure 13.2, to offer job-hunting advice and career development tips.

"Individuals needing advice and guidance in their career direction and job-search can come here for help from the experts," says

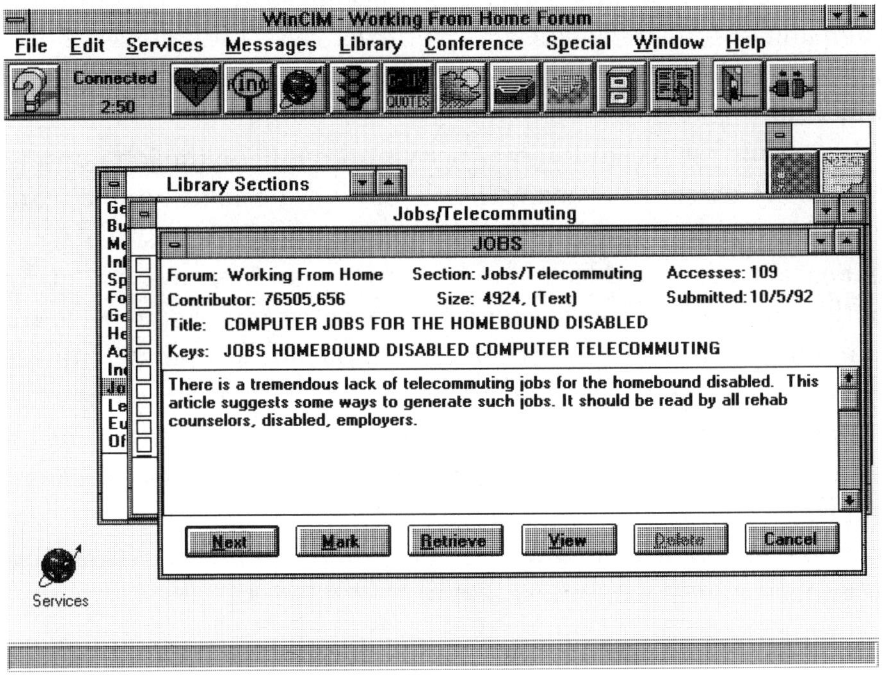

FIGURE 13.2: The Jobs/Telecommuting Section of CompuServe's Working From Home Forum

Steve Burt, the section leader and owner of Resume House, a home-based resume-writing service in Gainesville, Florida.

One successful online job-hunter is Dennis Hiel, a marketing major at Siena College in Albany, New York, who wasn't having much luck finding a job the old-fashioned way. With the economy still in the doldrums, he got no response from the big companies to which he had sent his resume, and none of the on-campus interviews he went on panned out. Eventually, though, Hiel did land a job—as a district manager for ADP in Clifton, New Jersey—through Career Network, an online employment service run by Information Kinetics, Inc. in Chicago. On Career Network, employers, job seekers and college placement officers can post and respond to job notices quickly and efficiently by using personal computers and modems.

"I figured that any way I could get my name out in front of companies would be beneficial to me," Hiel says. "I still think the best way to get a job is if you know somebody, but, if you don't, this is the way to go."

Despite the recent flurry of activity, though, online job hunting still hasn't entered the mainstream. Though no hard numbers are available, the pool of online resumes remains small, the result of technological barriers and lack of public awareness. Burt says that many of the University of Florida students whose resumes he prepares are still unfamiliar with computers and modems. Corporate human resources officers are leery of change as well. As a result, off-line job searching methods such as on-campus interviews, print media classifieds, and recruiters continue to dominate the employment industry.

"People want something to hold in their hands," Burt says. "You can't do that with a computer screen."

Search Tips

One key factor to consider before conducting an online job hunt—or recruitment if you are an employer—is cost. Some online resume services charge a fee to the job hunter, others charge the employer, still others charge both. CompuServe charges its standard connect-time rates to participate in its forums and search its Adnet database. Prodigy members can search its TPI Online Classifieds for no extra charge above the regular $14.95-a-month flat fee.

To save money, Burt, the CompuServe section leader, advises job seekers to "try to use as many free databases as you can. They may or may not be effective, but, if they're free, you might as well take advantage of them."

As for those databases that charge a fee, "try to find out the success rate others have had with that particular database," Burt suggests. "Ask for names of others who have used the database, and call them. Ask for the names of corporate subscribers, and ask them if they really do use the database for recruiting."

In addition to the online classified services offered on both CompuServe and Prodigy, there are dozens of independent bulletin boards and resumes services that exist solely to match up job-seekers and employers. Career Network, for example, uses Prodigy to bring together companies and college placement offices nationwide. Employers can post company profiles, up-to-the-minute industry news, and current job openings for both graduating seniors and alumni. An extensive electronic mail system lets users communicate with their colleagues throughout the nation. Fees are $50 for a three-month enrollment with 30 free e-mail messages a month.

KiNexus, a resume-only database produced by the same company, charges job seekers $19.95 a year and is offered free to recent and pending graduates through their college placement center. To contact Career Network, write to Information Kinetics, Inc., 640 N. LaSalle St., Suite 560, Chicago IL 60610, or call 1-800-828-0422.

Then there's Job Bank USA, an online resume service that targets small and mid-size companies, and charges $30 to enroll job seekers in its database for a year. Rather than allow employers to search the database directly, Job Bank USA staffers use specialized software to identify those candidates that meet the employer's criteria and then send the company a list of names—once the applicants have authorized their release. Job Bank USA charges employers up to $100 for this service. The company tries to forward between two and 10 screened applicants to the employer within 48 hours. To contact Job Bank USA, write to 1420 Spring Hill Rd., Suite 480, McLean VA 22102, or call 703-847-1706.

There's also The National Resume Bank, a service run by the Professional Association of Resume Writers, which lets job seekers post their resumes on line for $25 for three months under one of 22 job categories. Each additional listing is also $25. Employers can search the database for free. To contact The National Resume Bank, write in care of The Professional Association of Resume Writers, 3637 Fourth St. North, Suite 330, St. Petersburg FL 33704, or call 813-896-3694.

Professional Advice: Is There a Doctor (or Lawyer, or CPA) in the House?

While going online is a great way to drum up business, it's also a good way to get business advice—at a fraction of what you'd pay to consult with doctors, lawyers or accountants in their offices. Of course, you'll still need to see your doctor for your annual physical and meet with your lawyer to draft important legal documents, but the advice you get online can certainly help point you in the right direction.

Here's a sampling of the kind of advice you can get online for free (apart from connect-time charges).

LEGAL ADVICE

If you're in the market for a lawyer, there's plenty of legal advice available on CompuServe's Legal (Lawsig) and Working From Home Forums. Forum members who log onto Lawsig can browse through such library sections as Computer Law and Software and Lawyer-to-Lawyer, an information exchange for attorneys. In addition, you can post your legal questions on a bulletin board called Attorney Wanted, where lawyers answer your questions, giving tips and suggesting referrals.

And, unlike the advice offered by a lawyer in his office or a phone consultation, the online advice is free—apart from CompuServe's 22-cents-a-minute connect-time charge. At the same time, it's important to recognize that online legal advice has its limitations. While a lawyer may be happy to give you some general advice on a legal topic, he won't be able to offer a specific solution to your problem until he meets with you to discuss the case.

For more in-depth legal information, consider logging onto Dialog's Knowledge Index, which gives you access to over 120 Dialog databases during evenings and weekends at a reduced rate. Subscribers get access to the Legal Resource Index, which features articles from more than 750 law journals and reviews, and BNA Daily News, which offers daily news coverage of national and international government and private-sector activities.

TAX ADVICE

You can find plenty of tax advice online, too, just by logging onto one of the many money-related bulletin boards.

Prodigy's Money Talk bulletin board has a special section just about taxes (illustrated in Figure 13.3), where members can post notes under the headings Ask Julian Block, Ask Kiplinger, Ask the CPA, and Ask the Experts.

Here's a snippet of a recent exchange on Ask the CPA:

"I have been hearing about a new form of business that gives the owner the benefits of limited liability but is basically a sole-proprietorship," writes J. Patrick Cullen. "Does anyone know about this and what it is called?"

Responds Henry Klein: "Patrick, you may be referring to Limited Liability Companies (LLCs), a relatively new form of legal ownership that offers advantages and benefits that are not available to S-Corps or partnerships. The LLC combines the advantages of limited liability for all investors with the partnership tax advantage of maximum flexibility. A properly structured LLC will be a partnership for Federal Tax purposes—the unique advantage of LLCs is that

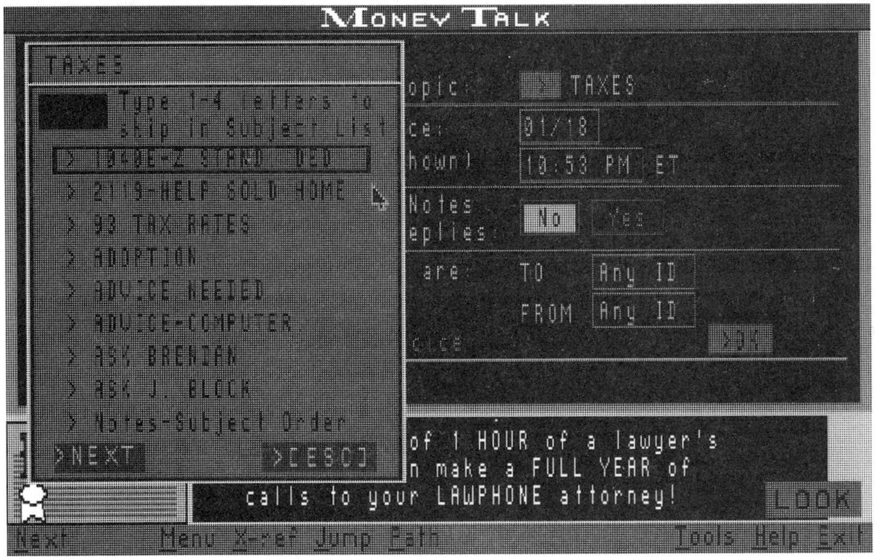

FIGURE 13.3: The Tax Section of Prodigy's Money Talk Bulletin Board

they can provide limited liability to all owners even if they fully participate in the management—and many of the restrictions that apply to S-Corps can be avoided."

CompuServe, for its part, not only offers tax advice on its various financial forums but also provides access to an H&R Block area, where you can find tax tips, tax news, tax-related articles, a calendar of important tax dates, and answers to commonly asked questions. (H&R Block, you'll recall, is the tax-preparation company that owns CompuServe.)

Here's a sample Q & A session from H & R Block:

"**Question**: I sometimes bring work home from the office. A home computer would help me on these occasions. If I buy one, can I deduct the cost as a business expense?

Answer: No. Your employer must require you to own a home computer as a condition for holding your job in order for its cost to be a deductible expense."

GETTING HEALTH ADVICE: AN OUNCE OF PREVENTION

Thanks to the rapidly expanding world of online health services, anybody with a personal computer and a modem can plug into a treasure trove of leading-edge health and medical knowledge for a fraction of the cost of a doctor's visit or a fancy health spa.

Connecting to CompuServe, for example, lets you peruse medical journals, order prescription drugs and even chat with other members about everything from exercise to cancer treatments. CompuServe's Health Database Plus lets you download articles from *American Health*, *Runner's World*, and *Psychology Today*, while the service's Court Pharmacy offers bargains at its online drug store.

Consider the case of Pete Crosta.

As weight-reduction strategies go, sitting in a comfy chair in front of a computer screen seems an unlikely way to shed one's excess baggage. But for Crosta, 38, a Nutley, New Jersey, high school teacher, a daily regimen of computer keystrokes was just what the doctor ordered. Since starting his online weight-loss program nearly two years ago, Crosta has slimmed down from 305 pounds to 245 pounds and tightened his belt by a full 12 inches.

Crosta, who now works out regularly at the local gym, admits he didn't do it with online exercises alone, but says the support and camaraderie of the people he met on CompuServe's Health & Fitness Forum played a key role in helping him lose those 60 pounds.

"It was this socialization that kept me going," Crosta says. "I became so addicted to the Health & Fitness Forum and going to the gym each day that if I did not do both, I got upset."

The Medsig Forum

CompuServe's Medsig Forum, sponsored by the American Medical Informatics Association, lets doctors, nurses, and other members of the medical professional swap ideas and information about medical topics. But it's also a good place for the lay person to look, and many of its messages and library files are useful and timely.

One recent file offered the full text of *The Low Fat Lifestyle Health Letter*, a monthly newsletter published by Dr. Robert C. Baker, medical director of the Low Fat Lifestyle Program in Pitman, New Jersey. Here's a sample of the good doctor's suggestions:

- "Many people eat only one fruit a day. Gradually increase that to 2 or 3 fruits a day. Fruit juices don't count—they lack the fiber, and do not satisfy hunger—in fact, they may stimulate the appetite in some people."
- "Try to eat a salad daily, using a no-fat salad dressing. Over several months, increase the size of the salad; then promote yourself to 2 salads a day. You will notice that you are acquiring a taste for vegetables that you never had before."

- "Peel bananas, freeze them, and when an ice cream craving attack occurs, run to the refrigerator and take out a frozen banana. Put it in the blender, with vanilla extract if you wish, and in minutes you have 'ice cream'—the low fat variety."

News Updates and Databases

If you're looking to tap into health news, there's plenty available online, from timely news updates to sophisticated research databases.

CompuServe, for example, offers Health Database Plus, which contains more than 48,000 articles on health, fitness, and nutrition from publications ranging from *Psychology Today* to *The New England Journal of Medicine*; HealthNet, a home medical reference library; PaperChase, a database of references to scholarly biomedical literature, and Physicians Data Query, which contains information about more than 80 types of cancer and the names of roughly 12,000 cancer specialists.

Prodigy doesn't offer the same kind of research databases that CompuServe does—it's a more consumer-oriented online service. But its Health News collection of trends, tips, and consumer reports is changed frequently to reflect up-to-the-minute health and fitness issues. Recently, the Health News main menu offered these six selections: Health Topics: No Such Thing as a Good Tan, Timely Topics: Insurance Woes, Consumer Reports: How to Live Longer, Health News: Daily News Update, Health Quiz: Are you Health Savvy?, and Keeping Fit: How-to Guide. Figure 13.4 illustrates a recent sampling of topics.

America Online's Issues in Mental Health area offers chats and conferences led by "Arrienn," a trained mental health professional experienced in crisis intervention, child advocacy, parenting and other family concerns. Regular features in the section include The Parenting Board, The Daily Living Board, The Relationships Board and The Teen Talk Board. The area's library contains transcripts of conferences, special feature articles and general information files pertaining to mental health.

FIGURE 13.4:
Prodigy's Health News

Support Groups

Online networking is also becoming increasingly popular with people who suffer from chronic illnesses and other disabilities—people who, in some cases, can't leave their homes or hospital beds to find the support and companionship they desperately need. Groups like these offers valuable—and inexpensive—resources if you own or work for a small company that can't afford its own employee assistance program.

CompuServe probably offers the widest assortment of support groups and resource centers of any online service. These include the Diabetes and Hypoglycemia Forum, the Cancer Forum, and the Living with AIDS Section of the Human Sexuality Forum, just to name a few.

"The typical reaction of new diabetics is basically one of horror and fear and uncertainty," says David Groves, a long-time diabetic and former bank executive in Bedford, Texas, who manages the Diabetes and Hypoglycemia Forum. "Our typical reaction is to be comforting. What we tell people is, no matter what you've heard about diabetes, you can take care of it and we'll help teach you how."

Groves' forum appears to be attracting a wide following. More than 5000 people have visited the forum so far from places as far afield as France, New Zealand, Japan and Belgium, and Groves estimates that 30 percent of the new members are people who have recently been diagnosed with diabetes.

CompuServe's Health & Fitness Forum, meanwhile, hosts regular meetings of Alcoholics Anonymous and Narcotics Anonymous in addition to the 10-week weight-loss program that Crosta joined.

"We have close to 300 people who access our forum on behalf of AA," says Allan Stevens, a Kettering, Ohio, consultant who runs the forum. Stevens adds, however, that the sessions are "supplemental, rather than taking the place of an in-person meeting. The people in that section really make you feel at home."

Figure 13.5 shows a recent sampling of topics on the Health & Fitness Forum.

Summary

In this chapter, you learned about "working the room"—how to drum up business and meet professional colleagues by joining online business clubs and bulletin boards. You also found out how to get professional advice and locate medical, legal and tax help online. In the medical area, you learned where to get the latest health news updates and medical research plus affordable health insurance and support groups for yourself and your employees.

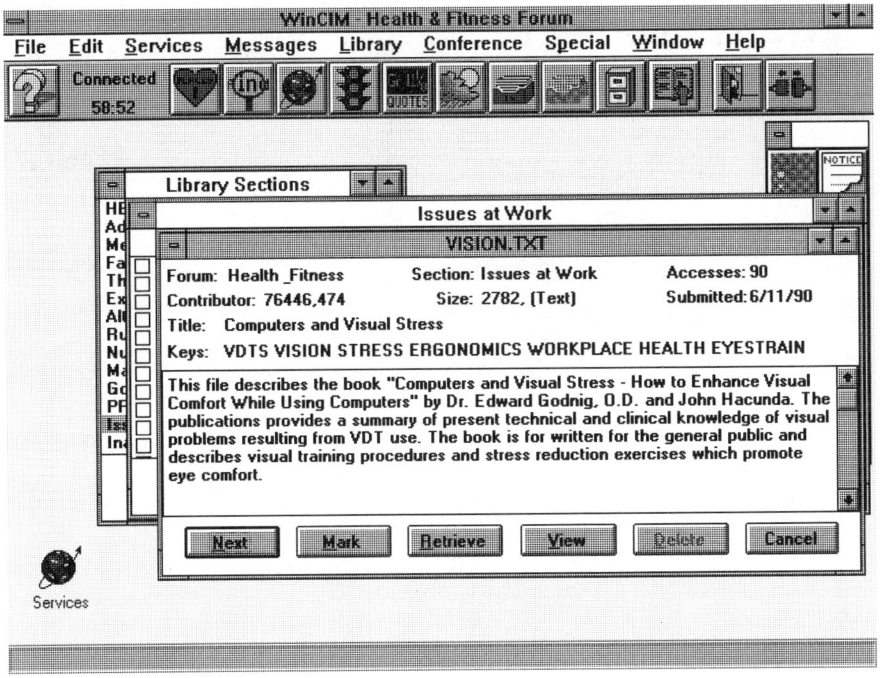

FIGURE 13.5: CompuServe's Health & Fitness Forum

In the next chapter, you'll find out how to stock your office—with everything from PCs to flowers—by shopping and ordering on-line. You'll get a quick tour of what the major services provide plus tips on how to comparison-shop through online databases filled with reviews and critiques from *Consumer Reports* and dozens of computer magazines.

CHAPTER 14

Stocking Your Office

In the last chapter, you learned about "working the room"—how to drum up business and meet professional colleagues by joining online business clubs and bulletin boards. You also found out how to get professional advice and locate medical, legal, and tax help online.

In this chapter, you'll find out how to stock your office with everything from PCs to flowers by shopping the electronic "malls" and ordering online. You'll get a quick tour of what the major online services provide plus tips on how to comparison-shop through online databases filled with reviews and critiques from *Consumer Reports* and dozens of computer magazines. You'll also learn about online ordering—and how to make it easy.

The Hassle-Free World of Online Shopping

If you run an office—either your own or somebody else's, you know the hassle of trekking out to the office supplies store to restock your supply of fax paper, scurrying from store to store to get the best deal on a new computer, and racking your brains at Christmastime trying to find the right gift for everyone on your holiday list. Not only do you waste valuable time driving, there's also the aggravation of waiting in line for a sales clerk to help you—only to be told that what you're looking for is out of stock.

Fortunately, there is a better way. Thanks to the convenience of online services, anybody with a computer and a modem can quickly and easily browse through hundreds of stores and thousands of products from computer software to gourmet cookies at some of the nation's leading department stores, discounters, catalog retailers, and specialty merchants—all without ever leaving the office. What's more, online malls stay open 24 hours a day, and there's never a hunt for a parking space. And unlike dialing an 800 number, online shopping doesn't mean waiting on hold for a clerk to take your order.

"In many ways, electronic shopping is the ideal medium for the 90s from both the retailer's and the consumer's points of view," says Regina Brady, CompuServe's director of customer promotion. "Consumers, particularly those who work full time, appreciate the sheer convenience of being able to sit down at their computers, at any time of the day or night, and order top-quality merchandise from well-known retailers."

While it's hard to know precisely how many people shop online or how much they spend there, Brady says that high-tech shopping does appear to be catching on among subscribers to CompuServe. For the first nine months of 1992, she says, the number of orders placed in the CompuServe Mall rose by 33.4 percent while sales shot up by 38.5 percent over the same period a year earlier. Approximately 3.8 percent of all visits to the Mall resulted in a purchase, Brady says, with an average sale of $75. Prodigy would not disclose its sales figures.

But online shopping is not only a convenience for the consumer, it's also a time-saver for small business owners, who often must act as their own purchasing agent in addition to the many other hats they wear. Thanks to online shopping, a company can restock its supply of copier paper, shop for a laser printer, even ship gourmet chocolates to an important client for a holiday treat. At Prodigy, for example, PC Flowers, an online flower delivery service, has blossomed into the fifth largest FTD florist worldwide.

"What we offer is one-stop shopping," says Ed Sessler, Prodigy's director of merchandise marketing. "Somebody owning or operating a small business does not have the time to run around to a lot of different places."

People like David Moskowitz, for one. Three years ago, the Norristown, Pennsylvania, computer consultant decided to buy a laptop computer to take with him on business trips. A savvy shopper, Moskowitz researched the market thoroughly before plunking down his money, reading up on makes and models reviewed in computer magazines and shopping the mail-order houses and computer stores. He even tried out a couple of laptops owned by business colleagues.

Finally, he settled on a Toshiba T1600/40—purchasing it not from a conventional retail outlet but from an online computer store that peddles its wares on CompuServe. The reason? An unbeatable price and the convenience of having the computer shipped directly to his door.

"I found a good price and it was better than anything else I'd seen, and I said, 'Do it!,'" recalls Moskowitz, owner of Productivity Solutions, Inc. "I got precisely what I wanted."

THE PROS AND CONS

But, while online shopping clearly has lots of advantages, it's still got a long way to go before it catches on the way automated teller machines (ATMs) have in the world of banking.

One problem is that, while online services occasionally provide on-screen illustrations of the products they sell, you still can't touch, smell, taste, or try on the product before you buy it. Another drawback is that placing an order online is often slower than dialing an 800 number because of the time it takes to transmit graphics and product information to your computer screen at 2400 bits per second, the modem speed at which most people currently log on. (Prodigy, arguably the slowest of the major online services because it depends so heavily on graphics, recently introduced 9600 bps access, which should help speed things up a bit.)

"I don't think you can say that electronic malls are catching on in a big way," says Chris Elwell, editorial director of Simba Information, Inc. in Wilton, Connecticut, which tracks the online services industry. "It's still probably a helluva lot simpler to call an 800 number and order Flowers Direct than it is to do it through Prodigy."

Elwell predicts that online shopping probably won't begin to replace off-line catalogs or 800 numbers for another five years—until subscribers can "call up an online catalog and see a multimedia image of a fashion model modeling a piece of clothing." Not only must multimedia computer systems first become more widely available to the public, he explains, but the copper wire that runs most telephone systems now may need to be scrapped in favor of cable or some other medium with a large enough bandwidth to accommodate the vast amount of data required to be transmitted.

Even people who regularly shop online say that online purchasing is not for everyone—or every purchase. Moskowitz, the consultant who bought the laptop, says the key to successful online shopping is to do your homework first—read magazines, chat with knowledgeable friends and colleagues, and maybe even test the product in person before making your buy. It's also important to find out about the merchant's or manufacturer's warranty and return policy.

"I wouldn't buy anything online that I hadn't researched thoroughly," Moskowitz says. "It's not a totally risk-free proposition."

On the other hand, he says, shoppers who subscribe to an online service do have a leg up on off-line shoppers—thanks to the vast array of bulletin boards and databases that many online services offer.

Both Prodigy and CompuServe offer access to an online version of *Consumer Reports*, the well-know buying guide. CompuServe, for its part, also offers searchable databases of full-text magazine articles; Computer Database Plus, for example, offers reviews of hardware and software products.

Moskowitz says he has also found it helpful to post notes on various online bulletin boards asking members to advise him on the best deals.

"If you're going to use an online service to buy something, then it makes sense to use the resources of the online service to help you," he says.

Cruising the Electronic Malls

While online services don't yet offer everything you can find in the off-line world of shopping malls, mail order catalogs, and specialty retail stores, they do offer a surprisingly varied selection—especially when it comes to computer hardware and software. But that's not all. Together, the four biggest online services—Prodigy, CompuServe, America Online, and GEnie—offer access to more than 200 retailers, from department store chains like JCPenney to specialty retailers such as Hammacher Schlemmer and Omaha Steaks.

(**Tip:** Many of the bigger and better-known retailers, such as The Gift Sender and Hammacher Schlemmer, are available on more than one online service. That's why, if you're planning to subscribe to more than one service, it pays to shop around. On Prodigy, shopping is included in the $14.95 monthly fee; on CompuServe, you pay no connect-time charges for the time you spend in the mall but will be charged 30 cents an hour to access the CompuServe network. GEnie lets you shop for free at night and on weekends but charges you $6 an hour to shop during business hours.)

COMPUSERVE

Introduced on CompuServe in 1985, the CompuServe Mall has more stores online—117—than any of its competitors. Though CompuServe admits that, at first, many subscribers were leery of buying items they couldn't see or try on and tended to restrict their purchases to books or computer software, the service says that today Mall sales are at a record high. Part of the Mall's appeal, explains Brady, can be traced to broader consumer acceptance of home shopping, the same trend that has triggered dramatic growth in catalog sales, direct mail, and toll-free telephone ordering.

CompuServe Mall merchants range from such well-known department stores as JCPenney to specialty stores hawking gourmet food, consumer electronics, pharmaceuticals, and pet supplies. Some car manufacturers, including Ford and Buick, make information about their products available through the Mall but do not offer direct ordering. Shoppers can access a particular store directly or browse by product categories such as Information/Services, Office Supplies, Computing, and Gifts/Flowers/Gourmet Foods.

Making a purchase on CompuServe is as easy as completing a simple online order form and receiving a confirmation number. Many merchants offer express delivery within 72 hours, and many will ship merchandise almost anywhere in the world. And if you can't find what you're looking for or have questions about a product, you can send an e-mail message to a merchant and get a prompt response. CompuServe also provides an online gift guide with a wide array of gift suggestions for men, women, IBM-owners, employers, employees, and devotees of gourmet foods.

Here's a sampling of what's available on the CompuServe Mall:

- Dalco Computer Electronics - PC components and supplies
- Desktop Direct From Digital - Computer products
- Direct Micro - Computer accessories and software

- Executive Stamper - Rubber stamps, engraved gifts
- Flower Stop - Flowers and gifts
- Gimmee Jimmy's Cookies - Cookies
- Hammacher Schlemmer - Gifts, unique and unusual products
- JCPenney Online Catalog - Department store
- JDR Microdevices - Values for the PC enthusiast
- The Laser's Edge - Laser discs and laser disc equipment
- MacWarehouse - Macintosh hardware, software & access
- MicroWarehouse - Hardware, software & accessories for PCs
- Mission Control Software - The newest software and accessories
- Omaha Steaks - Gourmet food
- Omni Technics - Computer peripherals and electronics
- PC Catalog - Mail order PC products
- Penny Wise Office Products - Discount office products
- Safeware Computer Insurance - Insurance
- Shareware Depot - Software
- Small Computer Book Club - Computer books
- Telebit Corp. - Transportable modems
- Walden Computer Books - Computer books & computer accessories

- Z Best - Discount electronics

Figure 14.1 shows an Electronic Mall News screen, a daily guide to new offerings from Mall retailers.

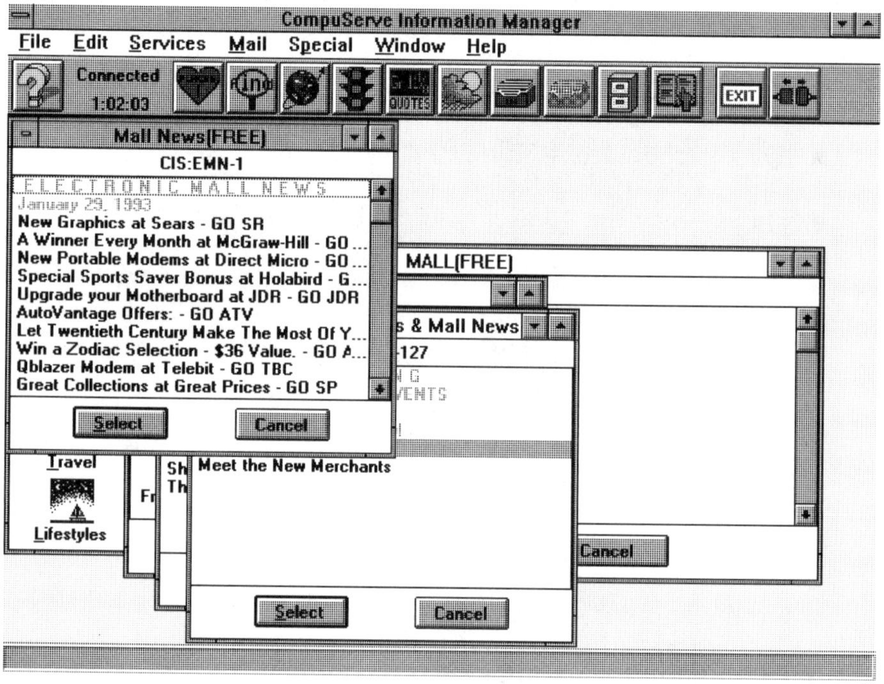

FIGURE 14.1: The CompuServe Mall's Electronic Mall News display

PRODIGY

One of the best-stocked shopping services online, Prodigy offers a cornucopia of goodies for both the consumer and the small business owner. The service's more than 70,000 offerings range from men's shirts and fine china to flower bouquets and postage stamps and include more than 3000 software titles, 30,000 compact discs, 4500 videos and 300 magazines. The Prodigy Mall houses 35 merchants in all. (That number includes only vendors from which you can order directly; it does not include companies that offer product information but not direct sales, which are counted by CompuServe and some of the other online services.)

Like CompuServe, Prodigy offers access to the JCPenney catalog in addition to leading hardware and software vendors such as Computer Express and Shareware Depot. Prodigy also offers a wide array of personalized shopping services, including online customer service, 48-hour order confirmation, and Gift Reminder, a service that lets you list up to 50 events such as birthdays and anniversaries and get a reminder notice delivered to your mailbox three weeks prior to each event. In addition, Prodigy guarantees all merchandise for 30 days from the date of receipt.

Recently, Prodigy has been making a major push to attract more shoppers to its mall. Apart from promotions offered by individual merchants, Prodigy itself has started running sweepstakes and offering free Air Miles to members who shop there.

Here's a sampling of what's available on Prodigy:

- Austad's Golf - Golf equipment, supplies
- CheeseBoard - Cheeses, pasta, paté
- Coffee Anyone??? - Gourmet coffee, teas
- Computer Express - Computer software
- Contact Lens Replacement Center - Contact lenses
- Gift Sender - Gourmet food, and gifts
- Hammacher Schlemmer - Unique items, gifts
- JCPenney - Department store
- Lands' End - Classic clothing for men and women
- Marymac - Discount Radio Shack products
- MOVIEWORKS! - 10,000+ video titles

- MUSICWORKS! - 30,000 CDs and tapes
- Ontrack - Protect data against PC viruses
- PC Balloons - Balloon bouquets
- PC Flowers - FTD fresh flowers
- PC Pens - Pens, art, drafting by HG Daniels
- Petworks - Unique pet products
- Shareware Club - Software subscription
- Shareware Depot - Software, less than $1 per program
- Spiegel - Apparel, home, electronics
- Sports Saver - Discount tennis/Athletic shoes
- The Sunglass Shop - Discounted top-name sunglasses
- US Stamp - US postage stamps

Figure 14.2 shows a screen from the Prodigy Mall.

Comparison Shopping

In addition to hassle-free shopping and ordering, online services offer something else that many conventional retailers do not—comparison shopping. By logging onto an online service, you can search dozens of databases for reviews, critiques, and feature articles about products you want to buy.

SEARCHING CONSUMER REPORTS

Both Prodigy and CompuServe offer access to an online version of Consumer Reports, the nationally known product buying guide. This database lets you search through electronic versions of the latest reviews of products and services from the pages of Consumer Reports

FIGURE 14.2:
The Prodigy Mall

magazine. Reports range from appliances and automobiles to electronics and insurance; they feature test results, ratings and recommendations as well as buying tips.

Let's say you want to buy a new answering machine. Here's how you would use CompuServe's Consumer Reports database to do your homework:

1. Select Go from the WinCIM Services menu or click the Go icon on the toolbar at the top of your screen. Type CONSUMER. Press ↵.
2. Double-click Electronics/Cameras.
3. Double-click Answering Machines.
4. Double-click one of the four options that appear on the next menu: 1) Intro/Overview (background information on answering machines in general), 2) What to Look For (desirable and undesirable product features and price ranges), 3) Recommendations (comparison of selected

models plus recommendations by Consumers Union), and 4) Models Tested/Ratings (price, description and ratings of tested models).

5. To find out more about Consumer Reports' ratings system, double-click 4) Models Tested/Ratings. Click Proceed, then double-click Guide to Ratings on the next menu that appears. Consumer Reports has five ratings categories, from ***** (excellent) to * (poor).

6. To see the ratings report for a particular model, just select it from the ratings menu.

Figure 14.3 shows the beginning of the Ratings display for answering machines.

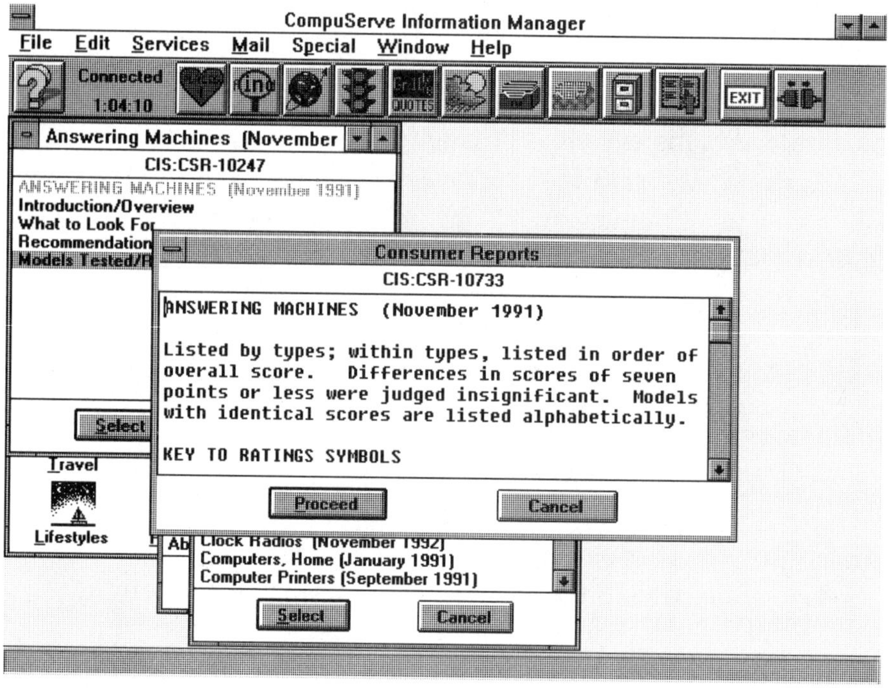

FIGURE 14.3:
Searching Consumer Reports on CompuServe

SEARCHING PC CATALOG

If you're in the market for a new computer or any of the trimmings, Prodigy's PC Catalog is a good place to go for some basic price and product information. A cross between a research database and a mail-order merchant, PC Catalog lets you select from eight product categories (computers, modems, monitors, printers, and so on), then compare features and prices by calling up a list of products on your screen. To learn more about a product, simply select the number next to it and press ↵. The phone number of each mail-order vendor is listed along with the price and product description.

Figure 14.4 shows the opening screen from PC Catalog.

FIGURE 14.4: Searching PC Catalog on Prodigy

Online Ordering

Once you've shopped the service and decided what you want to buy, online services make ordering a snap—after all, their merchants don't get paid until they ring up the sale. And, while online shopping may not yet be as simple as dialing an 800 number or picking a product off the shelf, it's getting easier all the time—thanks to online menus that prompt you every step of the way.

ORDERING THROUGH PRODIGY

Here's how to place an order on Prodigy's Computer Express, an online software vendor:

1. Log onto Prodigy, and choose JUMP from the bottom of your screen. Type **computer exp** in the JUMPwindow, and press ↵.
2. Select Store Directory, and press ↵.
3. On the next screen that appears, choose from the following four options under Main Store Menu: 1) Shop by Catalog, 2) Product Search, 3) New Products, and 4) Weekly Specials. To shop for, say, accounting software, choose Shop by Category, and press ↵.
4. The screen that appears next allows you to choose from software for different types of computers, such as Apple, Apple IIGS, Macintosh, and IBM PC. If your computer is an IBM PC-compatible, select IBM PC and press ↵.
5. Select Business from the next screen that appears, and press ↵. The menu also lets you choose Education, Games, Home Management, and Utility.
6. Choose Accounting from the next menu. Press ↵.
7. Shop from the alphabetical listing that appears on your screen. When you find a program that interests you, say, Meca's One Write Plus Accounting 3.0, press ↵. Product and price information will appear on your screen.

8. To make your purchase, choose ACTION from the bottom of your screen. Then type the quantity you wish to order and press ↵.

9. Review your order on the next screen that appears, and choose COMPLETE.

10. Prodigy's Easy Ordering menu, shown in Figure 14.5, prompts you for your credit card number, billing address, delivery address and other information. It also shows you the estimated price, including shipping.

11. To complete your purchase, choose SEND from the bottom of your screen. Choose CANCEL to cancel your order if you change your mind.

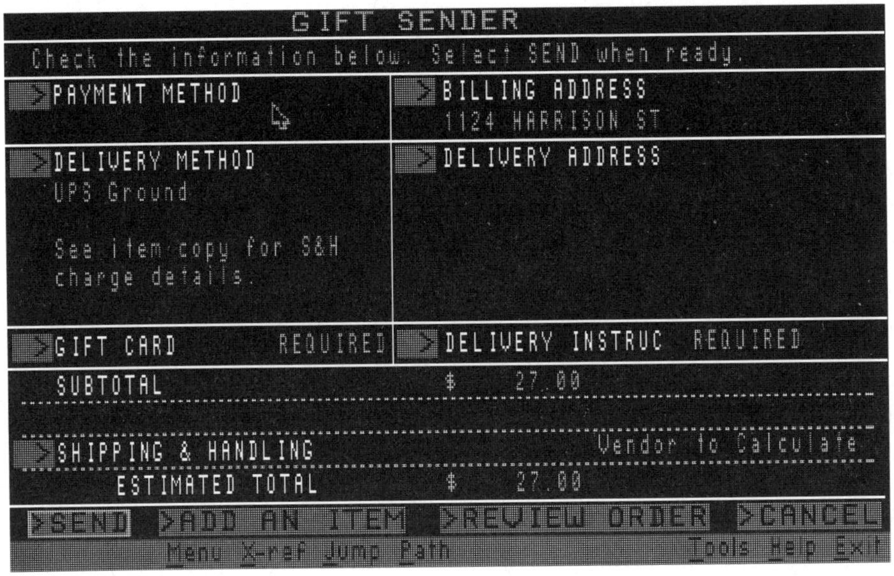

FIGURE 14.5: Using Prodigy's Easy Ordering menu to place an order with Gift Sender, an online vendor

Summary

In this chapter, you learned how to stock your office with everything from PC's to flowers by shopping the electronic "malls" and ordering online. You also got a quick tour of what the major online services provide plus tips on comparison-shopping and online ordering.

In the next chapter, we'll look at online travel—how to use online services to research trips, make travel reservations, even get airline tickets delivered to your door. You'll also learn how to access two of the online world's most popular reservations systems, Eaasy Sabre and the Official Airline Guides, and learn tips and tricks from experienced travelers to help save you time and money.

CHAPTER 15

Trains, Planes, and Automobiles

In the last chapter, you learned how to stock your office with everything from PCs to flowers by shopping the electronic "malls" and ordering online. You also got a quick tour of what the major online services provide, plus tips on comparison-shopping and online ordering.

In this chapter, we'll take a look at online travel—how to use online services to research trips; book flights, cars, and hotel rooms; and even get airline tickets delivered to your door. You'll also learn how to log onto two of the online world's most popular reservations systems, Eaasy Sabre and the Official Airline Guide, and learn tips and tricks from experienced travelers to help save you time and money.

Online Travel Services: Your Ticket to Ride

If you've booked a trip lately, you know that business travel is not as simple as it used to be. With millions of airfares, dozens of frequent flyer clubs and special deals on hotel rooms and rental cars, it's hard to know which way to turn. And, while a travel agent may be of some help, there's still the time and trouble of driving to the travel agent's office—or calling an 800 number and being put on hold—plus the unfortunate fact that many travel agencies are closed at night and on weekends.

That's where online services come in. Depending on what you're looking for and how much you're willing to spend, there's a wealth of travel advice and information as close as a phone call away. By logging onto an online service, you can research trips and make reservations with the same skill, speed, and acumen as a professional travel agent. On Prodigy, CompuServe, and several of the other major online services, you can dial up specialized bulletin boards to ask other members for travel advice, then log onto Eaasy Sabre, the consumer version of the reservations system that travel agents use to tap into a database of more than 45 million airfares, 20,000 hotels and 52 car rental agencies.

Making travel arrangements online has many advantages. Convenience, for one. Most off-line travel agencies are open only during standard business hours. Online travel services, by contrast, are open 24 hours a day and the line is rarely busy. Also, by logging onto an online travel service, you can comparison shop before you plunk down your money.

Even if you do use a travel agent, an online service can help make you a savvier travel shopper. In fact, some veteran online travelers say it makes sense to combine electronic and human travel resources, first doing your homework by computer, then calling your travel agent to actually book the trip. Not only do you get the reassurance of chatting with a fellow human being, but there's also someone to haggle with the airline or hotel if problems arise.

"Many of our members love doing their own research, finding their own bargains, and then turning it all over to their agent for review," says Jerry Schneiderman, a part-time travel agent and manager of CompuServe's Travel (Travsig) Forum. "When our members themselves find the best deal, they feel great. When their agent gets them a better deal, they feel even better. It's really the best of both worlds."

TRAVEL CLUBS

One of the best ways to plan your trip is to log onto an online travel club and read the messages left by other members there—or, better yet, post a message of your own. (For step-by-step instructions on how to do this, see Chapter 8.) Prodigy, CompuServe, GEnie and America Online all boast widely-trafficked travel clubs, or bulletin boards, that allow tourists, travel agents and even armchair travelers to exchange tips, trivia, caveats and personal experiences that other members can profit by. The Prodigy and CompuServe boards are especially well traveled, with members posting hundreds of messages a day from places as exotic as Bangladesh, Cambodia, and Hungary.

Lan Sluder, who manages the Caribbean Section of CompuServe's Travel Forum, is particularly enthusiastic. "Where else can a prospective visitor to the Caribbean ask a specific question and get answers from knowledgeable recent travelers to the island—in a few hours? I can't believe anyone these days would plan a trip to the Caribbean without asking frequent Caribbean travelers their opinions," he says.

Online travel clubs can also save you money.

When the nation's airlines unleashed a flurry of fare cuts in April 1992, for example, thousands of Americans scrambled to climb aboard. Within hours, phone lines to travel agents and airline ticket offices were jammed. For many travelers, booking a flight became difficult, if not impossible.

Amid the hubbub, Schneiderman, who manages CompuServe's Travel Forum (illustrated in Figure 15.1), advised club members to

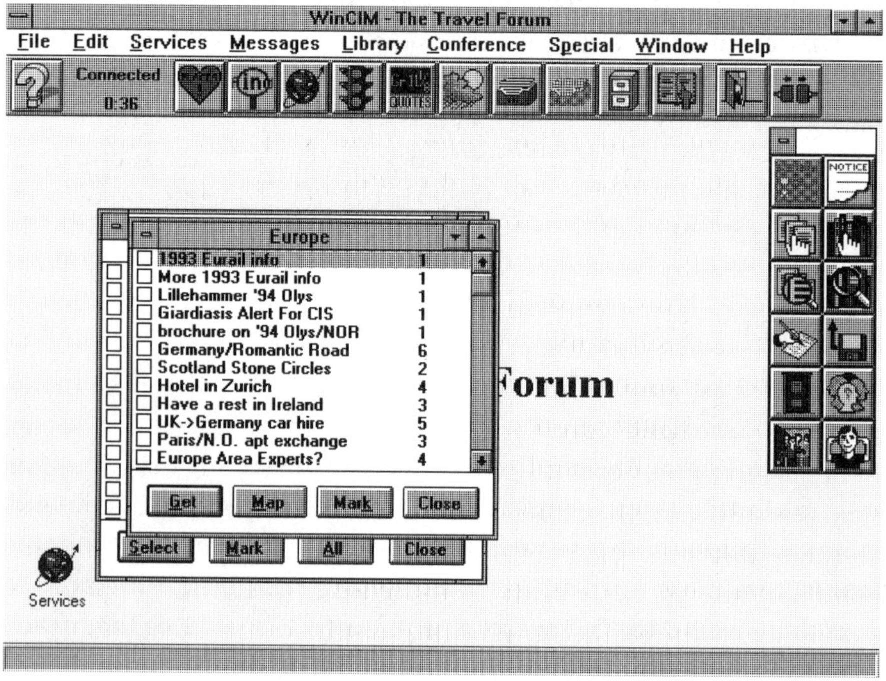

FIGURE 15.1: CompuServe's Travel Forum

log onto Eaasy Sabre, American Airlines' online reservations service, either very late at night or first thing in the morning. He also steered members toward a less heavily trafficked online travel reservations system called Travelshopper, which is also available on CompuServe.

"Travsig was probably responsible for hundreds of people getting half-price tickets who otherwise might have been shut out," Schneiderman says.

TRAVEL DATABASES

Apart from the travel clubs and reservations, both of the major online services offer a treasure chest of travel databases for the novice and experienced traveler alike.

Prodigy's well-stocked Travel section includes a series of City Guides to Atlanta, Boston, Chicago, Dallas, Los Angeles, Miami, New York, Philadelphia, San Francisco, and Washington; Travel Focus, which offers information about promotional discounts and frequent flyer clubs; the 1992 Mobil Travel Guide to thousands of hotels, motels, restaurants, events and attractions throughout the United States and Canada; a Travelog column that features reports from writers on their trips at home and abroad, and the Florida Vacation Guide to what's happening in the Sunshine State.

The City Guides, based on information collected from surveys of Prodigy members, can be especially helpful if you're visiting a place for the first time. Listen to what Prodigy members say about New York: "In New York, you not only don't need a car, you don't want a car. Parking in garages is expensive. On the street, almost impossible. Subways and buses go nearly everywhere, and taxicabs are plentiful. New York is also a great city for walking. But neighborhoods can change from gentrified to seedy in one block, so caution in exploring is a good idea."

Prodigy members from Texas advise a stop at Billy Bob's. "YEE HA! Billy Bob's of Fort Worth is by far THE place for country 'n' western 2-stepping," the entry reads. "For the real Old West, there's the nearby White Elephant Saloon. If you're not up for the drive to Cow Town, try Cowboys, Stampede or the Longhorn Ballroom in Dallas. For a good steak and family fun to boot, stop in at the Trail Dust."

Inveterate bargain hunters can also sign up for the Air Miles "frequent buyer" program through Prodigy and earn free mileage for shopping at the Prodigy Mall and using other Prodigy services. Prodigy members can also participate in American Airlines A-Advantage Travel Awards Program.

CompuServe also offers a wealth of online travel information. There's the ABC Worldwide Hotel Guide, which provides up-to-date listings of over 60,000 hotels worldwide. Within the ABC directory, information on each hotel includes the street address, distance from downtown, local and toll-free phone and fax numbers, number of rooms, rate guidelines (in both local currency and US dollars), sports facilities, business services, and types of credit cards accepted. The guide is updated four times a year to reflect changes in room rates, facilities and services and to include new hotel listings.

CompuServe also offers information on federal visa requirements, passport processing and travel document service fees in addition to specialized bulletin boards about the West Coast and Florida.

Reservations Systems

Once you've researched your trip, there's no need to call a travel agent to book it—unless, of course, you prefer to do it that way. As Schneiderman's experience shows, one of the big pluses to making travel plans online is the opportunity to log onto an online reservations system and book flights, cars and hotel rooms on your own. Eaasy Sabre, the most widely available of the online booking services, is accessible through all five major online services—Prodigy, CompuServe, GEnie, America Online and Delphi. It's cheap, too. Access to Eaasy Sabre is included in Prodigy's $14.95 monthly fee as well as in CompuServe's $8.95-a-month flat-fee plan.

But Eaasy Sabre isn't the only reservations system online. CompuServe also offers access to the Official Airline Guide, a highly sophisticated travel reservations system that includes certain specialized information and travel advisories that Eaasy Sabre does not. But OAG doesn't come cheap. Besides the CompuServe connect-time charge of 22 cents a minute, there's a $10-an-hour surcharge during evening hours and a $28 an hour surcharge during the day. CompuServe also offers access to Worldspan Travelshopper, a travel planning management service owned by Northwest Airlines, Delta and TWA.

So which reservations system should you chose?

Despite Eaasy Sabre's clear price advantage, some experienced online users prefer OAG. The reason? Ease of use, for one thing, according to Schneiderman, the CompuServe forum manager. Speed, for another.

"During a fare war, if you have to pay $4 to go through OAG [instead of Eaasy Sabre] to save $200 a ticket for yourself and your family, do it," Schneiderman advises. "You have to be careful in counting your pennies. Sometimes, it can cost you big dollars."

For many travelers, though, the question isn't choosing between Eaasy Sabre and OAG but deciding whether to book their trip online at all. That's because getting the most from Eaasy Sabre and the other online travel services requires a little more savvy about both computers and travel bookings than many novice users possess. In fact, a number of people on both Prodigy and CompuServe have run into reservations glitches and other problems online.

"The downside is that you're on your own," says Steve Gresham, a CompuServe member from Washington, D.C. "When I was trying to book some very cheap seats I had made but not confirmed, the connection broke down between CompuServe and Eaasy Sabre. I tried later and confirmed the reservation. Two days later, two nonrefundable tickets showed up in the mail.

"Eaasy Sabre said it was a problem to be dealt with by AA On-Line [American Airlines' online ticketing service]. AA On-Line said it was Sabre's problem. I called both of them and got little satisfaction, so I have sent them a note saying that I can't possibly use two tickets on the same flight on the same day.

"Who in their right mind would want to go to Albany, New York, twice anyhow?"

Prodigy members have had their share of problems, too. In response, Prodigy recently rolled out a new service called Book-a-Trip that combines the automated booking system offered by Eaasy Sabre with some human hand-holding by travel agents employed by Rosenbluth Travel, another Prodigy affiliate. Book-a-Trip lets you type in specific information about where and when you wish to travel and let the Rosenbluth agent create a customized itinerary that you can purchase, cancel, or change to suit their needs. The service is offered at no extra charge.

EAASY SABRE

There are two ways to access the Eaasy Sabre reservations system—the easy way and the quick way. If you're new to online reservations systems, your best bet may be to log on through Prodigy, which masks Eaasy Sabre with the same user-friendly front-end software that runs the rest of the Prodigy service. Another option is to log onto Eaasy Sabre through CompuServe Information Manager, CompuServe's front-end program, which lets you book flights, fares, cars and hotels using a Windows (or Windows-like) format.

Once you get more familiar with the system, you may want to sacrifice some ease of use for a lot more speed. The text-based version of Eaasy Sabre available on CompuServe, GEnie, America Online and Delphi rapidly leads you through a series of menus that let you type in your departure point, destination and travel dates. You also have the option of typing in special commands and codes if you want to go even faster (see below).

ACCESSING EAASY SABRE ON PRODIGY

Here's a step-by-step guide to using Eaasy Sabre to book a flight on Prodigy:

1. Log onto Prodigy. Then choose JUMP from the bottom of your screen and type **eaasy flights** from the JUMPwindow. Press ↵.

2. Type your Eaasy Sabre password. Press ↵. If you don't have an Eaasy Sabre password yet, you will be prompted to enroll in the program and may select your password at that time.

3. On the Flights Request screen, type your travel date and departure time and your desired departure and destination airports. (If you don't know the codes for them, select Codes from the bottom of the screen.) You can also type in a specific airline, booking class, connecting city, or any

combination. Eaasy Sabre will then narrow the field to only those flights that meet your requests. Press ↵ when you are ready to proceed to the Flight Availability screen, illustrated in Figure 15.2.

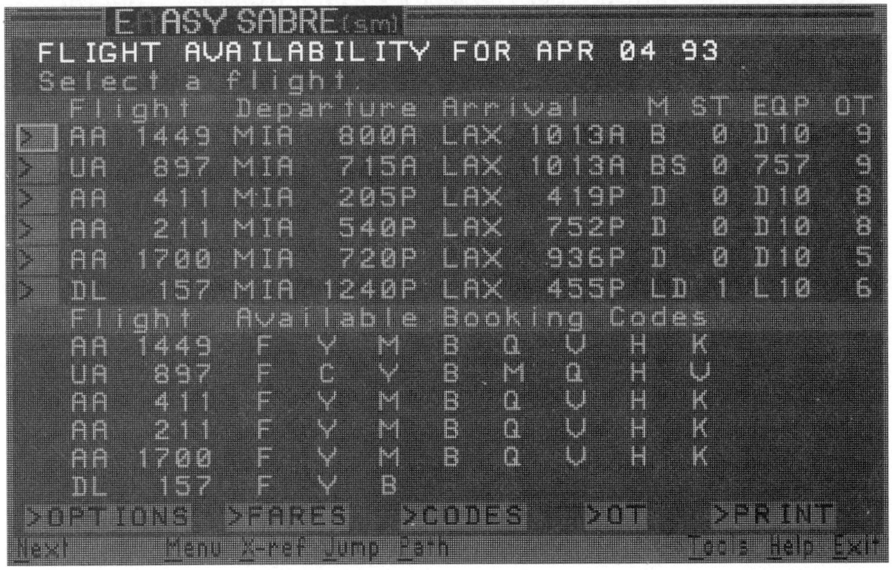

FIGURE 15.2:

Booking a flight on Prodigy's Eaasy Sabre reservations system

4. Listed on the screen are the flights that best match your travel requests plus any specifics you have noted, such as a particular airline, booking class or connecting city. The Flight Availability screen also displays information about meals served, number of stops en route, aircraft types and on-time rating for selected flights. If you'd like to know more about specific alphabetical codes that appear on the screen, you can select CODES on certain Eaasy Sabre screens.

   When you've found the flight you want, select the box next to it and press ↵. Then choose the type of fare you want—selecting Bargain Finder will locate the lowest fare—and press ↵. To make your reservation, choose the box next to Flight Selection Correct/Continue and follow the on-screen prompts.

5. If you need to change or cancel your flight, select ITINERARY REVIEW from the Eaasy Sabre reservations menu. You can also jump to the EAASY REVIEW menu. Always remember to write down the itinerary number for each reservation as you make it.

6. To begin your changes, select a specific itinerary from the displayed list. To change a reservation, simply select the itinerary number you want to alter and type in your changes. You can change part of the reservation or all of it.

7. To cancel a reservation, specify the itinerary number, then select the reservation you wish to cancel. Always cancel your existing reservation before making a replacement. Don't worry about canceling the wrong reservation—you need to confirm all cancellations before they're recorded by Eaasy Sabre, so it's hard to make a mistake.

8. Once your reservation is complete, Eaasy Sabre will charge your tickets on the credit card that you've specified in your travel profile when you originally signed up for the service unless you specify otherwise.

9. To receive your tickets, you can choose from a variety of delivery options including Federal Express, courier, local pick-up and US mail. Or you can pick up your tickets from a travel agency, an airport ticket counter or a local airline office and pay for them there.

Special Commands and Shortcuts

While Prodigy's Eaasy Sabre system is easy to use, it can also be painfully slow—the result of lots of fancy graphics being transmitted to your screen. Once you feel you know your way around, try logging onto the text-based version available on CompuServe and some of the other services.

Here are some time-saving tips to get you started:

- **Use keywords:** Keywords are one-word navigational commands preceded by a slash (/). For example, /AIR checks flight availability, /FARES checks flight fares and rules, and /CAR checks car rental avaiability.
- **Use Quick Path:** Quick Path entries allow you to skip time-consuming menus and prompts by combining information, separated by commas, into a single entry. Quick Paths can be used to check air fares, flight availability, cars and hotel rooms as well as to make reservations. For example, **DFW,TUL,JUN12,AA311,1,F** would book one first-class seat on American Airlines Flight 311 from Dallas to Tulsa on June 12.
- **Use Faasttrack:** Faasttrack uses a combination of keywords and Quick Path entries to let you access a certain part of the Eaasy Sabre system, such as flight availability, and make a reservations request all in a single entry. For example, **/AIR,DFW,MIA,08OCT,7A,1** would check flight availability for a single passenger flying from Dallas to Miami on Oct. 8 at 7 A.M.
- **Automate your sign-on:** Instead of waiting for the prompts, type **/SIGNON,AADVANTAGE NUMBER,PASSWORD** to log onto the Eaasy Sabre system.

ACCESSING THE OFFICIAL AIRLINE GUIDE ON COMPUSERVE

Another online reservations option is the Official Airline Guide. It's fast and easy to use, it gives you access to several travel databases, and it requires no special knowledge of computers or travel codes. It's also very current; in fact, airlines throughout the world electronically access and update their schedules on OAG's database. The OAG Electronic Edition available on CompuServe—OAG is available in printed form, too—lets you view worldwide hotel and motel listings, choose the most convenient schedule, find the lowest fare, view actual seat availability, book your flight and arrange for ticketing right from your computer.

Like Eaasy Sabre, the system prompts you for your departure city, destination, and preferred date and time of travel. The schedule information is then displayed for you chronologically by departure time, with fares from lowest to highest, for easy decision-making. OAG also offers access to databases packed with everything from travel news and tours, cruises and discount travel packages to frequent flyer/frequent lodger award programs. You can also call up US State Department Travel Advisories, ZapoDel's Adventure Atlas, Vacation Florida, Nationwide Intelligence, The Official Recreation Guide, CruiseStar Worldwide Cruises, All Cruise Travel, Cruise Marketplace, Ski Resort Information, Star Rated Restaurants & Hotels and actual Arrival/Departure Information for Chicago's O'Hare International Airport.

Here's how you would use OAG to find a hotel room in Philadelphia using WinCIM, as illustrated in Figure 15.3:

1. Log onto CompuServe, and click the Go icon on the toolbar. Type **OAG**. Press ↵.
2. Double-click on Access$.
3. From OAG's main menu, type 4 to choose Lodging and Dining. Press ↵.
4. Type 1 and press ↵ to choose OAG Electronic Edition. This will access the database of 40,000 hotels worldwide.
5. Type **/H** to display a listing of hotels and motels. Press ↵.
6. At the prompt that says *Enter city name or code,* type **Philadelphia**. Press ↵.
7. At *Enter a line number,* choose 1 City Center and Other to book a room in downtown Philadelphia. Press ↵.

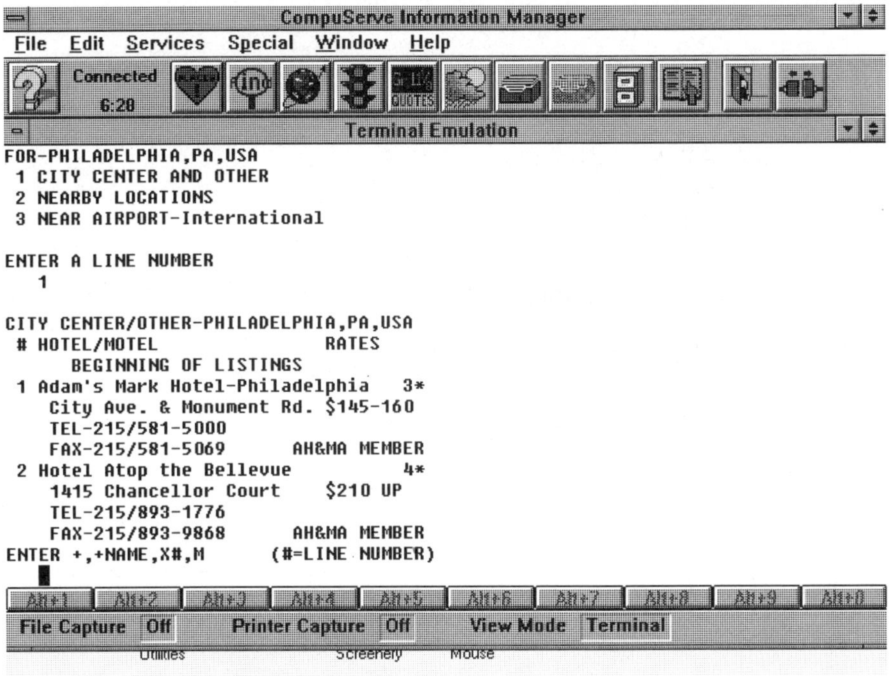

FIGURE 15.3:
Finding a Hotel Room on CompuServe's Official Airline Guide

8. To see more hotels, press ↵. To read more about a particular hotel, type **X** and the line number of the hotel listing; for example, **X1**.

9. When you've found the hotel you want, call the number listed in the hotel's entry. OAG does not allow you to book hotel reservations online.

Special Commands and Shortcuts

Like Eaasy Sabre, OAG offers slash (/) commands and other shortcuts to help you get around the system faster.

Here are some examples:

/S Begin schedules request

/M Display the OAG command menu

/F	Begin fares request
/H	Begin hotel/motel request
/C	Review or cancel a booking
/I	Information and assistance

OAG also offers some commands that may be unfamiliar to Eaasy Sabre users:

+	Next display
–	Previous display
A#	Display fares/seats available
B#	Book flight or connection
CX	Display connections
DF	Display direct flights
RS	Display return flights
RF	Display return fares

Here are some sample command lines:

Flight Schedules: /SCHI;NYC;15JUN8A

This tells OAG to search for flights that depart Chicago on June 15 at 8 A.M. and arrive in New York City.

Fares: /FDayton;Atlanta29AUG8A

This tells OAG to search for fares of flights that leave Dayton, Ohio, on Aug. 29 at 8 A.M. and arrive in Atlanta.

Ticket Deliveries

Once you've made your reservations online, getting your tickets is a snap—and much less expensive than you might think.

Prodigy, for example, offers QuikTix as part of its Eaasy Sabre service. Through QuikTix, you can get free overnight express delivery to your home or office if you order your plane tickets by 9 P.M. EST Monday through Thursday. There is a $12.50 surcharge for Saturday express delivery—though that fee is waived if the total value of your tickets exceeds $498. Depending on how much time you have before your flight leaves, you can pick up your tickets at one of 400 American Airlines City Ticket Offices nationwide or have the tickets delivered by courier for an additional $15. QuikTix is illustrated in Figure 15.4.

If you book your trip through CompuServe's OAG Electronic Edition, you can choose from one or more of the following delivery options: Let Thomas Cook Travel send your tickets, pick up your tickets at a local Thomas Cook office, let a DATAS II travel agency write your ticket, or pick up your ticket from the airline when you get to the airport.

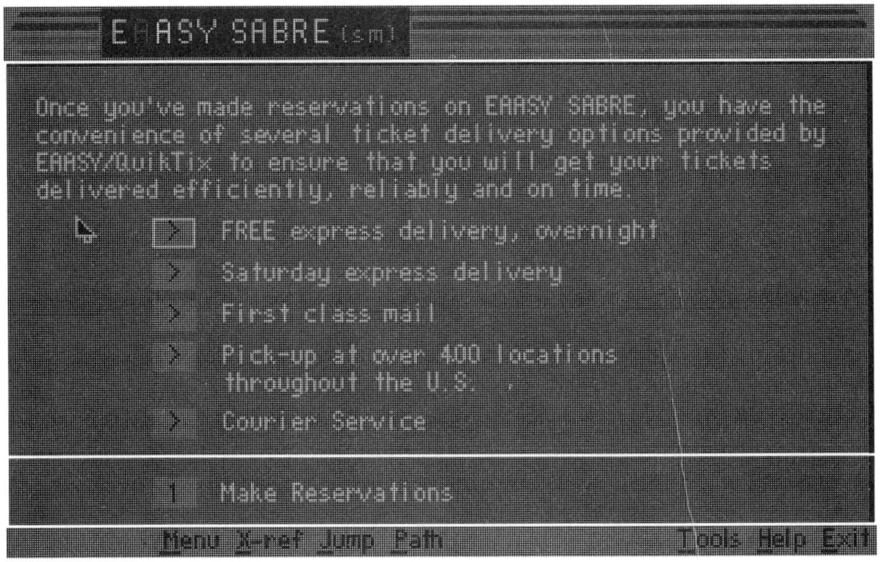

FIGURE 15.4: Prodigy's QuikTix ticket-delivery service

Summary

In this chapter, you toured the world of online travel—how to use online services to research trips, book flights, cars, and hotel rooms, even get airline tickets delivered to your door. You also learned how to log onto two of the online world's most popular reservations systems, Eaasy Sabre and the Official Airline Guide, and got some tips and tricks from experienced travelers to help save you time and money.

In the next chapter, you'll find out how to get technical support online—even if you don't know your RAM from your ROM.

CHAPTER 16

Technical Support for Non-Techies

In the last chapter, you toured the world of online travel—how to use online services to research trips, book flights, cars, and hotel rooms, even get airline tickets delivered to your door.

In this chapter, you'll find out how to get technical support online—even if you don't know your RAM from your ROM. In addition to a brief guide to the dozens of hardware and software support forums available on CompuServe, Prodigy and other online services, you'll get tips from other users on how to get the most from the tech support boards—and never waste your time on hold again.

Technicians Who Never Sleep

Unless you're a computer professional, chances are that all you know about computers is what you need to run your business. That's fine—except when something goes wrong with your computer and you need to go scrambling around trying to get help. And that often means a long-distance call to a technical support staffer in Seattle, a $75-an-hour "house call" from your local computer guru, or some other costly exercise in frustration.

Of course, getting technical support for your small business or home office doesn't have to boost your blood pressure—or drain your wallet. By logging onto a major online service like CompuServe, Prodigy, GEnie, or America Online, you can get fast, low-cost technical support that's only a phone call away. Simply tap into one of hundreds of tech help bulletin boards, and you can draw on a wealth of fast, free advice direct from the top hardware and software vendors themselves—IBM, Apple, Microsoft, Borland International, and dozens of others. There's also a knowledgeable network of thousands of fellow computer users who have been in your shoes and are more than willing to share tips and tricks from their own experience.

Especially if you own a small business, online technical support can be a real time-saver. That's because, unlike people who work for large corporations, people who work for themselves or for small companies rarely enjoy the benefit of on-site technical support staffs who can rush to the rescue at the first hint of trouble. Rather than waste valuable time sitting on the phone or paying a computer consultant big bucks just to tell you what the problem is, you can become a do-it-yourselfer, fixing your own PC problems with a little help from your online neighbors.

"I, like many others, have brought a PC into the house for business, family, and entertainment use," says CompuServe member Mike Brooks. "In the office, there are usually folks that have gone through the learning curve and are anxious to help out. In the home, you are mostly on your own. With the infinite number of programs, hardware and memory configurations out there, the first conclusion is that you need help."

For Brooks, help has frequently arrived in the form of the Microsoft support technicians who staff the company's technical support forums, or bulletin boards, on CompuServe. While Microsoft's telephone support lines are "friendly and backed by knowledgeable folks," Brooks says, "their operating hours, the length of wait to reach a tech rep and the telephone cost is discouraging.

"Conversely, the forum is reachable 24 hours a day, is serviced by Microsoft tech reps who usually will have an answer back to you within 24 hours, and is filled with knowledgeable people who will always jump in to help."

Other online subscribers, like Bob Bush of Prodigy's Computer Club, report fruitful experiences even with bulletin boards that are not staffed by professional support technicians. Prodigy's Computer Club, unlike the bulletin boards on CompuServe and several other online services, does not offer technical support directly from the software and hardware vendors themselves, though company technicians do log on from time to time. Prodigy does offer company-supported technical help boards for Packard Bell computers and for the IBM PS/1.

"I have received a wealth of valuable knowledge and help from a lot of people who frequent this bulletin board and would like to thank so many of you by name it would be next to impossible," Bush wrote in a recent message. "There are so many people out here like myself who are just beginning to grasp the method to all this madness, and we all greatly appreciate every little nugget of info we can gather. Thanks for the help."

Figure 16.1 shows the beginning of a Computer Club exchange.

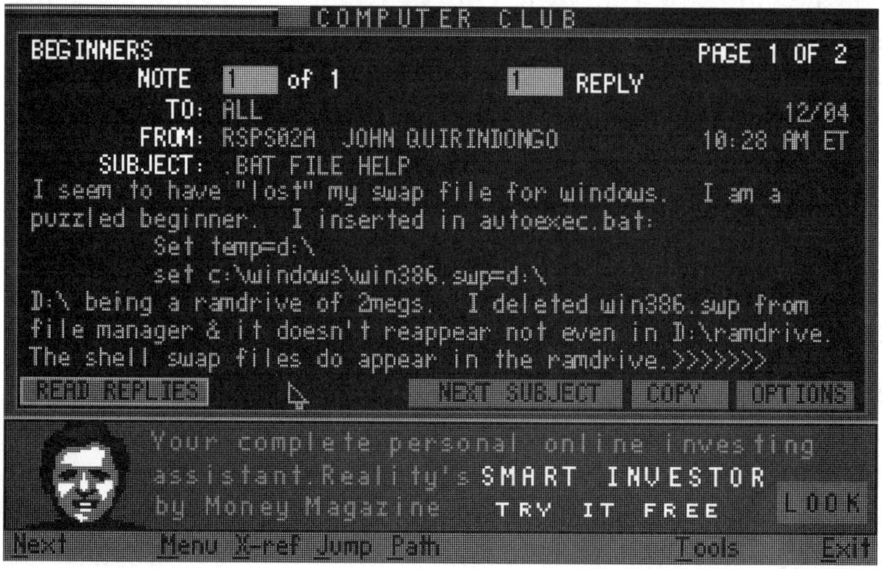

FIGURE 16.1: Prodigy's Computer Club

How to Get Help

While online help is plentiful, it can also be overwhelming—especially if you've never tapped into it before. After all, with dozens of bulletin boards supporting hundreds of hardware and software products, where do you even start?

WHERE TO START

If you're not sure where to go, try logging onto the online service's index and typing in the name of the hardware or software program you're having trouble with. If the computer or program is popular enough—like Windows 3.1 or DOS 5.0—chances are there's a bulletin board set up to deal with it. It's also a good idea to search the index under the manufacturer's name—IBM, Microsoft, or Borland, for example. Figure 16.2 illustrates a search underway on CompuServe's Microsoft forum.

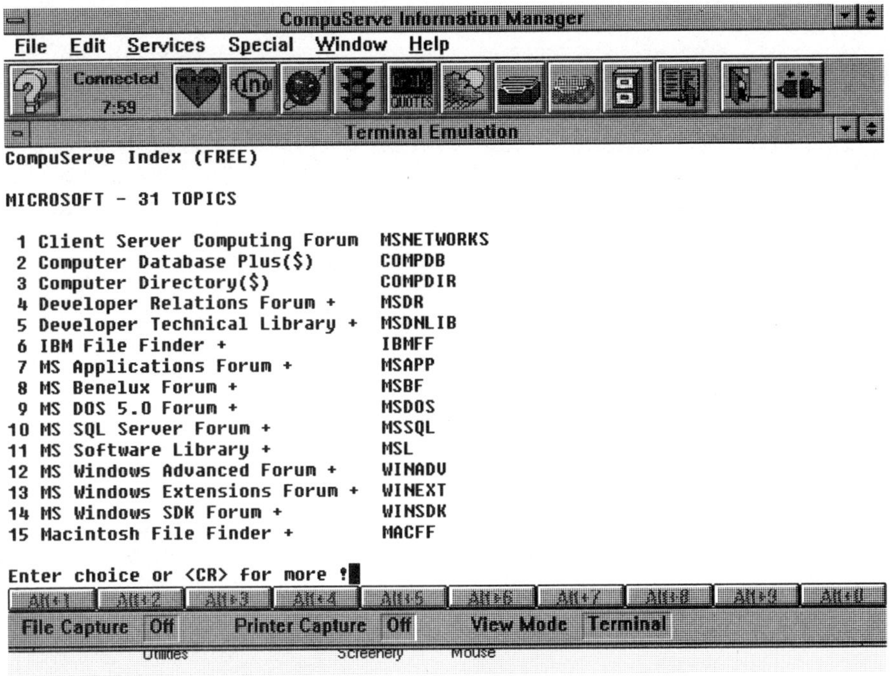

FIGURE 16.2: Searching for Microsoft support forums on CompuServe

Here's a sampling of the bulletin boards and their keywords available on the major online services.

On CompuServe:

- GO AMIGA (Amiga Forums)
- GO BORLAND (Borland International Forum)
- GO CBMNET (Commodore Users Network)
- GO HAYES (Online With Hayes Forum)
- GO IBMNET (IBM Users Network)
- GO MACINTOSH (Macintosh Forums)
- GO MICROSOFT (Microsoft Connection)
- GO WPSG (WordPerfect Users Forum)

On GEnie:

- AMIGA (Amiga RoundTable)
- COMMODORE (Commodore RoundTables)
- HAYES (Hayes RoundTable)
- IBMPC (IBM PC RoundTable)
- MAC (Macintosh RoundTable)
- MICROSOFT (Microsoft RoundTable)
- WP (WordPerfect RoundTable)

On America Online:

- [Amiga support available in the DOS hardware forum]
- BORLAND (Borland - Industry Connection)
- [Commodore support only on Q-Link]
- [Hayes support not available]
- IBM (Support available in the Computing & Software Department)
- MACINTOSH (Support available in the Computing & Software Department)
- MICROSOFT (Microsoft Support)
- WORDPERFECT (WordPerfect Support)

On Prodigy (does not offer direct support for Amiga, Borland, Commodore, Hayes, Macintosh, Microsoft or WordPerfect products):

- SOFTWARECONNX (Software Connexion - Publisher's Exchange)

- MANUFACT (Manufacturer's Corner)
- COMPUTER CLUB (Computer Club Bulletin Board)
- PB ONLINE (Packard-Bell Online)
- Prodigy also offers a technical support board for the IBM PS/1, available to PS/1 owners only

WORKING THE SYSTEM

Once you know where you're going, it's time to ask for help. The easiest way to do this is to post a note on the appropriate bulletin board and section—for example, the PS/2 Section of CompuServe's IBM Hardware Forum—and wait for a reply.

Tips: To expose your note to the widest possible audience, send it to all the members of the section. If you're using CompuServe, for example, type **all** at the *To:* prompt. It's also a good idea to give your message a heading that describes exactly what kind of help you're seeking. A message titled, "HELP!!!!," isn't specific enough to get the attention of the people who are likely to be able to help you. A message titled, "PS/2 Setup Problem," on the other hand, may be just what you need.

Within a day, you can expect to find a helpful reply from an online support technician and several more notes from other users who've encountered the same problem. Most hardware and software companies try to respond to help messages within 24 hours—though you may have to wait until Monday if you post a note on Friday afternoon or over the weekend. If your message touches a communal nerve—and many notes do, you may spark an online discussion that goes on for days or even weeks!

Here's an example of the kind of conversation you can expect to find on Prodigy's Computer Club bulletin board:

"I have a 286 pc at home with 1meg running DOS 5.0," writes club member Jim Moore. "What I want to be able to do is load mouse, smrtdrv.sys, etc. into high memory area. I'm now using himem.sys that came with DOS and am aware that DOS 5.0 won't allow the load-high command with a 286. Is there any cheap, or shareware utility that will allow me to do this?"

Less than two hours later, Moore got this response from Peder Thygesen, another member: "Jim, I recently (four days ago) upgraded to a 386SX for the same reason. I spoke to a local technician and was informed that, no matter what you do, there are a few things that a 286 won't do with DOS 5.0. I would suggest doing what I did—replace the motherboard. You would be really surprised how reasonable it is. Mine cost $150 for a 386-25, and I'm really happy with it. ... P.S.: You may want to get a second opinion. I'm no expert. I just know what I went through."

PROS AND CONS

Like any form of technical support, online help has its pluses and minuses. It's clearly less time-consuming than waiting for a technician to bail you out by phone—although, if you've got a problem that needs fixing right away, you may not want to wait the extra day to get an answer. And, while online help is often cheaper than dialing long-distance to the West Coast where many computer companies are located, logging onto an online bulletin board can be costly, too. CompuServe charges 22 cents a minute at 2400 bps to access its tech support boards (13 cents a minute on the flat-fee plan); GEnie charges 21 cents a minute during business hours.

Also, despite the many satisfied users, there are still some bugs in the system. Some veteran onliners complain that the help offered by their fellow users is sometimes of questionable value, while others gripe that the professional support technicians occasionally take too long to reply to their questions or fail to respond to their messages at all.

Even so, many veteran computer users say that online technical support is one of the best deals around—and that help can come in a matter of minutes. John Rigdon, president of Eastern Digital Resources, a software development and mailing list management firm in North Augusta, South Carolina, regularly hunts for technical support on both America Online and GEnie. Once, Rigdon recalls, he was helping a client install a CD-ROM drive on a Novell network running Ethernet cards. The problem: He couldn't manage to get both the drive and the network to work at the same time.

Stumped, Rigdon turned to America Online. Less than half an hour after posting a note on the service, he received an answer from another user—along with a software driver that immediately cleared up the problem as soon as he installed it on his client's system the next morning. Before he started tapping into online technical support boards two years ago, Rigdon says now, he probably would have had to write a software "patch" of his own to fix the problem.

"The responses I get online are almost always immediate," Rigdon says. "I have almost entirely gotten away from calling technical support lines."

Lee Hollander, a Naples, Florida, lawyer, says he relies on online technical support to help master the 386 computer he bought for the fledgling computer consulting business he runs from home. About a year ago, he says, he was having an unusual problem with his DOS shell program. Whenever he would boot up his system, the shell would come up black-and-white even though he had a color VGA monitor. Within five minutes of getting a reply from a Microsoft support technician on CompuServe, Hollander says, he was able to locate the problem and fix it.

"Normally, I hack out these problems myself," Hollander says, "but I was [on the bulletin board] reading messages, so I figured, 'Why not leave one?'"

Technical Support Databases

Besides the kind of interactive technical support offered through online bulletin boards, there are also plenty of online databases that let you search for your answer yourself. Online services also offers advice columns and other features of use to computer novices and experts alike.

BULLETIN BOARD MESSAGES AND LIBRARIES

One of the best places to search for online technical help is on the same bulletin boards where you post your help messages. After all, if you're having a problem with a certain hardware or software application, there's a good chance that other people are, too—and that somebody has already tried to help them. That's why it's a good idea to check the previous messages first before you post your own message online. CompuServe, for example, lets you search for message topics simply by typing in a keyword such as **modem** or **swapfile**.

You can search for library files the same way. CompuServe's bulletin boards feature online libraries that contain useful text files and software programs that you can download directly to your computer, often at no cost except for the 22-cents-a-minute CompuServe connect-time charge. Many boards also offer real-time conferences that let you pose your question—live—to a group of experts.

THE MICROSOFT KNOWLEDGE INDEX

In addition to its many forums, CompuServe also offers access to the Microsoft Knowledge Base, a searchable database that provides access to information previously available only to Microsoft's support engineers. With access to the company's support files, you can quickly obtain answers to your software questions any time of night or day (though you may need some technical savvy to put the information to use). Once you specify a search term, Knowledge Base sifts through more than 14,000 documents and retrieves all files relevant to your question or problem. If you still can't find the answer you're looking for, you can send an electronic message to Microsoft's Help Desk.

Microsoft Knowledge Base is also available on America Online and GEnie.

Here's how to access the Microsoft Knowledge Base using WinCIM:

1. Click the Go icon on the toolbar and type **MSKB**. Press ↵.
2. Double-click Search the Knowledge Base.
3. Select a search method. For example, type **1**, then press ↵, to search for words or phrases occurring anywhere in the database.
4. Type the word or phrase you're looking for. For example, **swapfile**. Press ↵.
5. Choose from the following options—display a list of documents, narrow your search, broaden your search or begin a new search. Type the corresponding number, and press ↵.
6. Type **/DOWN** to download a document to your computer.

Figure 16.3 shows the first screenful of topics related to swap files.

ADVICE COLUMNS

Some online services offer expert advice from the same well-known columnists who write for the glossy computer magazines that sell on the newsstand.

Prodigy's Computer Club, for example, features columns and advice by computing experts Larry Magid, former editor of *PC* magazine and Prodigy's resident authority on DOS and Windows, and Steve Rosenthal, Magid's counterpart on the Macintosh side. Magid and Rosenthal are also available to answer Prodigy members' questions via e-mail.

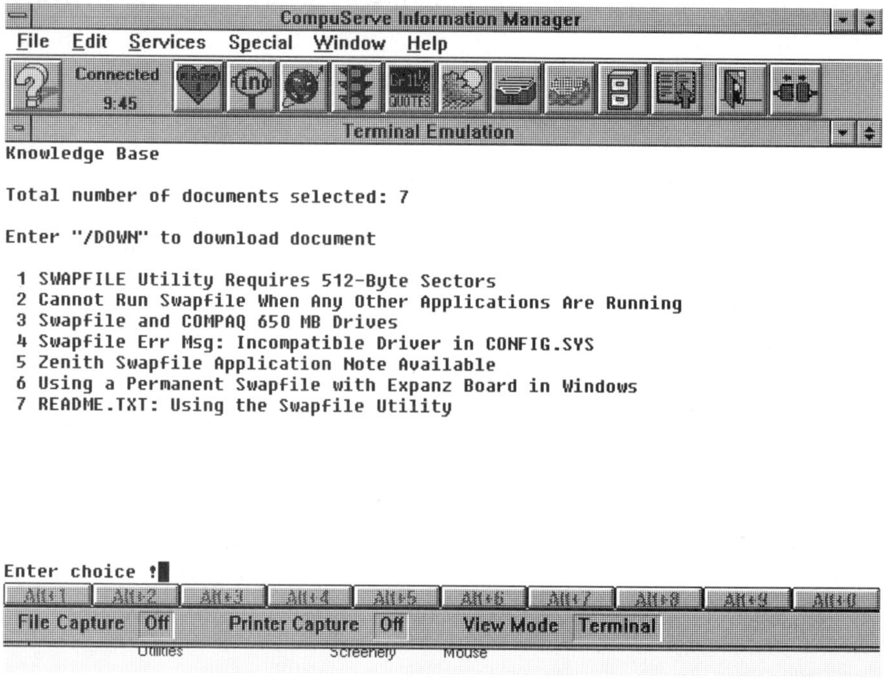

FIGURE 16.3: Searching the Microsoft Knowledge Base on CompuServe

Shopping for Help Online

It pays to shop around for online technical support, because not all services offer access to the same bulletin boards—although there is some degree of overlap, especially with CompuServe and GEnie. It's also important to find a board where the discussion is at a level you can understand—after all, the best technical advice in the world won't do you any good if it's too technical for you to understand. In fact, there are a few support boards, such as CompuServe's Microsoft Windows New Users Forum, designed specifically with the novice in mind. Others, such as Prodigy's Computer Club, offer a beginner's section.

PRODIGY

Unlike the other leading online services, Prodigy does not offer online technical support from computer industry leaders like Microsoft, Apple, and Hayes. Prodigy's real strength lies in its Computer Club bulletin board, which lets Prodigy's 2 million members swap notes and get help on a wide range of popular hardware and software. Topics include Beginners, Communications, Databases, Desktop Publishing, Financial Software, Hardware: Peripherals and Hardware: Systems.

Through its Software Connexion, Prodigy also offers access to The Publisher's Exchange, where members can send messages to participating software companies regarding technical support and other issues. Though the support itself is free, each message counts toward the 30 included in Prodigy's $14.95-a-month basic membership fee; additional messages cost 25 cents each. Participating companies include Access Software, Accolade, Buena Vista, DacEasy, Davidson and Associates, Diagsoft, Dynamix, Microprose, Mysoftware, Sierra On-line, T/Maker Co., Turbotax by Chipsoft, and Walt Disney Software.

Finally, Prodigy's Manufacturer's Corner lets you send messages directly to participating computer and peripherals manufacturers to get technical help. Like The Publisher's Exchange, the support itself is free, though each message sent counts toward the 30 included in Prodigy's $14.95-a-month basic membership fee. Hardware companies include Acros Computers, Packard Bell, Positive Corp., Premier Innov, KLH Computers, Tandon Corp., PC Brand, Leading Edge, Pionex and Professional PC. All companies have pledged to respond to questions within two business days.

Figure 16.4 shows the opening screen for Manufacturer's Corner.

COMPUSERVE

One of the premier clearinghouses for online technical support, CompuServe offers dozens of hardware and software bulletin boards,

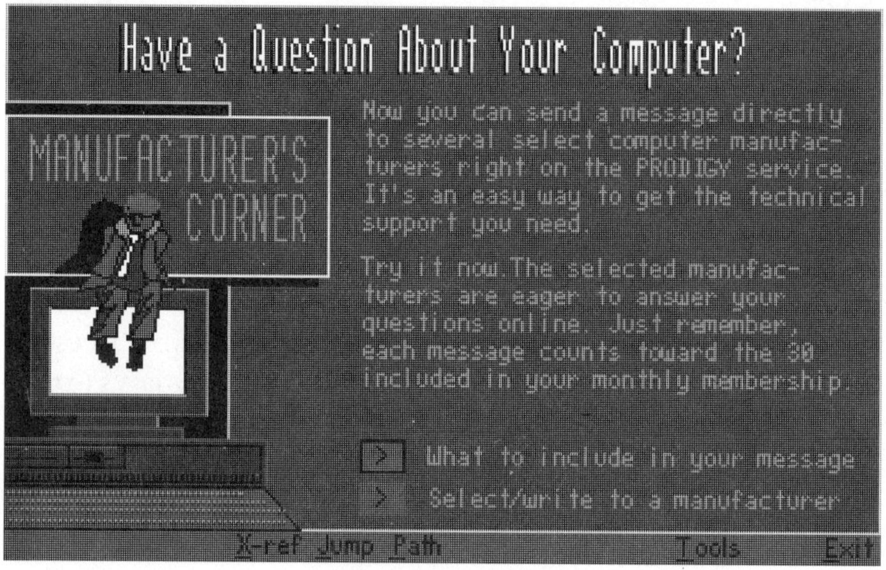

FIGURE 16.4: Prodigy's Manufacturer's Corner

most of them sponsored by the companies themselves and peopled by knowledgeable support technicians and experienced users. Among the participating companies are most of the computer industry's heavy hitters, including Microsoft, Borland International, DATASTORM Technologies, Lotus, Novell, Symantec, Apple, Epson, Hewlett-Packard, IBM, Tandy and Zenith. There's even a bulletin board called the Computer Club Forum to help users of hoary machines whose manufacturers have long since pulled their plugs.

CompuServe also offers forums for users with special needs and interests. The IBM European Users Forum, for example (illustrated in Figure 16.5), contains information on accessing the service from Europe, answers to questions about modem configurations and software needs, keyboard drivers, foreign-language characters, multilingual user problems and more. The forum also contains a helpful file called TRAVEL.KIT that spells out everything you need to know about telecommunicating from overseas. Likewise, the IBM/Special Needs Forum addresses all aspects of special education—from education of the handicapped to bilingual and vocational education,

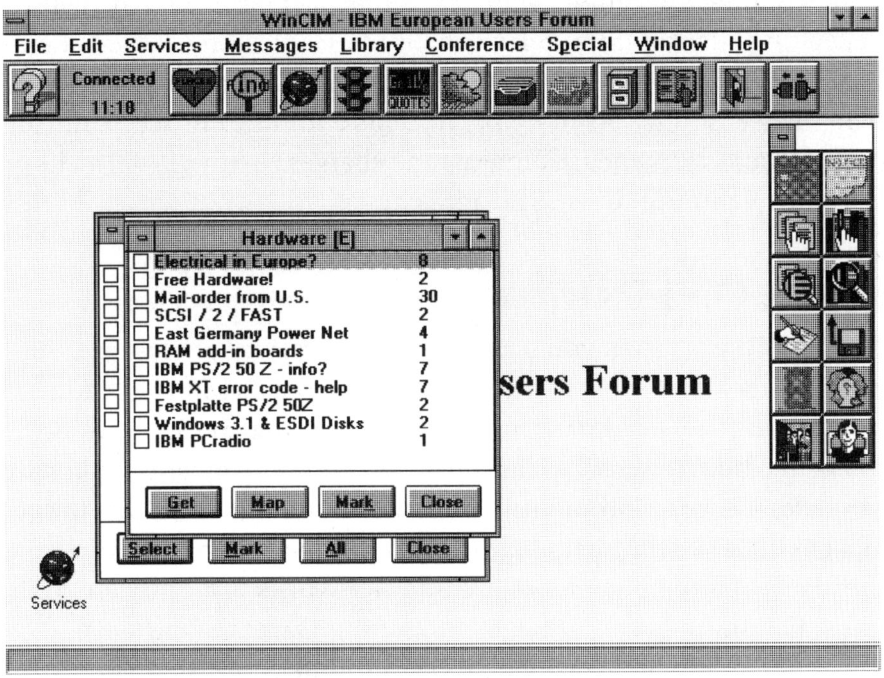

FIGURE 16.5:

CompuServe's IBM European Users Forum

from K–12 to adult literacy programs.

The only downside to accessing CompuServe's support boards is that they're not included in the service's $8.95 flat-fee plan. You're still stuck paying 22 cents a minute.

GENIE

Like CompuServe, GEnie also offers bulletin boards (known on GEnie as "roundtables") on personal computing and PC support. The boards, most of which are staffed by company support technicians, include Apple, Atari, Commodore & Amiga, IBM PC and Compatibles, Product Support, TI and Orphans, Database, Chipsoft, GeoWorks, Borland, Forth, Hayes, Microsoft, Qmodem, WordPerfect, and CE Software. Again like CompuServe, GEnie's bulletin boards include libraries filled with free and low-cost software and help files in addition to real-time conferences.

Scouting for online help on GEnie can be a real bargain—depending on what time of day you log on. While none of the bulletin boards are covered under the service's $4.95-a-month basic services plan, they cost only $6 an hour (10 cents a minute) to access during evenings and weekends. Connect-time charges rise to $12.50 an hour (21 cents a minute) during business hours.

AMERICA ONLINE

America Online gives you access to a wide variety of technical support boards with the click of a mouse. The service's Industry Connection feature (available through the Computing & Software area) offers technical support, new product announcements, software upgrades, demos, and monthly real-time conferences featuring special guests and developers of top-selling software and hardware.

Participating companies include GeoWorks, CE Software, DacEasy, Farallon, Leading Edge, Lucasfilm Games, OptImage, and Spectrum HoloByte. America Online also offers the Microsoft Solution Series forum, hosted by support technician Brian Kearns. The Microsoft staff says its goal is to reply to all direct messages within two business days. America Online's basic plan costs $7.95 a month, which includes two hours of connect time.

Summary

In this chapter, you found out how to get technical support online—even if you don't know your RAM from your ROM. In addition to a brief guide to the dozens of hardware and software support forums available on CompuServe, Prodigy and other online services, you also got tips from other users on how to get the most from technical support boards plus help in searching online databases that can speed help your way even faster.

This completes our tour of the world of online services—as it exists today. The Conclusion offers a brief glimpse of what the online world may look like in the decade to come.

CONCLUSION

The Future of Online Services

Just five years ago, fewer than 1 million Americans subscribed to mass-market online services. Prodigy, now the nation's largest online service, was in its infancy, and the online world was still largely the province of academic researchers, corporate librarians, and computer hackers.

Today, the nation's online services count close to 4 million subscribers, most of them personal computer users who log on for everything from sending e-mail to managing their investments and businesses. With online services like Prodigy and CompuServe now available to anyone with a computer and a modem for under $15 a month, the online world is in the midst of a population explosion. By 1996, close to 6 million people nationwide will subscribe to mass-market online services, according to Simba Information, a Wilton, Connecticut, market research firm.

In fact, a "virtual community" of online subscribers is already springing up nationwide. Online networking is fast replacing business lunches and face-to-face meetings, online malls are luring time-squeezed shoppers, online technical support is scrapping the need for long-distance phone calls and frustrating waits on hold, and online database research is making treks to the library unnecessary. Electronic mail links now connect millions of people worldwide.

But despite the rapid growth of online services, they're still far from a fixture in today's homes and offices. While nearly a third of all American adults use a computer at work, home, or school, and the number of personal computers worldwide has rocketed past 130 million, today's business community continues to rely on the communications and research methods of the past. Though the technology is here, postal mail, overnight delivery and faxes are still far more common than e-mail in the nation's homes and businesses.

Why? Technological barriers, for one. Personal computers and, especially, modems can still be difficult for computer novices to use, especially for people who grew up in the days before desktop computers caught on. For many people, it's easier to type or scribble a note and stick it in the office fax machine. For another, the online world, despite its fancy graphics and multiplayer games, can seem cold and impersonal to new users. When it comes to doing business, many people still prefer to communicate in person or by phone, rather than by sending electronic messages or participating in a real-time conference. When it comes to shopping, many people would rather see, touch, and smell what they're buying before they plunk down their money.

Even so, there are some encouraging trends that promise to open up the online world to people who have remained off-line until now:

- **Online services are getting easier to use.** As personal computer users continue to demand access to online databases and bulletin boards, even specialized online services like Dialog and Dow Jones News/Retrieval are introducing simplified systems to make their services easier for non-librarians to navigate. Front-end programs such as WinCIM (CompuServe Information Manager for Windows), with pull-down boxes and point-and-click mouse compatibility, eliminate the need for novice online users to master complex commands and menu structures. America Online has also just released Windows software, and in 1993, several other major online services, including Prodigy and Dow Jones News/Retrieval, are expected to follow suit.

- **Online services are getting faster.** Just a few years ago, modems that sent and received data at 1200 bits per second were considered leading-edge technology. Now, you'd be hard-pressed to buy one if you wanted to. These days, virtually every new modem sold is at least as fast as 2400 bps, and the three largest online services—Prodigy, CompuServe and GEnie—have already made 9600 bps access available. High-speed modems that transmit data at a lightning-fast 14,400 bps have also hit the shelves at computer superstores.

With higher-speed modems now available, "slow" services like Prodigy, which depends heavily on graphics, will move much faster, making online access easier and more enjoyable. Within the next five years, technologies such as cable and fiber optics may even make multimedia presentations a real-time reality.

- **Online services are getting cheaper—sort of.** Following on the success of Prodigy, all the major mass-market online services now offer some sort of flat-fee plan, most of them including a generous allotment of e-mail. At the same time, some services are finding ways to raise prices in other areas. For example, Prodigy charges extra for access to specialized databases like Ziffnet and Strategic Investor. Even so, you still have the option of declining those add-ons and paying only for what you want.

- **Online services are offering more for your money.** As more databases and interactive money-management tools go online, subscribers are getting far more than the standard news-weather-and-sport packages that they used to. Bulletin boards are proliferating, too, as online services compete to satiate their members' craving for chat. And, as more and more people go online, there's a growing community of people to chat with—especially now that most major online services provide links to the Internet.

So, while it may be some time before going online becomes as commonplace as reading the newspaper or dialing the phone, one trend is becoming clear. In the not-too-distant future, the competitive edge will belong to those people who are prepared to log on, tap in, and reach out.

APPENDIX

The Rest of the Pack

In this book, we've talked primarily about the Big Two—Prodigy and CompuServe; after all, these are the online services that most people use. But three other major online services—GEnie, America Online and Delphi—have also attracted large followings. While these services do not offer everything that CompuServe and Prodigy do, each has carved out a niche of its own—picking up members by offering unique features or low prices.

Here's a brief look at "the rest of the pack" and what they offer.

GEnie

Launched by General Electric Information Services in 1985, GEnie is the third-largest mass-market online service behind Prodigy and CompuServe. As of late 1992, GEnie had 350,000 subscribers, up from 285,000 the year before.

Unlike its two larger competitors, GEnie uses a "cable TV" approach to pricing—a low flat fee for basic programming and higher-priced tiers for premium services. GEnie's basic, or "star," services include unlimited access to hobby and leisure-time bulletin boards, the Eaasy Sabre travel reservations system, stock quotes, educational services, news, sports, weather, movie reviews and e-mail. GEnie's higher-priced "value" services include personal computing bulletin boards, software libraries, financial services, chat lines, real-time conferences and multi-player games.

GEnie subscribers pay $4.95 a month to access basic services during off-peak hours (6 P.M. to 8 A.M. local time Monday through Friday plus weekends and national holidays) and $12.50 an hour for basic access during daytime business hours. "Value" services cost $6 an hour during off-peak hours and $12.50 an hour during the day. There are also additional fees for "professional services" such as Charles Schwab Brokerage, Dow Jones News/Retrieval and the Official Airline Guide.

GEnie introduced its flat-fee plan in October 1990, following Prodigy's lead. The $4.95-a-month fee turned off some existing members but attracted many new ones, giving its membership a net boost. In late 1992, GEnie slashed its prime-time rates from $18 an hour to $12.50.

Clearly, one of GEnie's main attractions is price—as long as you log on at night and don't stray beyond the basic offerings. It also features a wide selection of multi-player games plus real-time chat sessions with well-known science fiction writers. GEnie also offers plenty of resources for the personal investor and the small business owner—investment- and business-related bulletin boards, hardware and software support "roundtables" (similar to CompuServe's forums), and an after-hours gateway to Dow Jones News/Retrieval's wealth of financial information. Then there's the GEnie Newstand, a searchable database of 12 daily newspapers and a total of 900 periodicals.

GEnie's main drawback is its complex menu structure, which makes the system difficult to navigate without its Aladdin front-end software (illustrated in Figure A.1). While the service does offer on-line help, its menus typically offer too many choices and the screen sequence can be confusing. Also, you can waste valuable time going back and forth between the basic, value and professional service areas, and GEnie doesn't tell you how much you've spent during the session once you've logged off.

More about GEnie:

- **Availability**:You can log onto GEnie through local access numbers in more than 600 U.S. and 14 Canadian cities as well as through the SprintNet and DataPac networks. The service is also available in eight countries outside the United States, including Austria, Australia and New Zealand.

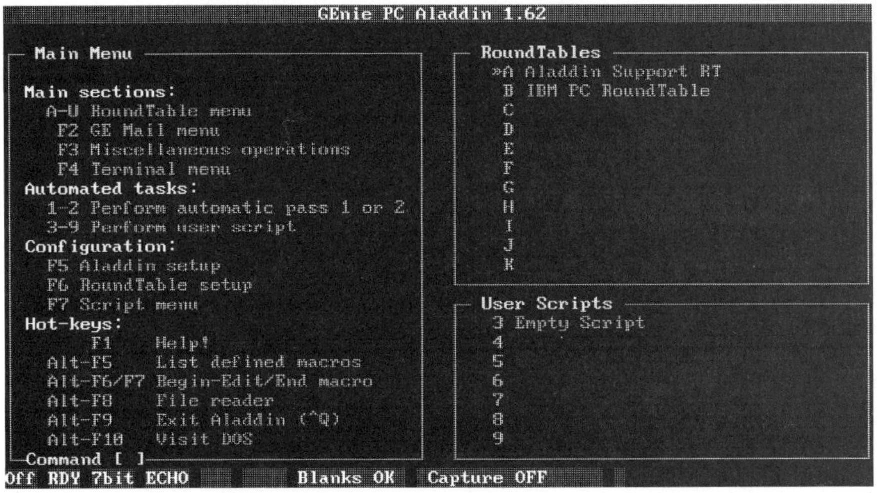

FIGURE A.1:

GEnie's Aladdin front-end software makes the service easier to navigate

- **Modem speeds supported:** 300 bps, 1200 bps, 2400 bps and 9600 bps (now available in about 100 U.S. and Canadian cities)
- **Computer platforms supported:** DOS, Macintosh, any ASCII-based computer terminal
- **Number of bulletin boards:** Over 100
- **Address:** General Electric Information Service, 401 N. Washington St., Rockville MD 20850
- **Phone number:** 1-800-638-9636

America Online

The nation's fourth largest online service, America Online combines the ease of Prodigy with the communications power of CompuServe. A snap for anybody who knows his way around a Macintosh or Microsoft Windows, America Online lets you quickly and easily dash off an online message, join in a real-time chat session or download free and low-cost software—simply by clicking an icon with your mouse.

America Online's $7.95-a-month flat fee includes two free hours of connect time; additional hours are billed at 10 cents a minute.

Founded in 1985, America Online now boasts over 200,000 members, up from 143,000 subscribers in 1991. Actually, America Online is not one online service but four: Q-Link for users of the Commodore 64 and 128 computers; PC Link, for Tandy MS DOS-based computer users; America Online, for users of Macintosh, Apple II, IBM PCs and PC-compatible computers, and Promenade, for IBM PS/1 computers.

Considerably smaller than Prodigy, CompuServe and GEnie, America Online has grown by going where the big guys aren't. Rather than try to be the USA Today of the online world, America Online positions itself as a series of specialized magazines catering to niche markets. For example, the service, in connection with the Tribune Co. newspaper company, recently spun off a local version of itself called Chicago Online.

The best thing about America Online is that it's fun to use. And, while it offers many of the same kinds of investment and small-business bulletin boards, brokerage services, and databases that its competition does, the online ambiance tends to be a little friendlier and more relaxed. The service even has a unique feature called Members Helping Members that lets you chat about everything from online ethics to billing and pricing to how to run America Online under Windows—for free. America Online also lets you scoot about the service under an alias or "screen name" that lets you interact with other members without disclosing your true identity.

Earlier this year, America Online released a Windows version, making the service even more accessible. America Online for Windows features a "flashbar," similar to CompuServe's WinCIM toolbar, which lets you click a row of icons at the top of the screen to access news stories, stock market information, the Download Manager, and other service features. Also similar to WinCIM is a "mobile access" feature that lets users who travel frequently program in multiple phone numbers to log on from. And, for those who like to hear their computers "talk," America Online for Windows lets you transmit sounds while chatting with other members and hear special noises when a download is complete or a message arrives in your mailbox. There's even an electronic voice to greet you when you log on and off.

The major drawback to America Online is that it lacks some important features that personal investors and business users need—namely, access to a broad range of newspaper and magazine databases and in-depth financial information. What's more, the bulletin boards offered on the service tend to focus primarily on personal interests, resulting in far fewer networking opportunities than exist on CompuServe. It's also quite easy to rack up hefty connect-time charges on America Online. America Online only recently introduced a "Download Manager" that lets you save money by selecting a group of files, downloading them all at once and logging off.

More about America Online:

- **Availability**: You can log onto America Online through approximately 500 local access numbers nationwide.
- **Modem speeds supported**: 1200 bps, 2400 bps and 9600 bps (to be announced in 1993)
- **Computer platforms supported**: DOS, Macintosh, Commodore, Windows
- **Number of bulletin boards**: Over 500
- **Address:** America Online, 8619 Westwood Center Dr., Vienna VA 22182
- **Phone number**: 1-703-448-8700

Figure A.2 shows America Online's main menu screen.

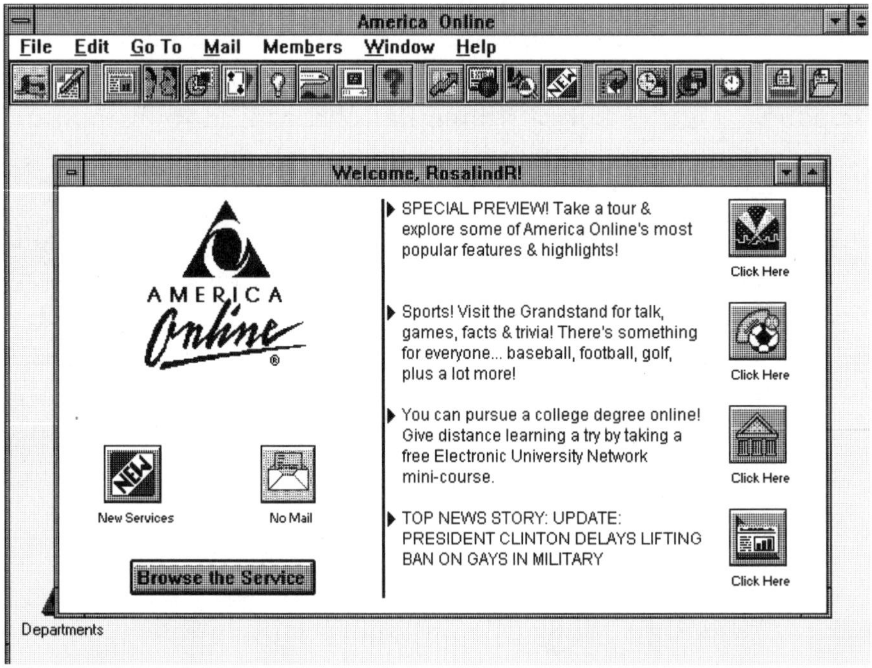

FIGURE A.2: America Online lets you scoot around the service by clicking icons with your mouse

Delphi

A distant fifth in terms of membership, Delphi offers one of the best values of any mass-market online service, plus some unique features that its bigger competitors don't have.

With fewer than 100,000 subscribers, Delphi offers the same mix of e-mail, real-time chats, downloadable software libraries, stock quotes and multi-player games that most other online services do—but for far less than the other pay-as-you-go plans. Under Delphi's 20/20 Advantage Plan, you pay only $20 a month (plus a $19 one-time enrollment fee) for 20 hours of usage. Delphi's 10/4 Plan charges a $10 monthly fee for the first four hours of evening and weekend use and includes free access to help files, billing information and other support services; additional connect time costs just $4 an hour. CompuServe, by contrast, charges $12.80 an hour for 2400 bps access; GEnie charges up to $12.50 an hour during weekdays.

For just $3 a month more, Delphi lets you tap into the Internet, a global communications network with links to millions of computer users, and send e-mail to people who use other online services. Delphi is the only major commercial online service that offers access to the Internet's full range of database and file-transfer capabilities in addition to worldwide e-mail.

Delphi offers some other pluses, too—a simplied menu-based command structure, foreign-language translation services, and access to Latin America through its Delphi/Argentina and Delphi/Miami international gateways. Delphi also provides a wealth of trip-planning services, including Commercial Sabre, the professional version of the Eaasy Sabre service offered by the rest of the online pack. (Delphi offers access to Eaasy Sabre, too.)

Delphi's biggest drawback is that you get what you pay for—and, in the case of business information, that's not much. Though Delphi does offer stock quotes, commodities prices and several stock-tip newsletters, the service doesn't have much in the way of business-related databases or bulletin boards. And, unless you go through Delphi's Dialog gateway, there are no newspaper or magazine archives to search. Accessing Dialog costs $35 an hour for Delphi subscribers with extra fees for access to databases and articles retrieved.

Another drawback to Delphi is its lack of local access numbers—unless you live in the Delphi's hub cities of Boston and Kansas City. Anywhere else, you've got to log on through a telecommunications network, such as Tymnet or Sprint, adding as much as $9 an hour to your bill during business hours. (Other services, such as America Online, also must be accessed through a telecommunications network, but include the network charge in their monthly access fees.)

More about Delphi:

- **Availability**: You can log onto Delphi through the more than 600 local access numbers offered by Tymnet and SprintNet. Local access is available only in Boston and Kansas City.
- **Modem speeds supported**: 300 bps, 1200 bps, 2400 bps
- **Computer platforms supported**: DOS, Macintosh, any kind of ASCII-based terminal
- **Number of bulletin boards**: 35
- **Address**: General Videotex Corp., 1030 Massachusetts Ave., Cambridge MA 02138
- **Phone number**: 1-800-695-4005

Figure A.3 shows Delphi's Business and Finance menu.

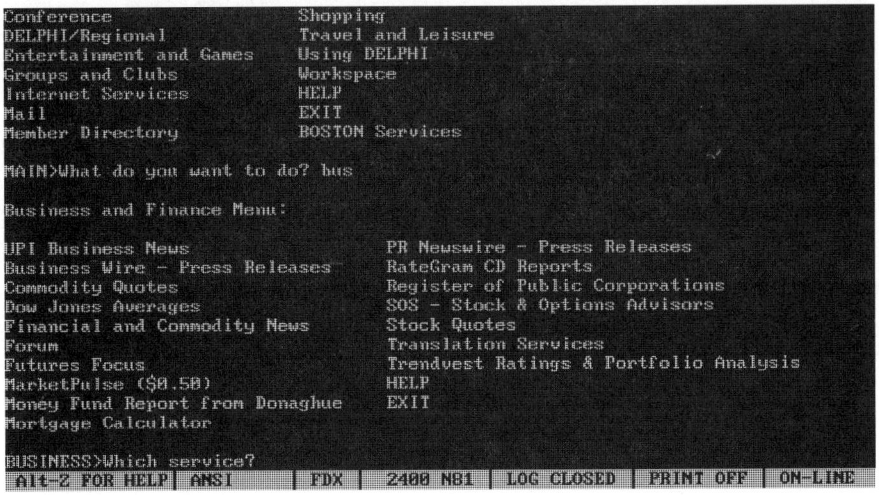

FIGURE A.3:

Delphi's 20/20 Advantage Plan gives you 20 hours' usage for only $20 a month

INDEX

Symbols

+ (plus sign), 268
- (hyphen), 268
/ (slash), 148, 265, 267, 268

A

access fees, network, xxi, 69, 73–74
  definition of, 71, 73
accessing
  America Online, 25
  CompuServe forums, and TAPCIS, 77–78
  CB Simulator, 135–36
  Computer Database Plus, 146–47
  Official Airline Guide, 265–68
  Consumer Reports, 246–48
  databases, online, vs. online overload, 140–42
  databases, overview of, 139–54
  D&B Dun's Market Identifiers, 140, 150, 152
  Eaasy Sabre, on Prodigy, specific steps for, 262–65
  encyclopedias, 142–44
  Favorite Places, 44–45
  financial information, with CompuServe and Prodigy, 195–98
  Microsoft Knowledge Base using WinCIM, 283–84
  WinCIM, 44–45. *See also* access fees, network; downloading; searching
Accessories window, 42
accountants, 228, 229–30
Account Menu, 79
ACORN target marketing, 151
acronyms, 100–101
Acros Computers, 285
Add, 60, 87, 95
address book(s), 29, 31, 91
  basic description of, 94
  and CompuServe features, overview of, 181
  creating an, with CompuServe, specific steps for, 95–96
  creating an, with Prodigy, specific steps for, 96–97
  and searching forum membership directories, 133
Adnet, 226
advertisements, 99
  classifieds, 12–13, 224, 226–27
advice
  accessing professional, 228–34
  columns, and technical support, 283–84
agreement numbers
  and logging onto CompuServe, 44
Agrochemicals Handbook, 6
AIDS, 233
Alcoholics Anonymous, 234
American Airlines, 5, 184, 258, 259, 261, 265, 269
American Demographics, 11, 201
American Health, 230
American Heart Association, 14
American Medical Informatics Association, 231
America Online, xxi, 4, 25
  basic description of, 298–300
  and bulletin boards, 123, 133
  cost of, 76, 48, 298
  and financial information, 207, 212, 216
  and the creation of front-end programs, reasons for, 43
  and the future of online services, 290
  Industry Connection feature, 288
  and the Internet, 207
  Investor's Network forum, 216
  Members Helping Members, 299
  and online shopping, 241
  and other online services, comparison of, 175, 176
  Service Corp of Retired Executives, 223
  special software required by, 40
  and technical support, 274, 278, 281, 282, 288
  and travel services, 257, 262
  and Windows-like features, 28
Amiga, 123, 277–78

Analyzer menu, 196–97
Apple computers, 18, 214, 250, 298
and technical support, 274, 285, 286, 287. *See also* Macintosh
Arbitron ratings, 151
Article Types, 146
ASCII-base terminals, 302
ASCII characters
components of, 33, 106
ASCII files, 117
and logging on overseas, 162
reading of, 104–5, 113
and uploading text files, using WinCIM, 104–5
AT&T, 153, 181
Atari, 287
Atlantic, The, 145
attorneys, 223–24, 228
autodial directories, 36, 39
setting up, specific steps for, 34–35
AVEL.KIT, 160, 161, 163, 286

B

B (back), 56
Backspace key
and editing e-mail messages, 88
Baker, Robert C., 231
bar graphs, 108
Barron's, 201, 213
Basic Services, 45
batch files
transfer of, 117
baud rates
definition of, 33
and logging onto CompuServe, 44
Begin Download, 114
bibliographic citations
and surcharges, 50, 73
billing, 195, 251, 264
binary data
definition of, 106
binary files, 105, 106. *See also* graphics files
BondText, 206
Borland, 184, 276, 287
BORLAND, 278
Borland International, 274, 277, 286
bps rates
and America Online, 300
and CompuServe and Prodigy, comparison of, 179, 186, 187, 189
definition of, 22, 32–33
and Delphi, 302
and the future of online services, 290–91
and GEnie, 298
and logging onto CompuServe, 42
and online shopping, 240
and technical support, 280
brokerages, 177
Charles Schwab, 212, 296
description and comparison of, 212–13, 215–16
and making a trade, specific steps for, 213–15
Browse, 169
Browse Library, 108, 129
Browse list, 58
Browse Messages, 128
browsing
for bulletin board messages, 128–29
and downloading text files, 108
through forum libraries, 108, 129
and retrieving e-mail messages, 92
bugs
and uploading program files, 106
and WinCIM, 31
bulletin boards, xxi, 3–4
and CB Simulator, 134–36
and CompuServe and Prodigy, comparison of, 179, 180, 181, 184–85, 186, 189
and conference rooms, 130–32
cost of, 142–45, 186
and "finding kindred spirits," 132–33
general overview of, 120–37
"hanging out at," 122–23
investor, basic description of, 216–17
and logging on overseas, 166
and low-cost ways to search for information, 142–45
"major," sticking with, 124
and the message board, basic description of, 125–29
and online shopping, 240
and posting a message, specific steps for, 125–27
and reading a message, specific steps for, 128–29
and responding to a message, specific steps for, 127
and "screen names," selection of, 133
shopping for, 284–88
systems, basic description of, 122–23
and technical support, 274–81, 282, 284–88

and travel clubs, 257–58
and tuning in to online chat boards, 122, 133–36.
See also forum(s); forum libraries
Business & Finance Report, 11, 201
business directories, 152–54
business letters
utility of e-mail for, 87
"Busy" signal, 36

C

Cancel, 92, 95
canceling
airline reservations, specific steps for, 264
cancer, 232, 233
capturing
text files, 109–11
Career Network, 225, 226
CE Software, 287, 288
Census Bureau, 150
Charles Schwab, 212, 296
Chipsoft, 285, 287
choosing
a file transfer protocol, 115–17
chronic illness, 233
Citizens Band radios, 134
classifieds, 12–13, 224, 226–27
clicking
and front-end software, 25
Clipboard
and logging on through Windows, 28
closing
the Terminal window, 43
Command mode
and abbreviated menus, 62, 63
Commerce Business Daily, 141–42
Commerce Department, 13
Commodities, 140
Commodore, 277, 278, 298
Commodore & Amiga, 287
Commodore RoundTable, 278
Commodore Users Network, 277
communications ports
and logging onto CompuServe, 42–43, 44
and setting up your software, 34–35, 36
communications software, xxi
as a basic tool, 18
cost of, 24–25
design of, purpose of, 24
and disk space, 26
and ease of use, 26
learning the lingo of, 32–34
multipurpose vs. front-end, 24–26
and off-the-shelf programs vs. shareware, 23–24, 26–27
and protocols, function of, 116
selection of, 23–31
setting up, 32–37
troubleshooting, 36
communications tool kit, 158, 161–63
CompuServe, xx, xxi, 4
accessing financial information with, 196–97, 198, 199
and the Adnet Online Employment Advertising Network, 224
and bps access, faster, 291
and bulletin boards, 123–25, 128–32, 134–36, 184–85
and *Consumer Reports*, 241, 246–48
cost of, 7, 8, 9, 31, 48, 50, 70–77, 81, 167–68, 176, 289, 301
creating an address book with, 95–96
creating a public message on, 98, 99
and the creation of front-end programs, reasons for, 43
databases, overview of, 181–84
dialing, specific steps for, 34–35
and downloading financial information, 210
and electronic mail, 75, 86, 89–90, 92–93, 95–96, 98–99, 181
and encyclopedias, 142, 183–84
evolution of, 176–80
and flat-fee plans, 48, 50
four ways of navigating, summary of, 56
future of, 189–90
getting billing information on, 81
getting rate information on, 74
and hard disk storage, 26
and health advice, 72, 230–31, 234, 235
and the Internet, 207
and job searches, 224
local access number, 42
logging off, 45–46
and logging on, basic description of, 40
and logging on overseas, 159, 163–69
and logging on through Windows, 28–32
logging onto, using Procomm Plus, 41–42
logging onto, using WinCIM, 43–46
manual, 41
navigating, basic commands for, 55–57
and online brokerages, 212, 213, 215–16

and online networking, 222–25, 226–28, 231–35
and online shopping, 238, 241, 242–44, 245
and other online services, comparison of, 175–90, 299
and overseas phone numbers, compiling, 165
and postal mail, sending, 90–91
and posting a bulletin board message, 125
and Prodigy, comparison of, 180–88
receiving a message from, specific steps for, 92–93
rules and regulations, display of, 42, 44
sending an e-mail message on, specific steps for, 87–90
sending a fax on, specific steps for, 89–90
and shortcut commands, 57–59
subscribers, number of, 176
and support groups, 233–34
and tax advice, 230
and technical support, 273–75, 277, 281, 284, 285–87
and terminal emulation mode, 64–65
and travel services, 256–61, 265–68, 269–70
and Windows-like features, 28. *See also* CompuServe (features)
CompuServe (features)
1-800 service, 40, 74, 153
ABC Worldwide Hotel Guide, 259–60
address book. *See* address book(s)
AMIA Medical Forum, 184
Amiga Forums, 277
Borland International Forum, 277
Business Database Plus, 73, 145, 197
Cancer Forum, 233
CB Simulator, 134–36
classifieds, 12–13, 224, 226–27
Commodore Users Network, 277
Company Analyzer, 196–97
Compuserve magazine, 71–72
Computer Club Forum, 286
Computer Consultant's Forum, 184, 222–23
Computer Database Plus, 50, 107, 145, 146–47, 182, 241
Court Pharmacy, 230
D&B Dun's Market Identifiers, 140, 150, 152
Desktop Publishing Forum, 128–29, 184
Diabetes and Hypoglycemia Forum, 233, 234
E-Trade Securities, 215, 216
Executive Service Option, 49, 186
Favorite Places, 29, 44–45, 59, 61–62
Financial Forums, 217
GIF (Graphics Interchange Format), 31
Health & Fitness Forum, 231, 234, 235
Health Database Plus, 73, 230, 232
Human Sexuality Forum, Living with AIDS Section, 233
IBM European Users Forum, 159, 160–61, 163, 286
IBM Hardware Forum, 279
IBM Users Network, 277
Information Manager. *See* WinCIM (CompuServe Information Manager for Windows)
Information Service, 28, 177
International Entrepreneurs' Network, 184
Investext, 206
Investor's Forum, 124, 129, 130, 184, 216
IQuest, 149–50, 182, 199
Journalism Forum, 124
Legal Forum, 184, 228
Macintosh Forums, 277
Magazine Database Plus, 73, 145
Mall, 185, 238, 242–44
Medsig Forum, 231–32
Microsoft forums, 131–32, 276–77, 284
NAIC Forum, 14, 218
Newspaper Library, 145, 182
Official Airline Guide (OAG), 252, 255, 260–61, 265–68, 269, 270, 296
Online With Hayes Forum, 277
Practice Forum, 65
Private Investigator's Forum, 12
Quick & Reilly, 216
Spear & Rees, 216
Travel Forum, 256, 257–58
WordPerfect Users Forum, 277
Working from Home Forum, 5, 99, 107–11, 124, 222, 224–25, 228
Worldspan Travelshopper, 260. *See also* CompuServe
Computer Club Bulletin Board, 279
Computer Express, 245
conference(s)
and e-mail, 99
and erasing things you've typed, 65
rooms, 125, 130–32
connect charges, 69, 71–72, 228, 282
definition of, 70, 71
"Connected" message, 45
Consumer Reports, 184, 235, 237, 241, 246–48
conversion plugs, 162
copying
addresses, and address books, 95
and downloading on Prodigy, 111, 112

and downloading the Ziffnet Download Manager, 114
and downloading vs. printing, 118
and WinCIM, 77
Copy Options, 111, 112
CPAs (certified public accountants), 228, 229–30
creating
an address book, with CompuServe, 95–96
an address book, with Prodigy, 96–97
a bulletin board message, on CompuServe, 125–27
a CompuServe Favorite Place list, 61
e-mail messages, on CompuServe, 87–89
a Prodigy pathlist, 59–60
a public message, on CompuServe, 99
a public message, on Prodigy, 98, 99
Create Mail, 87, 95
Create Message, 126
credit information, 141, 182
cross-referencing, 143, 189
Ctrl-C
description of, 64
Ctrl-O
description of, 65
Ctrl-Q
description of, 64
Ctrl-S
description of, 64
Ctrl-U
description of, 65
customization
and CompuServe and Prodigy, comparison of, 181
and navigating, 59–61
overview of, 185–86
and service options, 40, 49
Custom Choice, 114
customer presentations, 159
cut-and-paste
and editing e-mail messages, 88
CX (command), 268
Cypress, 203

D

DacEasy, 285
Dalco Computer Electronics, 242
D&B Dun's Market Identifiers, 8, 140, 150, 152
Database (company), 287
data bits, 32
definition of, 33
and logging onto CompuServe, 42
DataPac, 165, 297
DATAS II, 269
Data-Star, 4, 140
Automotive Industry News, 205
basic description of, 204–5
Drug News Daily, 205
Tradstat, 11, 140, 205
DATASTORM Technologies, 286
Davidson and Associates, 285
decoders
and WinCIM, 31
decompression programs, 113
default settings
WinCIM, and downloading, 110
deleting
addresses, in address books, 95
and editing e-mail messages, 88
e-mail messages, 92
listings, on CB simulator, 136
messages, on CompuServe, 26
Delphi, 4, 176, 262
basic description of, 301–3
and bulletin boards, 123
Business and Finance Menu, 302–3
cost of, 301, 302
and the Internet, 207
and other online services, comparison of, 175
Delta, 260
demodulation
definition of, 18
demographic databases, 150–52
desktop features
and the Desktop Publishing Forum, 128–29, 184
and Desktop Direct from Digital, 242
and WinCIM, 29, 31
detectives, 12, 17
DF (command), 268
Diagsoft, 285
dialing
auto-, 45
command suffixes, 164
and logging onto CompuServe, 45
and logging on overseas, 163–64
and network charges, 73–74
pulse vs. tone, 163–64
and reprogramming your modem, 164
specific steps for, 34–35
and troubleshooting, 36. *See also* dialing directories

dialing directories
autodial, 34–36, 39
enhanced, 27
and full duplex and half duplex modes, 32
and local echos, 32
Procomm Plus, 35
and setting up your software, 35
Dialog, 4, 6, 149, 176, 198–99, 204, 209
accessing, for Delphi subscribers, 302
basic description of, 200–201
and the future of online services, 290
Information Services, 140
Knowledge Index, 7–8, 48, 200–201, 228
dictionary
of e-mail lingo, 100–101
diets, 230–32
Digital Express Group, 209
directories
AT&T's toll-free, 153
forum membership, searching of, 132–33
specification of, and downloading text files, 108
See also dialing directories
disabled persons, 233, 286
Disclosure, 8, 197
Disclosure II, 49, 73, 182
diskettes
and logging onto CompuServe, 44
Doctors. *See* medical advice
DOS
and CompuServe, 28–31, 177
and Delphi, 302
and the Desktop Publishing Forum, 128
and front-end programs, compatibility of, 28
Procomm Plus for, 34–35
prompt, returning to, 35
and technical support, 276, 278, 279–80, 281, 283
and WinCIM, 28–31
Dow Jones News/Retrieval, 4, 6, 10, 290
basic description of, 201–3
Company News, 195
cost of, 7, 8, 48–50, 194, 198, 199, 202–3, 209
and downloading financial information, 210
and the DowQuest menu system, 202
Forecasts & Analyses, 203
General Interest, 203
and GEnie, 296, 297
and the Internet, 207
and logging on, basic description of, 40
and logging on overseas, 159
and logging on through Windows, 28
News & Quotes, 203
and off-peak plans, 48–49
and online brokerages, 212, 216
downloading, 102–18
on America Online, 299
and "capturing" text files, 109–11
and choosing file transfer protocols, 115–17
cost of, 72
and decompression programs, 113, 114
definition of, 4, 23, 103
financial information, 193, 210–11
forum files, 107–11, 129
from the Microsoft Knowledge Base, 283
and modems, 23–24
program and graphics files, 113–15
search results, 152
a text file, specific steps for, 107–12
and WinCIM, 29
the Ziffnet Download Manager, 114
Download Manager, 299
DowQuest menu system, 202
Dun's Electronic Business Directory, 152
duplex mode
full and half, 32–33
Dynamix, 285

E

Eaasy Sabre, 5, 184, 255–56, 258, 269, 270
accessing, specific steps for, 262–65
and Delphi, 301
and GEnie, 296
and online shopping, 252
overview of, 260–67
and shortcut commands, 59
EAASY REVIEW menu, 264
Eastern Digital Resources, 280–81
echos, local, 32
definition of, 33
Economic Bulletin Board, 13
editing
address books, 95
and CompuServe features, overview of, 181
e-mail messages, 88
listings, on CB simulator, 136
Edit menu, 31, 88
electronic mail (e-mail), xxi, 4
advantages of, 86–87
and browsing through "message threads," 98
and CompuServe, 25–26, 29, 31, 86, 88–90, 92–93, 95–96, 98–99, 177, 179, 180, 181, 189

cost of, 10, 75, 186
and the future of online services, 289, 291
and the Internet, 207
lingo and "etiquette," 99–101
and logging on overseas, 159, 164
and logging on through Windows, 28
and Mailing Lists, 97
overview of, 84–101
and private and public messages, 97–99
and Prodigy, 48, 86, 91–94, 96–99, 179, 180, 181, 189
and sending and receiving messages, 86–92, 97
and retrieving an electronic message, 92–94
and saving time with an address book, 94–97
and sending the same message to a group of people, 97
and technical support, 283
and user ID numbers, 87, 89, 91, 95, 97
and WinCIM, 29, 31
Electronic Funds Transfer, 81
e-mail. *See* electronic mail (e-mail)
employment
searching for, 224–27
encyclopedias
and CompuServe and Prodigy, comparison of, 179, 183–84
Grolier's Academic, 142–45, 183–84
and low–cost ways of searching for information, 142–45
Epson, 286
errors
in data transmission, 33
checking for, and protocols, 116, 117
and dialing, 164
and logging on overseas, 164
Ethernet cards, 281
Excel, 196, 210
exiting
address books, 95
CB Simulator, 136
CompuServe, 43, 44, 45, 147
Procomm Plus, 35
Prodigy, 114

F

faxes
and CompuServe, 89, 177, 181
and the future of online services, 290
and logging on overseas, 159–60, 162, 165, 166
and modems, 11, 20, 22–23
sending a, on CompuServe, specific steps for, 89. *See also* electronic mail (e-mail)
Fidelity, 212
Fidelity Investors Express, 216
Fidelity Online Xpress, 212
File, 42
File It, 92
File menu, 43, 44, 93, 118
file size
and uploading text files, 105
Filing Cabinets, 29, 31
accessing, 44–45
storing e-mail messages in, 93
Find, 58–59, 66
flat-fee plans, 69, 72, 89, 179, 180
and CompuServe and Prodigy, comparison of, 186
and financial information, 198, 199, 203
and the future of online services, 291
vs. pay-as-you-go plans, 75–76
Flight Availability screen, 262
flow control
and logging onto CompuServe, 42
Ford Motor Company, 242
foreign language
Education Forum, 160
translation services, 301
formatting
and ASCII files, 105
Fortune 500 companies, xx, 200
forum(s)
basic description of, 177–78
and CompuServe and Prodigy, comparison of, 184–85
cost off, 76, 77
definition of, 123
files, downloading, 107–11, 129
messages, and WinCIM, 29, 31. *See also* bulletin boards; forum libraries; message boards
forum libraries, 125, 129–30
and logging on overseas, 160–61
organization of, 129
and WinCIM, 29
frequent-flyer programs, 259
Friends, 136
Friends List box, 136
Front Porch Computers, 12
Frost & Sullivan, 206

G

GEnie, xxi, 4, 7, 40
and 9600 bps access, 291
Alladin software, 297
basic description of, 296–98
and bulletin boards, 123
Computer Press Association Roundtable, 223
cost of, 9, 48, 76, 296, 301
and electronic mail, 91
and financial information, 198, 203, 207, 212
and the Internet, 207
Newstand, 297
and online shopping, 241
and other online services, comparison of, 175, 176
and technical support, 274, 278, 281, 282, 284, 287–88, 287
and travel services, 257, 262
General Electric Information Services, 296, 298
General Videotext Corporation, 302
GeoWorks, 287, 288
Get All, 93, 94
Get New Mail, 25, 45, 92, 169
getting around. *See* navigating
GIF (Graphics Interchange Format), 31
Go, 46, 66
accessing, 44–45
and ease of use, 187
and navigating, 57–58, 59
and retrieving e-mail messages, 92
graphics files
downloading, specific steps for, 113–15
storage of, in forum libraries, 125
uploading, specific steps for, 106
Grolier's Academic American Encyclopedia, 142–45, 183–84. *See also* encyclopedias

H

Hammacher Schlemmer, 185, 241, 243, 245
H&R Block, 177
handles
and CB Simulator, 134, 135, 126
hard drives, xx
and composing mail and forum messages, 31
disk space on, 26
and logging onto CompuServe, 44
saving text onto, and stopping online operations, 64
and shareware, 27
and TAPCIS, 78
and uploading and downloading, 103
and WinCIM, 31
Hayes Microcomputer Products, 21
Hayes-compatible modems, 19, 78, 21–22, 163–64
Hayes RoundTable, 278
and technical support, 278, 285, 287
health advice, 228, 230–34
HealthNet, 232
help (technical support), xxi, 65, 273–88
accessing, where to start, 276–77
and advice columns, 283–84
and America Online, 274, 278, 281, 282, 288
and Apple Computer, 274, 285, 286, 287
bulletin boards, lists of, 277–79
cost of, 280, 282, 285, 287, 288
and CompuServe, 273–75, 277, 281, 284, 285–87
context-sensitive, 27, 29
and GEnie, 274, 278, 281, 282, 284, 287–88, 287
how to get, overview of, 276–81
and IBM, 274–76, 278, 279, 286, 287
and logging on overseas, 166
and Microsoft, 274, 275, 276, 277, 278, 281, 282–83, 285, 286, 287
and navigating, 65
and Prodigy, 273, 274, 275–76, 278–79, 283, 284, 285–86
pros and cons of, 280–81
and searching databases, 149
and shopping for help online, 284–88
and setting up your software, 36
and technical support databases, basic description of, 281–84
and Windows, 276, 283
and WordPerfect, 277, 278, 287
Hewlett-Packard, 286
home business owners
and the Working from Home Forum, 5, 99, 107–11, 124, 222, 224–25, 228
and online networking, overview of, 222–24
how-to files, 99

I

IBM (IBM computers), 12, 18, 176, 250, 298
and bulletin boards, 123
Communications Forum, 113

and CompuServe and Prodigy, comparison of, 178–79
and CompuServe forums, 184
and downloading financial information, 210
European Users Forum, 159, 160–61, 163
and modems, 18, 21
PC RoundTable, 278
Special Needs Forum, 286
and TAPCIS, 78
and technical support, 274–76, 278, 279, 286, 287
Users Network, 277
import/export information, 140, 145, 198
In-Baskets, 29, 31
and retrieving e-mail messages, 92
storing e-mail messages in, 93
Infonet, 165, 166, 167, 169
Information Kinetics, 225, 227
Information Manager. *See* WinCIM (CompuServe Information Manager for Windows)
Input Box, 131, 135
installation
"sign-up" portion of, 44
of modems, 19–20
of Procomm Plus, 34
of WinCIM, specific steps for, 44–46
Institutional Brokers Estimate System, 49
instruction manuals, 41, 123
Internet, 86, 291, 301
basic description of, 207–9
cost of, 208–9
and CompuServe and Prodigy, comparison of, 181
and financial information, 203
Internet Guide for New Users, The (Dern), 208
Investext, 206
investment clubs
basic description of, 218–19
Investor's Business Daily, 49, 195
I/Plus Direct, 199
basic description of, 206–7
IQuest, 149–50, 182, 199
IRS (Internal Revenue Service), 9

J

JCPenny, 241, 242, 243, 245
JDR Microdevices, 243
jobs
searching for, and online networking, 224–27
Jump, 59, 66
JUMP, 93, 114, 143, 189, 214, 211, 250, 262
and navigating Prodigy, 54, 56
and sending e-mail messages with Prodigy, 91
JumpWindow, 59, 61, 250
and navigating, 54–55
Jumpwords, 54, 59

K

Kermit, 116
key combinations
and logging onto CompuServe, 56
keywords
and reservation systems, 265
and searching for files in forum libraries, 129
and technical support, 277–79, 282
KiNexus, 227
KLH Computers, 285
Knight-Ridder Publishing Company, 140, 200, 204
Konexx Koupler, 163

L

Laplink, 159
Laser's Edge, 243
Leading Edge, 285, 288
legal advice, 184, 223–24, 228
libraries, online
and CompuServe and Prodigy, comparison of, 182–84
and downloading text files, 107–11
forum, 29, 125, 129–30, 160–61
and getting decompression programs, 113
legal, 228
and technical support, 282, 287
Library menu, 109
LLCs (Limited Liability Companies), 229–30
loading
script-reading programs, 164
local echos, 32
definition of, 33
Lockheed Missiles & Space, 176, 200
logging. *See* logging off; logging on; logging on overseas
logging off
America Online, 299
CompuServe, 42, 45–46
and creating e-mail messages, 89

and getting help, 65
logging on, 36
basic description of, 40
and changing your password, 46
CompuServe, 28–32, 45, 56, 62
with a front-end program, 43–46
with a multipurpose program, 41–43
Prodigy, 54
through Windows, 28–31
with Windows Terminal. *See also* logging on overseas
logging on overseas, xxi
and anticipating disasters, 158–60
and backup plans, 166–67
and bps rates, 187
and "braving the risks," 159–60
and communications tool kits, 158, 161–63
cost of, 159, 163, 165, 167–69
and CompuServe, 168–69, 188
and Delphi, 301
and electronic mail, 89, 99, 159, 164
and faxes, 159–60, 162, 165, 166
and getting help, 166
and loading script–reading programs, 164
and local access numbers, 165–66, 167
and modems, 158, 159, 163–64, 167
overview of, 156–70
and preparing for pitfalls, 160–66
seven tips for, 160–66
and technical support, 286. *See also* logging on
Lotus, 184, 286
Lotus 1-2-3, 196
and downloading financial information, 210
Low Fat Lifestyle Health Letter, The, 231
Low Fat Lifestyle Program, 231

M

M (menu), 56
Macintosh, 56, 243, 250, 298
and bulletin boards, 123, 277–78
and Delphi, 302
and technical support, 277, 278, 283
version of CompuServe, 177
macros
and logging onto CompuServe, 56
Mailing List, 97
Mail menu, 87, 89, 92, 95, 105
Main Menu
CompuServe, 178, 189, 232
and navigating, 54–55
Prodigy, 54–55, 180
Managing Your Money, 196
markets, 145
and tapping into databases, 140–41
targeting, specific steps for, 143–44
MarkIntel, 206
MarkIntel Master, 206
MCI Mail, 86, 95, 181
box, sending a message to a, 90
and financial information, 202, 203
Meca Software, 212
medical advice, 228, 230–34
memory
requirements of CompuServe, 31
menus
abbreviated, 61–63
returning to the previous, 56
shortcutting complex, 28. *See also* specific menus
message(s)
private, 98, 127
public, 98
threads, 129
message boards
basic description of, 125–29
division of, into three parts, 125. *See also* bulletin boards
Micronesian Investment Quarterly, 200
Microprocessor Report, 200
Microsoft, 184
Connection, 277
graphical Windows environment, 24
Knowledge Base, 282–83
RoundTable, 278
Small Business Center, 223
Solution Series Forum, 288
Support, 278
and technical support, 274, 275, 276, 277, 278, 281, 282–83, 285, 286, 287. *See also* Windows (Microsoft)
Mission Control Software, 243
Mode menu, 63
modems, xxi, 11, 116
and America Online, 300
basic description of, 18
command options for, changing, 164
and "command sets," 21
and communications software, selection of, 23–24
cost of, 19
and data compression, 22

and Delphi, 302
and dialing directories, 23
and error correction, 22
and GEnie, 298
Hayes-compatible, 19, 78, 21–22, 163–64
installation of, 19–20
internal vs. external, 19–20
and logging on, 39
and logging on overseas, 158, 159, 163–64, 167, 208
and low-cost ways of searching for information, 145–54
and protocols, function of, 115
reprogramming your, 163–64
and sending faxes, specific steps for, 89
speed of, 22–23. *See also* bps rates
and TAPCIS, 78
troubleshooting, 36
types of, selecting, 19–20
modular plugs, 161
modulation
definition of, 18
Money Highlights menu, 54–55
monitors
and technical support, 281
mouse, xx
and bulletin boards, 124
and getting around Prodigy, 54, 55
and CompuServe and Prodigy, comparison of, 177
and logging onto CompuServe, 56
and setting up your software, 34, 36
and WinCIM, 29, 45
moving. *See* navigating
multiple files
transfer of, 117
multitasking
and WinCIM, 31

N

N (next), 57
Narcotics Anonymous, 234
NASA (National Aeronautic and Space Administration), 200
National Association of Investors Corporation (NAIC), 218
National Resume Bank, 227
navigating, 53–66
bulletin boards, 123–24
CompuServe, 55–57, 61, 189
and customizing services, 59–61
and getting online help, 65
and the Main Menu, 54–55
Prodigy, 54–55, 59–60
and "putting on the brakes," 64–65
and saving time with abbreviated menus, 61–63
and saving time with shortcut commands, 57–59
TAPCIS, 77–78
and using Find, 58–59
and using Go, 57–58
NetCom, 209
networking
and CompuServe, 222–25, 226–28, 231–35
for fun and profit, 222–27
and getting professional advice, 228–34
and health advice, 230–34
and home business owners, 222–24
and legal advice, 223–24, 228
and looking for a job, 224–27
and the Medsig Forum, 231–32
and news updates and databases, 232–33
overview of, 221–35
and Prodigy, 226, 224, 226–27, 229–30, 232, 233
searching tips for, 226–27
and support groups, 233–34
and tax advice, 229–30
New, 42
New England Journal of Medicine, 232
New Mail, 96
NewsFlash, 203
NewsNet, 4, 149
basic description of, 203–4
cost of, 199
New York Times, The, 207, 213
Next, 108
Nigeria, 223
"No Carrier" signal, 36
Northwest Airlines, 260
Novell, 281, 286

O

office
stocking your, 236–52. *See also* shopping
oil industry, 43–44
online services
the "Big Two," comparison of, 180–88

doing business on, individual examples of, 12–15
evolution of, 176–80
future of, 289–92
multiple, signing up for, 8–9, 25
options for, summary of, 48–50
selecting, 6–11, 175–76
time spent learning about, planning of, 9–10
Ontrack, 246
optical scanners, 36
OptImage, 288
Options menu, 63
ordering, online, 237, 249–51
Other Location, 60
Out-Baskets, 29, 31, 88, 105
OzCIS
and logging on overseas, 164

P

Packard Bell, 275, 279, 285
PACs (political action committees), 183
paging
through business directories, 152–54
Panix, 209
PaperChase, 232
parity bits, 32
definition of, 33
passwords, xxi, 39, 40
changing of, 36
and logging onto CompuServe, 42, 45, 168
protection of, 46–47
and sending e-mail messages with Prodigy, 91
and reservation systems, 262
temporary, 42
Paste From, 31
pasting
and WinCIM, 77
pathlists
Prodigy, creation of, 59–60
pay-as-you-go plans, xxi, 70, 176
vs. flat-fee plans, 75–76
PCFN (Personal Control Financial Network), 212
PC Magazine, 5, 283
People menu, 136
phone numbers, 18, 32
local access, 165–66, 167, 188, 200
compiling a list of, 165–66
and logging on overseas, 165–66, 167
and logging onto CompuServe, 42, 45
Phone menu, 43
Physicians Data Query, 232
Pioneer Online Investment Club, 14, 218
Pionex, 285
plug adapters, 161
postal mail
and CompuServe and Prodigy, comparison of, 181
sending, specific steps for, 90–91
posting
a bulletin board message, 125–27
Practical Peripherals, 20
practicing skills, 65
Preferences, 110, 135
Print, 93, 118
Print from the File menu, 110
printing
vs. downloading, 111, 118
e-mail messages, 93, 118
and stopping online operations, 64
Procomm
and hard disk storage, 26
shareware version of, 25, 27
Procomm Plus
and abbreviated menus, 62
and changing modem command options, 164
dialing, specific steps for, 34–35
logging onto CompuServe using, 41–42, 56
and logging on through Windows, 28
protocols offered by, 116
version 2.0, 24
version 2.4.3, 27
Prodigy, xx, xxi, 4, 10, 295
access to *Consumer Reports*, 246–48
accessing financial information with, 195–96
and bulletin boards, 123, 124, 125, 132, 184–85
and bps rates, faster, 291
command structure of, plain-English, 10
and CompuServe, comparison of, 180–88
cost of, 8, 9, 25, 48, 73, 76, 79–80, 113, 176, 289
and the cost of financial information, 199
creating an address book with, 96–97
creating a public message on, 98, 99
and the creation of front-end programs, reasons for, 43
and customized plans, 49
databases, overview of, 181–84
and downloading, 103–4, 107, 111–14, 113
and e-mail, 86, 91–94, 96–99, 181
and encyclopedias, 142, 143–44, 183–84

evolution of, 176–80
future of, 189–90, 289
getting billing information on, 79–80
and hard disk storage, 26
and the Internet, 207
logging onto, 28, 54, 167
making a trade on, 214–15
membership database, 132
navigating, 54–55
online classifieds, 224, 226–27
online ordering through, 250–51
and online networking, 226, 224, 226–27, 229–30, 232, 233
and online shopping, 179, 238, 239, 240, 241, 244–48, 250–51
and other online services, comparison of, 175–90
pathlist, creation of, 59–60
and protecting your password, 46
receiving a message from, specific steps for, 93–94
and the rule against advertising, 99
and searching for a job, 224
sending an e-mail message on, specific steps for, 91–92
and sending files, general description of, 11
software, selection of, 24–25
subscribers, number of, 176
and tax advice, 230
and technical support, 65, 273, 274, 275–76, 278–79,
283, 284, 285–86
toll free number, 40
and travel services, 256, 258–61, 262–65, 269
and Windows-like features, 28. *See also* Prodigy (features)
Prodigy (features)
Ask the CPA, 229
BillPay USA, 183
Book-a-Trip, 261
Business & Industry News, 195
Careers, 184
City Guides, 259
Computer Express, 250
Computer Club, 274, 275–76, 279, 283, 284, 285
Custom Choices, 49, 113, 185, 186
Easy Ordering menu, 251
Environment, 185
Florida Vacation Guide, 259
Gift Reminder, 245
Gift Sender, 251
Health News, 232, 233
Investors Business Daily, 183
Mall, 244–46, 259
Manufacturer's Corner, 285, 286
Money Highlights menu, 55
Money Talk, 5, 184, 188, 195, 216, 217, 229
Network Golf Tour, 185
PC Catalog, 249
PC Flowers, 239
PCFN (Personal Control Financial Network), 212, 213, 214–15
Political Profile, 183
Quote Check, 195, 210
Quote Track, 195, 210–11
Science & Technology, 185
Service Clubs, 185
Strategic Investor, 49, 183, 185, 186, 188, 195, 196, 291
Tavelog, 259
TPI Online Classifieds, 99
Travel Focus, 258–59. *See also* Prodigy
Prodigy Service Highlights, 54
Professional Association of Resume Writers, 227
Program Manager, 42
and logging onto CompuServe, 44
program files
downloading, specific steps for, 113–15
storage of, in forum libraries, 125
uploading, specific steps for, 106
prompt mode
and abbreviated menus, 62, 63
protecting
passwords, 46–47
protocols, 107, 115–17
Psychology Today, 230, 232
public messages
definition of, 98
Publisher's Exchange, 285

Q

Quick Path, 265
QuickTix, 269

R

R (resend), 57
Radio-Suisse, 11, 140, 205

reading
  ASCII files, 104–5, 113
  a bulletin board message, specific steps for, 128–29
  files in forum libraries, 129
Reality Technologies, 212
receiving, 102–18
  on America Online, 299
  and "capturing" text files, 109–11
  and choosing file transfer protocols, 115–17
  and decompression programs, 113, 114
  financial information, 193, 210–11
  forum files, 107–11, 129
  from the Microsoft Knowledge Base, 283
  and modems, 23–24
  program and graphics files, specific steps for, 113–15
  search results, 152
  a text file, specific steps for, 107–12
  and WinCIM, 29
Recipient List, 87, 105
Record in File, 109, 110
reservation systems, 5, 7, 58–59, 177, 184, 260–69
  commands and shortcuts for, 264–65. *See also* travel services
Retrieve, 108
Retrieve All, 109
Retrieve Marked, 108
retrieving
  files in forum libraries, 129
  forum messages, 77
  a message from CompuServe, specific steps for, 92–93
  a message from Prodigy, specific steps for, 93–94
returning
  to the main menu, in forum libraries, 129
  to the previous menu, 56
  to the previous page or screenfull of text, 56
RF (command), 268
roundtables
  definition of, 123
RS (command), 268
rules
  and CompuServe's CB Simulator, 135
  and e-mail, 99–101
  and logging on overseas, 158
  for making airline reservations, 265
  for searching online databases, 147–49. *See also* protocols

S

saving
  e-mail messages, 93
  and logging onto CompuServe, 44
  passwords, 47
  settings, 43, 44, 47
  and stopping online operations, 64
screwdrivers, 158, 160, 162–63
script-reading programs, 164
Sealink, 116
searching
  for bulletin board messages, 128–29
  business directories, 152–54
  Computer Database Plus, 145, 146–47, 148
  Consumer Reports, specific steps for, 246–48
  databases, overview of, 139–54
  and the DowQuest menu system, 202
  for financial information, cost-cutting tips for, 209–10
  forum membership directories, specific steps for, 132–33
  full-text databases, overview of, 145–50
  and getting help, 149
  and letting your keyboard do the walking, 152–54
  and logging on overseas, 159
  for a job, and online networking, 224–27
  the Microsoft Knowledge Base, 283-84
  and mining your modem for money, 145–54
  and online access vs. online overload, 140–42
  and search words, characteristics of, 144–45
  and targeting your market, specific steps for, 143–44
  tips for, 147–49, 209–10
  and tracking people trends, 150–52
  and "wildcards," 148
Search Methods menu, 146
Search Summary menu, 147
Sears, 178
SEC (Securities and Exchange Commission), 11, 73, 201
Security
  protecting passwords, 46–47
Send, 92
Send File, 105
sending
  a bulletin board message, using WinCIM, 128
  and choosing a file transfer protocol, 115–17
  an e-mail message, and address books, 95–97
  an e-mail message, basic description of, 86–87
  an e-mail message, on CompuServe, 87–90

an e-mail message, on Prodigy, 91–92
an e-mail message, to a group of people, 97
a fax, with CompuServe, 89
how-to files, 99
postal mail, specific steps for, 90–91
and printing text from the screen, 118
program and graphics files, 106
a TELEX transmission, 90
a text file, specific steps for, 104–6
serial numbers
and logging onto CompuServe, 44
Service Highlights menu, 54–55
Services menu, 30, 57–58, 59, 247
Session Settings, 28–29, 44, 46–47, 169
set up
for communications software, 32–37. *See also* installation
Settings menu, 42
Shareware, 24
Shareware Club, 246
Shareware Depot, 243, 245, 246
shopping, online, xxi
and *Consumer Reports*, 241, 246–48
"comparison," 237, 246–51
and CompuServe, 177, 181, 185, 238, 241, 242–44, 245
and cruising electronic malls, 241–46
and flat-fee vs. pay-as-you-go plans, 75
and the future of online services, 290
hassle-free world of, 238–41
for help, 284–88
and online ordering, 249–51
overview of, 236–52
and Prodigy, 179, 181, 238, 239, 240, 241, 244–48, 250–51
pros and cons of, 239–41
shortcut commands
saving time with, 57–59
Sierra On-line, 285
sign-ons
automation of, 265
Simba Information, 240, 289
Small Computer Book Club, 243
Smart Investor, 212
SMSA (Standard Metropolitan Statistical Area), 151
Social Security, 182
Software Connexion, 278, 285
Special menu, 46, 109–10, 132, 133, 135, 169
specification
of directory paths, 112
speed. *See* bps rates
spelling
of search words, 144
spreadsheets, 104, 193
downloading data to, specific steps for, 210–12
Sprint, 302
SprintNet, 71, 199, 200, 297
Standard & Poor's Register, 140, 182, 197
Start-up kits, 40, 46
Statement, 79
Statement Help, 79
Steel Hector & Davis, 160
stop bits
definition of, 33
and logging onto CompuServe, 42
stopping
online operations, specific steps for, 64
Subject Headings, 146
SUPERSITE, 150, 151–52
support, technical. *See* technical support
support groups, 233–34
surcharges, xxi, 50, 69
and accessing financial information, 198, 199
for Computer Database Plus, 147
definition of, 70, 72–73
for demographic databases, 150–51
for IQuest, 149
and logging on overseas, 165
surge protectors, 158, 159, 161, 162
Switzerland, 11, 140
Symantec, 286

T

T (top)
description of, 56
and getting online help, 65
Tandy, 18, 286, 298
TAPCIS
cost of, 70, 77–78
and e-mail, 87
Forum, 160
and logging on overseas, 160, 164, 165
tax advice, 9, 229–30
technical support, xxi, 65, 273–88
accessing, basic description of, 276–81
and advice columns, 283–84
and America online, 274, 278, 281, 282, 288
and Apple Computer, 274, 285, 286, 287
bulletin boards, lists of, 277–79
cost of, 280, 282, 285, 287, 288

and CompuServe, 273–75, 277, 281, 284, 285–87
databases, basic description of, 281–84
and GEnie, 274, 278, 281, 282, 284, 287–88
and IBM, 274–76, 278, 279, 286, 287
and Microsoft, 274, 275, 276, 277, 278, 281, 282–83, 285, 286, 287
and Prodigy, 273, 274, 275–76, 278–79, 283, 284, 285–86
pros and cons of, 280–81
and shopping for help online, 284–88
and setting up your software, 36
and "technicians who never sleep," 274–76
and Windows, 276, 283
and WordPerfect, 277, 278, 287
Telebase Systems, 149
TELEX transmissions, 181
sending, specific steps for, 90
terminal emulation mode, 64–65, 81, 110
definition of, 64
getting online help in, 65
Thomas Cook Travel, 269
Thomas Register Online, 152
Thomson and Thomson, 199
Thomson Financial Networks, 206
ticket deliveries, 264, 269
toolbar, 299
and logging off of CompuServe, 45–46
and logging onto CompuServe, 44
and shortcut commands, 57–58
tool(s)
adapters, 158, 161
acoustic couplers, 161, 163
alligator clips, 158, 161, 162, 162
kits, communications, 158, 161–63
screwdrivers, 158, 160, 162–63
voltage converters, 158, 161, 162
TOOLS menu, 112
Toshiba, 239
Trade Data Exchange, 13
trademark availability, 141
translation services, 301
travel services
basic description of, 256–60
and CompuServe, 256–61, 265–68, 269–70
cost of, 75, 260–61
and earning free mileage, 259
and Prodigy, 256, 258–61, 262–65, 269
and reservation systems, xxi, 5, 7, 58–59, 177, 184, 260–69, 296
and ticket deliveries, 264, 269
and travel clubs, 257–58
and travel databases, 258–60
Traveling Software, 159
Travelshopper, 258
Trax Software, 203
Treasury bonds, 215
troubleshooting
your modem and communications software, 36
TRW Credit Reports, 182
TTY mode
description of, 25
Tymnet, 199, 200, 209, 302
and logging on overseas, 167
and network charges, 71, 73–74
typos, 131

U

Unlimited Systems, 163
upgrading, 31
uploading
and binary files, 105, 106
and choosing a file transfer protocol, 115–17
and CompuServe, 104–6, 177, 181, 186
definition of, 23, 103
and modems, 23
how-to files, 99
overview of, 102–18
and printing text from the screen, 118
and Prodigy, 111, 177, 181, 186
program and graphics files, specific steps for, 106
a text file, specific steps for, 104–6
US News & World Report, 145
user ID numbers, xxi, 39, 40
and address books, 95, 97
and e-mail, 87, 89, 91, 95, 97
and logging onto CompuServe, 41, 43, 44, 45, 168
and searching for files in forum libraries, 129
and searching forum membership directories, 133
and sending faxes, 89
and setting up your software, 33

V

Value Line, 182, 197
View, 108
Viewpath, 59, 61
voltage converters, 158, 161, 162

W

Walden Computer Books, 185, 243
Wall Street Journal, 10–11, 100, 201, 217
wildcards, 148
WinCIM (CompuServe Information Manager for Windows)
  and abbreviated menus, 62
  and accessing *Consumer Reports*, 246
  and accessing the Official Airline Guide, 266–67
  and accessing Eaasy Sabre, 262
  and accessing Internet, 207–8
  and accessing IQuest, 150
  and accessing the Microsoft Knowledge Base, 283–84
  and accessing rate information on CompuServe, 74
  and America Online, similarities between, 299
  and bulletin boards, 125–29, 131, 133–36
  and CB Simulator, 135, 136
  and "capturing" text files, 109–11
  changing your password using, 46
  Channel Selector grid, 135
  and CompuServe Favorite Places, creation of, 61
  and CompuServe features, overview of, 181
  cost of, 31, 74, 77–78, 81, 186
  downloading a text file using, specific steps for, 107–11
  and ease of use, 187
  and electronic mail, 77, 87–88, 90–95
  and the future of online services, 290
  Get All, saving time with, 93
  and getting billing information, specific steps for, 81
  installation of, specific steps for, 44–46
  logging on with, 43–46, 168, 169
  mailing a paper letter using, specific steps for, 90–91
  and navigating CompuServe, basic commands for, 56–57
  online help, 65
  and pay-as-you-go plans, 75–76
  participating in a conference on, specific steps for, 131
  and posting a bulletin board message, 125–27
  and protocols, 116
  and reading a bulletin board message, 128–29
  and responding to a bulletin board message, 128
  and retrieving a message, 92–93
  and searching Computer Database Plus, 146–47
  and searching forum membership directories, 133–34
  sending e-mail messages, 87–88, 90
  Sessions Settings box, 28–29
  and shortcut commands, 57–59
  and uploading program and graphics files, 106
  and uploading text files, 104–5
Windows (Microsoft), xx, 298
  logging on through, 28
  and reservation systems, 262
  and technical support, 276, 283
  Terminal, 27, 28
  version 3.0, 25, 42
  version 3.1, 27, 42
  version of the Dow Jones News/Retrieval service, 202.
  See also WinCIM (CompuServe Information Manager for Windows)
WordPerfect, 277, 278
Words in Article Text, 146
WordStar Forum, 126–27
Works, 27

Z

Zenith, 286
Ziff-Davis, 180
Ziffnet, 180, 183, 291
  Contents menu, 114
  cost of, 185
ZIP codes, 151, 153